THE RED FORT

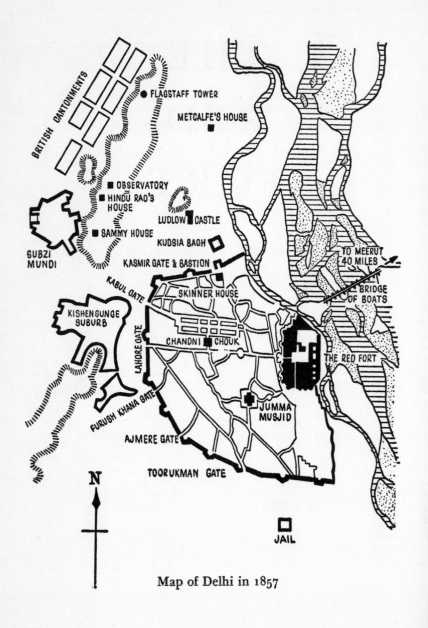

BRITISH CANTONMENTS

● FLAGSTAFF TOWER

■ METCALFE'S HOUSE

■ OBSERVATORY
■ HINDU RAO'S HOUSE
■ LUDLOW CASTLE
■ SAMMY HOUSE
KUDSIA BAGH
KASMIR GATE & BASTION

SUBZI MUNDI

KABUL GATE
SKINNER HOUSE

KISHENGUNGE SUBURB
LAHORE GATE
CHANDNI CHOUK

FURUSH KHANA GATE

AJMERE GATE

TOORUKMAN GATE

TO MEERUT 40 MILES
BRIDGE OF BOATS
THE RED FORT

✠ JUMMA MUSJID

N

□ JAIL

Map of Delhi in 1857

THE
RED
FORT

The Story of the Indian Mutiny of 1857

by

JAMES LEASOR

REYNAL & COMPANY

NEW YORK

Library of Congress catalog card number: 57-8322

PRINTED IN THE UNITED STATES OF AMERICA
AMERICAN BOOK–STRATFORD PRESS, INC., NEW YORK

To
Roland and Dora Bevan

ACKNOWLEDGMENTS

MY THANKS are due to Miss Mary Cosh for the research she has undertaken and for other assistance in the preparation of this book, and to the librarians and staff of the British Museum Reading Room, the India Office Library, and the Public Records Office. I would also like to acknowledge my indebtedness to the staff of the National Archives, New Delhi; to Miss E. Rendall, Archivist of the Society for the Propagation of the Gospel in Foreign Parts; and to the many people in England and India who were kind enough to let me see letters, papers, records and other documents from relations who served in India during 1857. When several conflicting accounts have existed of some episode, a mean has been struck between them. Any errors are my own.

J. L.

Contents

List of Illustrations

Introduction to the American Edition

COLUMBUS DISCOVERED AMERICA by mistake. He was not searching for a new country or a new world in the West, but for a route to the old world—the Indies and the Far East. In those days the Eastern World was synonymous with wealth; it was an irresistible magnet to the Western merchants. Hence their attempts to find new and speedier routes to Sumatra, China and India. Their thoughts were ever where the treasure lay.

English and French merchant adventurers formed private syndicates to sail ships to the Indian ports of Bombay and Calcutta. The voyage was as long as it was dangerous; they had no compasses worthy of the name, no proper charts, no maps. Pirates often robbed them as they returned heavily laden and were almost within sight of home. They earned the great profits made when their voyages were successful.

Their stories of the style and wealth of the Oriental princes became common in Europe, and their trade increased. By arrangement with local Indian rulers, the English and French established trading posts—called "factories"—in India, and they recruited young Indians to act as guards for these outposts, to protect their goods in transit by caravan and the stores they held in their warehouses.

These sepoys, as the guards were called, (from the Persian *sipahi*, meaning a horseman or a soldier) wore uniforms to give them authority, and were armed. At first their uniforms were made to the design or whim of the Europeans in charge of the factories, but gradually they came to be based on the uniforms of European soldiers. They were drilled on the same model, too, and these Company soldiers multiplied as trade grew and, with it, the number of trading posts to be protected.

Where there is great wealth there is also great greed and envy. As the English and the French wanted to be the only foreigners with trading concessions in India, the sepoy armies were used to continue on Indian soil battles that had begun between their masters in Europe. In these the English were victorious, and so their trading company—the East India Company—became in virtual control of the Indian sub-continent. They entered into agreements and treaties with the Indian kings and maharajas, much as today the American oil companies in the Middle East enter into business agreements with sheiks and other Arab rulers.

The world then was a far larger place than it is today. News of the Company's actions in India took months to reach London. The men on the spot were to all intents and purposes their own masters. Thus some tended to work for their own gain rather than for the gain of the Company that employed them.

Their temptations were enormous: position and affluence for life in return for a few unscrupulous years in India. In their eagerness to get rich quickly, they whittled down traditional rights and privileges of the sepoys. Some Indians feared that English missionaries were about to convert them forcibly to Christianity. No one told them differently, and so rumour and lying report won an easy victory, as so often they do. The result was the Indian Mutiny of 1857, with which this book is concerned.

The Mutiny marked the end of gross exploitation in India,

and the beginning of British rule under the British Crown. In the ninety years—until 1947—of direct British rule, reforms were undertaken in India that had never been attempted before. It was a time not without its glory.

Today, a hundred years after the Mutiny, when it is easy to ignore the brash new imperialism of the great oil companies and to view with indignation the older British imperialism in the East, many people forget that out of this older, wiser policy much good came. Ancient abuses were stamped out; the foundations of Parliamentary government and a system of law were laid; millions were educated. Many races have conquered India over the centuries, but none have left such positive results as memorials of their stay.

Under the old British Empire, there is no case recorded where Indians wished to become known as "Britons"—as subject races had hoped to be called "Romans" in the days of the great Roman Empire. The British achievement was, in fact, far greater.

They taught the Indians a new pride in being themselves.

THE RED FORT

CHAPTER I

Sunday in Meerut

THE DAY WAS ALREADY too warm for comfort by the time the church bell began to ring for morning service. As the Rev. James Rotton, the Chaplain at Meerut, looked out of his vestry window across the brown, baking dust of the road beyond the clusters of houses and the thatched barracks, he could see the mango groves that ringed in the garrison parade ground shimmering with heat. This was always a sign of an unpleasantly hot day.

A few kite-hawks turned and wheeled in the burnished air, and dived like plummets over the regimental cook-houses. Here and there he saw the small signs of Sunday morning activity: an Indian servant salaaming; a *syce* leading in a horse for an officer; a sweeper raising his brush of branches to his head in salute as an English family passed him by. Their carriage pulled a plume of dust across the whole hazy picture.

No more Europeans remained in this East India Company station about forty miles north-east of Delhi than duty compelled to. All who could had already left to spend the hot weather elsewhere. For several weeks past, long trains of wagons and donkey carts had carried the soldiers, their families and their baggage from the British cantonment up to bungalows at Simla and elsewhere in the hills, where the air

17

was cool and life was more bearable. No one saw the need for many troops to stay in Meerut during the worst of the hot weather; all the campaigns in the past had been fought in the cooler months of the year, and on the Indian frontiers, hundreds of miles away. And so, although the ratio of European troops to Indian sepoys had been fixed by Lord Cornwallis at one to three, "but not less than one to four," by that Sunday of 10 May 1857 it had sunk as low as one to six.

The garrison had been further weakened recently when some British regiments had gone back to Britain, their service overseas finished; and others posted to Persia in the previous year had still not returned. Although several troopships had been arriving at Bombay with new drafts, many of them were fresh-faced youngsters on their first foreign tour. Meerut was not a place for trouble, anyway. It was a place for pleasure, the scene of many gay balls and parties during the year, and a likely garrison for rapid advancement, since several of the finest regiments in India were stationed there.

The Rev. James Rotton, gazing down the wide, dusty road that led to his church, could see a sprinkling of distant figures in dress uniforms walking leisurely or riding in open carriages towards his doors. Two officers were only a hundred yards away, and behind them, amid the thick plantations of palm trees and mangoes and sugar cane, the roofs of the European cantonment stood in sharp outline against the hard blue sky of an Indian morning. Smoke curled up lazily from kitchen chimneys; there was no wind.

As he watched the familiar scene, Rotton suddenly remembered an incident which had occurred that morning as he was preparing to leave home to take the service. An Indian woman-servant had approached him silently, bowed and had been about to speak, and then, as if unnerved by some second thoughts, she suddenly turned and ran out of the room. For a moment the chaplain had thought of following her, then decided against it; one could not follow one's native servants to their quarters, however odd their behaviour might seem. But, for no reason that he could name, the memory of the incident made him feel vaguely uneasy; as though it possessed some hidden importance which he should have understood.

The two officers he had seen in the front of the group on their way to church were nearer now, and he recognized one as Lieutenant Hugh Gough, a nineteen-year-old subaltern of the 3rd Light Cavalry. The officer with him, a good-looking young man, was a stranger, evidently a new arrival. Rotton nodded to them both.

Gough introduced his companion as Lieutenant McNabb, and the three of them stood on the steps talking, while above them the great bell boomed and the air grew steadily hotter and drier. Both the officers looked uncomfortably warm, although they were wearing the undress summer uniform, with frock-coats and white overalls.

Rotton noticed that McNabb was dressed in alpaca bordered with a different lace braiding from that worn by the rest of the regiment. He knew that old General Hewitt, the Divisional Commander, was fastidious in the style of clothing worn by those in his command. He had an acid word for officers, whether new arrivals or seasoned soldiers, who did not know his idiosyncrasies of taste. Obviously, McNabb was very new to the station, or his uniform would not have passed the scrutiny of the 3rd Cavalry's Commanding Officer, Lieutenant-Colonel Carmichael Smyth, who equally unhesitatingly found fault when his officers appeared to be taking sartorial licence which he felt the General would not welcome. Hewitt was over seventy, with fifty years of Indian service behind him; he had reached the age when matters of dress and turnout were of supreme importance.

The two youths were discussing Gough's small private zoo. He kept, for his amusement, a leopard and two bears; he was explaining how he had to shoot one of the bears recently because it became too savage, when the bell stopped ringing. The service was due to begin. They had to separate before

Rotton could find an opportunity of mentioning the affair of his native servant. The officers might have understood its significance—if indeed there was any. As Gough used to say, "The perils from the climate were far greater than from any visible enemy"; and everyone agreed. Nevertheless, things were not as peaceful as they had been. For some months a faint undercurrent of unrest had been spreading, even to such a peaceful station as Meerut. And from other parts of the country, reports described the desire for change that had gripped some Indian regiments.

There was the recurring belief, for instance, that a new issue of cartridges from the Company's arsenal at Dum Dum, near Calcutta, had to be greased with cow's fat and pig's lard. Since Hindus held the cow as sacred, and all Mohammedans abhorred the pig as unclean, this rumour caused tremendous alarm among soldiers of both religions. It had arisen when the Company's army, in place of the old-fashioned smooth-bore muskets, began to be issued with Lee-Enfield rifles, which had a much closer fit of cartridge and ball, and so the cartridges had to be smeared with grease before they could be rammed into the barrel. Some commanding officers paraded their troops and assured them that the rumours were untrue; but no soldier will readily accept an official assurance on any subject if this contradicts a barrack-room rumour. The sepoys in 1857 were no exceptions to this rule.

Then there had been some unusual happenings, the sort of thing that people talked about quietly after dinner, when the Indian servants had been dismissed and the punkahs were still and the heavy-bodied night moths bumped into the globes of the oil-lamps. Headmen of villages—so the stories went—would be called to meet a stranger, and the stranger would give him four chupatties (pancakes made with wheat flour) and urge that four similar cakes should at once be made and sent on by the village watchman to the next village. These strangers would speak as in a parable. "From the north to the south, and from the east to the west." The message was always the same, until all India would be alive to the news that really was no news at all, but rather a vague feeling of unease, a portent of some unknown disaster.

And there were tales of Indian soldiers who awoke in their barracks to find that, in the night, someone had placed near their leader a lotus flower—the symbol of regeneration to Hindus. Yet no one knew who could have crept in past the sentries, or why indeed they should bother to do such a thing.

Others told of uprisings quickly suppressed, and sometimes, even as they spoke, their servants would rush in, greatly alarmed, to report that their own thatched houses were ablaze. Arrows had been dipped in oil and lit, and sent on their way—by soldiers, so it was said. In the safety of the dark one blazing arrow could bring down a whole house or even a barracks, for after the heat of afternoon the thatch was dry and hot and burned easily.

Finally, there had been the terrible business culminating in Meerut only the previous day—so recent, in fact, and so unexpected, that Mr. Rotton did not like to remember it, and instinctively glanced at the youngsters, Gough and Mc-Nabb, sitting near Hervey Greathed, the Commissioner of Meerut, and his wife, both old friends of Hugh Gough.

The Colonel of the 3rd Light Cavalry—one of the crack regiments of the East India Company's army, which Gough would insist was far smarter on parade than the cavalry regiment of the Queen's army, also stationed at Meerut—had heard rumours of discontent at the issue of these new cartridges and resolved to stop them at once. Colonel Carmichael Smyth had only returned from leave in April, and he was in no mood to endure what he called "this folly" of the cartridges, so he ordered on parade the skirmishers—picked sepoys, the élite of the corps, who were armed with carbines —with the intention of showing them that the grease was quite harmless.

He wished to explain that there was in any case no need to bite the cartridges with their teeth as they had been doing with some earlier issues of cartridges; they could tear these with their fingers. Thus, even if the grease *were* cow's fat or pig's lard (which it most certainly was not), they would not defile themselves. He had demonstrated this new way of loading to the Havildar-Major and his orderly at his house; that night the Havildar-Major's tent was burned down, and the orderly, presumably as a protest, "fired off a carbine twice."

"But," as Gough noted later in his diary, "only five would accept the cartridges served out to them, although they were out of the magazine." The other eighty-five men "respectfully but firmly" refused to touch them.

For Colonel Smyth this was an unheard of position. What was he to do? He stood the parade at ease and called over his officiating Adjutant, Lieutenant Melville Clark; the regular Adjutant was away on leave. Together they discussed the situation in undertones, trying not to look concerned. On the face of it, their duty was plain. The eighty-five men had refused to obey an order; they must therefore be made an example of before others could follow their lead.

The easiest course was to take the names of the five loyal skirmishers and then dismiss the parade. Since all the others had disobeyed the order, they could be arrested at any time, and one by one if need be. Before the Colonel actually took this step, however, he would have to consult General Hewitt, for on such a scale as this nothing could be done without his authority.

So the men were dismissed and filed off the parade ground, chattering excitedly at the unexpected result of their defiance. They had bluffed the British, and the bluff had not been called. That night the story of this strange parade spread through the bazaars, embellished and altered to something nearly unrecognizable, but always ending on a note of victory for the stalwart eighty-five.

That night, too, Colonel Smyth's account went up to the General, who passed it back to Army Headquarters, who replied with the only possible advice: an immediate court martial for the mutinous men.

The whole business irritated old General Hewitt intensely. He was an obese officer who had been posted to Meerut from Peshawar because he was "too inactive." He was so fat that he could no longer mount his horse, but had a buggy specially made for him in which he would inspect or review his troops. The Commander-in-Chief of the Bengal Army, General the Hon. George Anson, had only recently been promoted from commanding the Meerut Division, and Hewitt was annoyed that such an untoward event as men refusing to obey an order should occur so soon after he had assumed command. General Anson might think that he was no better in his new appointment than he had been in his previous one. At this thought his irritability increased; these men, if found guilty, must be punished with the utmost severity.

The eighty-five men were arrested easily enough, but it was found that no local gaol could accommodate so many. They were thus confined in an old hospital building near their lines, and guarded by a company of 60th Native Rifles —an action which the Governor-General, Lord Canning, was later to call "a folly that is inconceivable."

The court martial was arranged for Friday, 8 May, which was as soon as various Indian officers could be summoned from Delhi. The Superintending Officer, however, was British, and, so Gough believed, "his advice and legal knowledge probably considerably influenced their opinions."

There was some doubt in Meerut whether so many men could be court-martialled at the same time, for no barrack-room seemed available, and then someone suggested the large mess-room of the British cavalry regiment, one of the few buildings not roofed with thatch, because of fire risks.

The Court sat at a long, scrubbed Army mess table on trestles, and because the Indians then towered above them, they were also allowed to sit. There were no chairs—all the mess forms had been removed for the trial—and so they sat cross-legged on the hard earth floor.

Gough watched their faces as, one after the other, they pleaded "Not guilty."

The older men, and especially those with medals for long and good service, looked worn and anxious. If found guilty, they faced the loss of their pensions, for which they might already have served anything up to twenty years. The younger sepoys were doing their best to look unconcerned, and succeeding fairly well. Most of them looked sullen and resentful, determined to stand on what they imagined were their rights.

The court martial began. The Colonel explained what had happened. So did the acting Adjutant, Melville Clark, and while he was speaking some of the sepoys in front jumped up excitedly.

"Did the Adjutant *sahib* say *that?*" asked one. Clark replied rather testily that he had. And at once the cry came from all round the room: "It's a lie! It's a lie!"

The President of the Court banged the table for silence, and waited, looking from one sepoy to the next until all the murmuring ceased and the only sound in the mess-hall came from the creaking ropes on the punkah over their heads.

"Pray proceed," he said coldly.

It was all over very quickly, for, on the evidence, the case could have only one outcome. As the Indian guards marched their fellow-countrymen back to their temporary gaol in the old hospital, everyone must have realized this. All were, of course, found guilty, and details of the sentences were telegraphed to General Anson in Simla for his approval.

As soon as they had been confirmed, General Hewitt called a special parade for early the next morning. He regarded the whole affair almost as a personal insult, and with the sudden, irrational anger of an old man, ever conscious of his dwindling physical authority and energy, he decided to make an example of the stubborn eighty-five: their shame would be shown to the biggest audience he could muster.

On parade that Saturday, the English and the Indians fell
in to make three sides of a hollow square. The General was
supported by his Staff. Brigadier Archdale Wilson of the
Bengal Artillery was in command, with two batteries of the
Artillery, the 6th Dragoon Guards and the Queen's 6oth
Rifles, and the Indian regiments: the 3rd Light Cavalry
(without horses) and the 11th and 20th Native Infantry. The
European troops faced each other across the parade ground,
while the Indian regiments made up the third side of the
square, facing the General and the senior officers. They had
been issued with their arms, but with no ammunition, while
the British troops had loaded rifles. Artillery was also placed
so that "the least movement of disaffection or insurrection
would have been followed by instant slaughter."

Solemnly, first in English and then in Hindustani, the
sentences on the mutineers were read out. Severity had been
expected, but the prisoners found no comfort in having their
worst forebodings realized. The older soldiers received either
transportation or life imprisonment; the younger men were
sentenced to ten, fifteen, or twenty years in gaol.

As the last sentence was read out, no one spoke; no one
moved. Already the day was growing warm. A kite-hawk
screamed throatily in the sky, and the noise broke the tension. A few men scraped their boots uneasily on the ground.
The prisoners stood firm. And then, from beyond the parade
ground, a small group of men came marching, carrying coils
of chains and leg-irons; they were the armourers and smiths
of the Horse Artillery. The eighty-five men were ordered to
remove their boots, and as they stood barefoot on the hot, dusty
earth their uniforms were torn off their backs and fetters
hammered round their ankles. It was a slow and clumsy business that lasted for several hours.

At last, by midday, the prisoners were led off, stumbling
as they tried to march. Some of them threw their boots at
Colonel Smyth as they passed him, cursing him loudly in
Hindustani. The Colonel took no notice. General Hewitt

looked away; the heat was tiring and he wished he were elsewhere. That night, in his report to Army Headquarters, he
noted that "the majority of the prisoners seemed to feel
acutely the degradation to which their folly and insubordination had brought them."

The Indian troops watched in a taut and oppressive silence, until one of the eighty-five marching off suddenly
cried out loudly, "For the faith!"—and the other prisoners
took it up in a defiant chorus: "For the faith! For the faith!"
It was a cry that would echo across India many times before
the year was out.

Some of the Indian troops moved restlessly as the prisoners
shouted, "Remember us! Remember us!" while they were
marched off, but an officer called the British regiments to
attention, and the knowledge that their rifles were loaded
prevented any gesture of sympathy with the eighty-five.

Gough was a kindly young man and a good soldier—he
was awarded the newly instituted Victoria Cross a few
months later—and on that Saturday he felt his place was with
the men who had been sentenced. So, with some other officers
of the regiment, he went to see them, to settle their accounts
and problems of pay, and to help them in any way he could.

They were confined together in one of the largest wards
of the hospital, and although he knew most of them quite
well, and all at least by name, they gave him no welcome.
The prisoners squatted sullenly on the floor as Gough set
up a table and began to arrange little piles of rupees for
paying them out. Then, suddenly, they realized that this
would be their last pay-parade; after this, they would not be
old soldiers, but ex-soldiers, discharged with ignominy from
an honourable service into which many of them had been
born, and their fathers before them. At the knowledge, they
began to weep and beseech Gough for a mercy that was not
his to give, beating their heads against the ground and kiss-
ing his boots, until, as he admitted later, "I believe I was

weak enough almost to share their sorrow. They, at any rate, knew but little of the events that would follow. . . ."

The older soldiers were in the worst extremity, for their punishment was transportation across the *kali pani*—dark (deep) water—to the penal settlement that had been formed in 1789 in the Andaman Islands, 600 miles out in the Bay of Bengal. The thought of this terrible end, rotting away in the company of the depraved in that settlement, cast a gloom on them all that nothing could lift.

This atmosphere of misery affected Gough to such an extent that even when he returned to his bungalow he found it hard to shake off. Brooding over the day's events, he sat out on his veranda that evening until the attentions of the mosquitoes became unpleasant. He was just on the point of going inside and calling for his bath to be drawn, when from the outer darkness of the compound he heard a whisper.

"*Sahib!*"

"*Kya bat hai?* (What is it?)," he asked, half expecting a beggar or some mendicant, rotten with leprosy, to drag his ruined body in and beg for alms. A man stepped up into the half-light of the veranda, and Gough saw with surprise that he was one of his own native officers, a subahdar.

"What do you want?" he asked. The man paused for a moment.

"It is the accounts, *sahib,*" he said. "I have come to see you about the accounts."

"But we dealt with all those this afternoon, Subahdar *sahib,*" replied Gough rather irritably. "Can it not wait until Monday?"

"No, *sahib.* It cannot wait. It is very important."

The subahdar was very close to Gough now; he could see the whites of the man's eyes faintly luminous in the sudden Indian dusk.

He was whispering again, his voice trembling with the weight of his message.

"It is most important, *sahib.* The Native Infantry and

Cavalry are in a turmoil. The events on parade today annoyed them. They have been telling the people in the bazaars
about them. They are in an ugly mood, *sahib*. They mean to
release the prisoners."

"When?"

"Tomorrow, *sahib*. When the British troops are at church."

"Nonsense!" Gough tried to sound convincing. "You are
joking, Subahdar *sahib*."

"Indeed I am not, *sahib*. But I have done my duty. *Salaam,
sahib*."

"Salaamaji."

The man melted away and left Gough to the night and the
tiny clockwork twitterings of crickets and tree lizards and
the drone of little winged things. Although he shrugged off
the news as bazaar gossip, Gough felt uneasy; he had heard
so many stories of unrest—at Barrackpore, at Berhampore,
and elsewhere. The more he considered the news, the more
serious did it seem.

At last he decided to tell his Colonel about it.

Colonel Smyth was annoyed at being disturbed with such
a cock-and-bull story.

"He reproved me for listening to such idle words," wrote
Gough afterwards, remembering the brief interview; but still
some sense of the Subahdar's urgency stayed with him. He
risked a reprimand by going above the Colonel's head and
seeing Brigadier Wilson.

The Brigadier was equally incredulous. The whole thing
was impossible, he said, stroking his thin beard.

"The General is quite satisfied," he pointed out carefully,
passing the responsibility. So Gough returned to his bungalow, but he still felt that some person in authority ought to
treat his story seriously. After the morning service on Sunday he had a word with his friend Mrs. Greathed, wife of the
Commissioner, about the events of the previous day, as they
stood talking at the church door with the Chaplain and some

others. He hoped she would tell her husband, but whether she did or not he never found out.

After lunch, while some of his more energetic colleagues played a stiff game of racquets in the heat of afternoon, Gough went to bed. To pull the shutters, undress as far as your underpants and then lie on the sheets and doze—that was the accepted way of spending a Sunday afternoon. Gough felt he needed the rest; he was Orderly Officer and went on duty at five o'clock. He wanted to be fresh for the task ahead of him. He had no idea how long that day's task would last.

While the English slept, the sepoys were restless. Some squatted on their haunches in groups, on the shady side of the barracks, passing the mouthpieces of their big hubble-bubble pipes from hand to hand, discussing with many shakings of the head the unnerving events of the previous few days. Others wandered off to sit in the little thatched huts of the bazaar-wallahs, drinking the black, bitter tea of the hills, and telling again the story of the indignity thrust upon their comrades.

It was not a happy afternoon. After a time some of the prostitutes in the bazaar even began to taunt men of the 3rd Cavalry Regiment.

"The British are coming!" they jeered. "We shall see who the men are *then!*"

This was a foolish remark, but it was heard, repeated, and embellished, until some of the simpler soldiers were running back to camp convinced it was the truth, and that the British were about to attack them as they sat unarmed at their ease.

To the groups of sepoys still in the garrison this was the spark set to the warm tinder of their discontent. No one ever knew who first stood up, or who ran for his horse before the rest, but within minutes the camp was in confusion. Troopers mounted their horses, infantrymen seized rifles or stakes of wood, and, riding or running, they converged on the focal point of their grievances—the hospital that imprisoned their friends.

Even then they might have been stopped; but none were there to stop them. The English were abed and snoring, heads turned away from the hard, terrible light of the afternoon and the deeds of folly that were about to be committed in the name of freedom.

Gough stood up and opened the shutters. The woodwork was warm to his touch, and the afternoon outside seemed as hot as ever, but with the deceptive warmth of early evening in northern India.

Soon it would be dark, and the air would suddenly grow colder, heavy with the rich scents of the night-blooming flowers; as though there had been no cruel heat, no blinding sunshine. The musky smell of early evening, the glitter of stars in a sky suddenly turned cold, these were the things you remembered about India when you had left her shores; not the irritations, the loneliness, the feeling of being unwanted and alien.

A voice disturbed him, and he heard the pattering of his servant's bare feet. He turned, and the door opened behind him. His bearer rushed in, eyes wide with fright.

"*Sahib! Sahib!*" he cried. "The lines and the *sahibs'* bungalows are on fire!"

Gough, still heavy with sleep, repeated the words, unable to grasp their significance. As he stared at the man he heard a galloping of hooves outside, and saw an Indian officer and two men reining in their foaming horses under his window, shouting: "*Sahib! Sahib!*"

Still in his underwear, and pulling a shirt over his head as he ran, Gough rushed out on to the veranda. The officer was the same Subahdar who had come to warn him the previous evening.

"What's wrong, Subahdar *sahib?*" he asked.

"*All* is wrong, *sahib*. The Native Infantry are in open mutiny. They are murdering the officers. Our own regiment is arming and mounting!"

As he spoke, a rattle of musketry fire came from the sepoy lines, and clouds of black smoke drifted up behind the bungalows beyond the parade ground. Gough raced back into his house, shouting for his groom to saddle his black charger.

By the time Gough was ready and dressed, the *syce* had his horse at the front door. The beast, half Arab, half Waler, pawed the ground nervously and tossed back his head until the *syce* held a bunch of lucerne under his nose, which calmed him. The horse took a bite at it, and for the first time since he had owned him, Gough was able to mount the spirited beast without trouble. And—as Gough liked to tell friends later— ever afterwards that horse was perfectly behaved, until a few months later he "succumbed to hard work" outside Delhi.

The men who had come to warn Gough were not at all keen on accompanying him, but he persuaded them, and together they galloped off towards the scene of violence.

What was, in Gough's words, "usually a scene of perfect discipline and neatness, with rows of mud barracks neatly thatched, with a quarter-guard ready to turn out and with groups of well-dressed and happy, contented sepoys lounging about," was now a shambles. Men raced from hut to hut with burning brands, throwing them up on to the roofs and into windows, shouting and screaming like madmen. Others rushed hither and thither with rifles and belts of ammunition, "dancing and leaping frantically about, calling and yelling to each other and blazing away into the air in all directions, maddened and thirsting for their officers' blood."

Gough was appalled. The scene was beyond his comprehension, and he paused, reining in his trembling horse, wondering what to do. At that moment they saw him and rushed towards him, firing wildly and indiscriminately as they ran, screaming curses at him.

"Leave him! Leave him or we'll kill you, too!" they shouted to his escort.

The Subahdar turned to Gough.

"You must leave at once, *sahib*. We will *all* be killed."

It was sound advice. As they turned, a volley of shots whistled over their heads. Gough had the idea of rousting out his own troop to try to steady the others, and accordingly they galloped to their billets on the right of the lines. But here the confusion and disorder was just as great as in the place they had left. A large body of men had stormed the magazine and were dragging out crates of ammunition. Nobody paid any attention to Gough, shouting orders on horseback.

"I felt myself most unmistakably *de trop*," he admitted later, recalling the scene, but soon he was recognized. At first no one offered to harm him, although he heard shouts of *"Maro! Maro!* (Kill! Kill!)" and someone fired a pistol, "mostly at random." One shot pierced his saddle, but hurt neither him nor his horse.

As he sat helpless with his escort on either side, another European came galloping up, pursued by Indian horsemen with their swords drawn in their hands. He was Quartermaster-Sergeant Cunninghame.

"Lay down your arms!" shouted Gough, but the only answer came back louder than before: *"Maro! Maro!"*

"For God's sake don't stay here," gasped Cunninghame. "They're out to murder us all!"

Gough swung round and saw that his little party was almost surrounded by the group of Indian cavalry who were advancing with their swords drawn. An orderly seized the bridle of Gough's horse, twisted its head in the direction of the British cantonments, and punched the animal on the mouth. The terrified beast bolted, and Gough was almost unseated as he galloped over the hard ground, while Cunninghame spurred his own horse and rode by Gough's side. Behind them, their escort threw down their arms and joined the mutineers.

All the roads seemed blocked by burning buildings. There was only one way left—through the bazaar. Here the streets were thick with people shouting and carrying iron-bound cudgels or *tulwars*, the sabre-like blades of northern India. Most of the men were chewing betel nut, and in the shuddering glare of their torches the red juice they spat seemed like blood. As they saw the two Englishmen ride towards them, a tremendous roar went up and they surged at them, waving their clubs.

Lying forward on their horses' necks, Gough and Cunninghame drove through the crowd, who cut and tore at them as they passed. This reception from the polite stallholders and shopkeepers, "who had hitherto always *salaamed* to almost all the Europeans," shocked Gough almost as much as the terrible sight of his own troopers running amok. Here was a world gone made, a nightmare come to life.

At last they were through the worst danger; Gough recognized some landmarks, and knew he was near the Greatheds' house. He decided to go and see how his friends were faring and if they had any news about the extent of the mutiny, which seemed almost universal. He wanted to speak to someone in authority, to be reassured, to be with his own countrymen again and away from this naked Oriental rage so alien to everything English.

He and Cunninghame reached the bungalow gates just in time, for the *budmashes* and the lay-abouts and thieves of the bazaar were also advancing on the house. The two riders galloped up the path and beat on the front door. Two of the Commissioner's servants met them and refused to let them in.

"They are not here, *sahib*," said one of them, and went on to explain that their master and mistress escaped in their carriage. They did their best to hurry Gough and Cunninghame away again, insisting that both the Greatheds were safe. There was nothing to be gained by staying, so Gough galloped over to the European lines, and Cunninghame went off on his own.

In fact, the Greatheds were still at home. The Commissioner's faithful servants had persuaded them to go up on the roof, knowing that they could not prepare their carriage to get them away in time. They were holding the front door to mislead the mob, who arrived just after Gough left, screaming for the blood of the English.

From their rooftop the Greatheds had seen Gough arrive and leave, and could not understand why he had not come up to them. For a moment they thought that their servants were treacherous, but this the servants denied, and swore to save them, pointing out the impossibility of escape while the house was surrounded by shouting, drunken rioters waving torches and swords and clubs.

At last the mob broke into the house, and, because they could find no victims, they sacked the place, smashing everything they could see, and tried to set it on fire.

As soon as they went away, the servants persuaded the Greatheds to come down from the roof of the burning building and hid them in the garden. Some of the mob, learning that they were still about, came back to search for them, but without success. The Greatheds escaped in the morning.

About all this, of course, Hugh Gough knew nothing as he galloped on, escorted unexpectedly by an Indian officer and two sowars (cavalrymen), who loomed out of the darkness and joined him. As they did not offer him violence, he assumed they were still loyal, and so was surprised when, as soon as they reached the Artillery lines, they left him. The officer explained almost apologetically, that "his duty was with his regimental comrades."

Gough never saw him again, and efforts to trace him failed, but he remembered with gratitude the Indian's personal courage and his loyalty. Other Europeans had similar experiences and escapes through the loyalty of native officers and men. Elsewhere, the story was different.

The Artillery lines were a mass of burning houses and massacred Europeans, and full of rumours and refugees. No one knew how widespread the mutiny might be, and no one seemed keen on finding out. Night was now near, yet the British had made no move to help the wounded or avenge the dead. The mutineers ran wild, and no one tried to stop them. Gough noted bitterly that "There appeared to be a general paralysis."

General Hewitt was completely unmanned by the events of

the day. He delegated his authority to Brigadier Archdale Wilson, the next senior officer on the staff, and in shirt and pyjamas, watched the destruction of the garrison from his bungalow window. He showed no emotion at all, although afterwards he blamed Wilson for this chaos in Meerut and the fact that no troops pursued the mutineers when they headed for Delhi, "on the grounds that the movement of the troops depended on him."

As commander of the whole Meerut Division, which included the great station of Delhi with its tremendous magazine —one of the largest in the Empire—General Hewitt's responsibility was enormous; but, as a subsequent report on his conduct explained, he thought "only of the safety of the place in which he himself resided. . . ."

He had a dislike of anything that might cause provocation which in turn might lead to the need for a decision to be made. Accordingly, at Meerut there was, as Kaye and Malleson describe in their history of the Mutiny,

> a state of utter unpreparedness for action. There were troopers without horses, troopers that could not ride—artillerymen without guns, artillerymen who did not know a mortar from a howitzer, or the difference between round-shot and grape. . . .
>
> When an officer of Artillery commanding one of the Meerut batteries sought permission, a few days before the outbreak, to load his ammunition-wagons that he might be ready in case of accident for prompt service, he was told that such a step would excite suspicion among the natives. . . .

Wilson, like Hewitt, was a cautious officer. He was a thin, spare man in his middle fifties, with nearly thirty years of service in India, and although noted for his strategy as a whist player, some friends held that he was "not a very brilliant man." And since he had just recovered from a severe attack of smallpox, he was certainly not at his best.

But he was not only physically weak at this moment; he was weak in men to command. He could count only on a troop of

Horse Artillery, a Field Artillery battery, the 6th Dragoon
Guards (Carabineers), and the 1st Battalion of the 60th Rifles.
These represented the total of his European troops. Most of
the Indians had become mutineers within the space of an
evening.

However, he did what he could. He ordered the Artillery
to parade, and galloped out bravely to lead them himself. Then
it was discovered that there were no Indians left in the ammunition stores to issue them with cartridges, and since they were
useless with empty rifles, the parade had to be dismissed.

By now most of the mutinous Indians had disappeared; no
one knew where they might be. Some British troops had up to
twenty rounds of ammunition in their bandoliers, and they
started out on a rather faint-hearted search for mutineers.
They could find no mutineers in the barracks and so they
marched round the parade ground and fired several rounds
into a clump of trees, where someone thought he saw movement, and also into the sugar cane on the edge of the cantonment. This exercise aroused the wrath of a certain Lieutenant
Galloway, who was hiding in an outhouse and was mistaken
for a mutineer. Such was the aiming, however, that he was
unhurt.

One officer did take out a mounted party with the intention
of clearing the cantonment of any mutineers who might still
be there, and also to rescue any survivors. But the officer detailed to guide them unaccountably lost his way, and led them
dangerously far out into the dry plains outside Meerut, which
were criss-crossed with deep cracks and *nullahs*. Eventually
they only found their way back again by riding in the direction of the blazing houses. They had seen nothing and accomplished nothing.

Major Rosser of the 6th Dragoon Guards "earnestly im-
plored" Brigadier Wilson to allow him to take his squadron
and a couple of Horse Artillery guns, and chase the mutineers
"even to the walls of Delhi." The offer was not accepted.

At last, weary with nothing to do, with their barracks de-

stroyed and no plans for action, the British troops paraded
again—and bivouacked for the night on the barrack square.

Earlier that evening, Lieutenant Mackenzie of the Cavalry
had been sitting in his bungalow with his feet up, reading a
book, when his bearer, Sheodeen, rushed into the room excitedly.

"*Sahib! sahib!* there's a riot going on in the lines," he cried.
"The sepoys have mutinied and are murdering the *Sahib
logue* (people)!"

As Mackenzie swung his feet down on to the floor, he heard
the distant rattle of musket fire, and at once he knew that
something must be dangerously amiss; there was no target
practice on that Sunday in Meerut.

His first thought was that the men of his own regiment—the
3rd Bengal Light Cavalry—were attacking the Native Infantry
as a reprisal for remarks the infantry had made about their
unwillingness to break ranks and "rescue" the mutineers when
they had been shackled on parade.

"I would greatly have rejoiced to see the insult avenged,"
Mackenzie admitted later, but at the time his position was
clearly with his men, whatever the rights or wrongs of the
affair.

He grabbed his uniform, buckled on his sword and jumped
on his horse. As he reached the gate of his compound he saw
his Quartermaster-Sergeant—an Englishman—running towards
him from his own house in the lines. In one hand he held a
rifle; in the other, a sword.

"Oh, God, sir!" he sobbed. "The troops are coming to cut
us up!"

"Let us then stick together," replied the Lieutenant crisply.
"Two are better than one." He had no idea what the man
meant. Why should their troops want to cut them up? His
common-sense reply rallied the Sergeant for a moment, and
then he looked fearfully over his shoulder. Some way behind
him a cluster of galloping horses raised a cloud of dust that

rapidly drew nearer. The sight overcame the Sergeant's courage. Without another word, he fled through the gate into Mackenzie's compound, jumped the wall and disappeared into the garden of the next house.

Mackenzie watched him in amazement and was astonished to see a small mob of *budmashes*—local bad characters—"prominent among whom I recognized my own night watchman," leaping at him with sticks and clubs. The *chowkidar* actually lunged at the Sergeant with a spear as he was halfway over the wall and caught him on the mouth. The Sergeant rammed his rifle into the man's chest and shot him dead. As the others cowered back, he dropped to the ground on the other side of the wall and dashed into a room of the bungalow.

The two young officers who lived there were taking their Sunday rest. They were astonished at his arrival, streaming blood and panting for breath, but they did not stop to ask questions. They buckled on their arms and all three ran for the stables, where they kept three horses. They arrived in time to see a groom running away with a saddle on his head, but they still had two saddles and three bridles, so they all mounted —the Sergeant bare-back—and raced for the gates. Here the mutineers had anticipated them. The gates were locked and too high to jump. For a moment the three men paused, irresolute, and then from behind them came a cautious call: *"Sahib! sahib!"*

Their sweeper, the menial who emptied the privies, who swept the dust from the compound, who belonged to "the lowest and most despised caste of Indian domestics," was beckoning to them. He led them at a run behind some outhouses up to a gap in the compound wall, which the servants had made for their own convenience, and which the officers did not even know existed. Through this they went in single file, dodged a hail of shots from mutineers, and then galloped off towards the barracks of the 6th Rifles. The sweeper had no horse, and he was not fleet of foot. Within seconds, the infuriated mob had cut him to pieces.

But Mackenzie did not hear of this until later. At that moment he was fully engaged, for an infantry sepoy, armed with
an officer's sword, suddenly rushed at him out of the bushes
and tried to cut off his head.

Mackenzie whipped out his own sword, dug the spurs in his
horse's flank and rode at the man—a manoeuvre which he said
afterwards, with the understatement of the time, "spoilt his
stroke." The sword whistled through the air and cut Mackenzie's right shoulder cord. As he turned his horse again, the
sepoy jumped over the wall and fled.   ,

By now, the distant cloud of dust which had so alarmed the
Quartermaster-Sergeant was much nearer and Mackenzie saw
that it was raised by his own Cavalry troopers, galloping
towards him. They made a magnificent sight, stirrup to stirrup, swords and lances glittering in the sunlight, pennants
streaming in the wind.

"Even then it did not occur to me that they should have
any hostile intent towards myself, so I shouted to them to halt,"
Mackenzie noted afterwards in his diary. "This they did, and
surrounded me; and before I knew what was happening I
found myself warding off as well as I could a fierce onslaught
from many blades."

He parried the strokes like one in a daze, going through
the reflexes automatically from years of training, but still
quite unaware of any reason for his men to attack him so
furiously. Was he mad or were they? Was it all a dream?

He shouted for an explanation, but no one heeded him;
only the bright, sharp blades went up and down, and the
dark, contorted faces shone and ran with sweat.

So many cavalrymen surrounded him and pressed in so close
to each other that their numbers defeated their endeavours.
Each in his eagerness to kill the officer impeded a comrade,
but even so it seemed only a matter of seconds before Mackenzie would be cut down.

Suddenly he saw another European officer, Lieutenant
Craigie, ride out of his gate a little farther down the road and

gallop over to him, sword drawn. Some of the troopers saw
him, too, and they all galloped off past them both towards
the lines of the Europeans, waving their swords in the air.

"What's wrong?" Mackenzie asked, amazed at the state of
affairs.

"It's mutiny," replied Craigie briefly. "Mutiny. My wife
and your sister are together in my carriage," he went on.
"They were going to church."

Mackenzie looked at his watch.

"They should have arrived there safely by now. We'll have
to chance it, anyhow. Our place is on the parade ground."

Together they galloped towards their lines and found that
instead of the usual deserted expanse, the place was a scene
of uproar. Mackenzie noted that "hundreds of men were already mounted and riding to and fro, shouting, waving their
swords, firing carbines and pistols into the air. Others on the
edge of the ground were saddling up their horses as fast as
they could."

In and out of the groups rode British officers "trying to
restore order with entreaty and threats." But although they
were not molested, their advice was ignored. One Indian
shouted at Mackenzie, "The Company's *Raj* is over for ever!"
At this a great cheer went up.

Some of the men rallied to Mackenzie and Craigie as they
rode on together, and Craigie, who was an excellent linguist,
managed to persuade forty or fifty troopers to one side. They
told him that the gaol was even then being attacked and the
mutineers would be freed.

"Then our place is at the gaol," said Mackenzie at once.
With Lieutenant Melville Clark, who had also arrived, they
raced off towards it.

No one had any clear idea how a decisive attack on the
gaol could be stopped, but clearly they could do more good
there than by riding about aimlessly on the parade ground.

The roads were packed thick with excited natives, all waving sticks and flaming torches. The three officers rode side by

side and as they forced their way through this mass of shouting Indians, a great roar of approval went up from the bystanders. Mackenzie explained later: "They evidently did not distinguish the British officers in the dusk, and took the whole party for mutineers."

Although the disturbance was only a few hours old, the sepoys and the mob had already ruined the greater part of the garrison. Houses blazed on either side of the trunk road and clouds of thick black smoke poured sparks high up into the night sky.

The telegraph line which linked Meerut and Delhi had been cut, and a slack wire, hanging down across the road, caught Mackenzie in the chest and spun him off his horse into the dust. Had it touched him a few inches higher he would probably have lost his head. Fortunately, he was only winded and otherwise unhurt, and he lay on his back gasping in the dust while the horsemen thundered by.

Painfully he remounted and soon caught up with the column. As they came to a wider part of the road, they were astonished to see a palanquin-*gharry*—a box-shaped, Venetian carriage—rushing driverless towards them. By its side rode a trooper of the 3rd Cavalry, leaning in through the open window, stabbing his sword into the body of a dead European woman passenger.

So intent was he on this mutilation that he did not even look up as Mackenzie's column approached. Craigie brought down his sword across the back of his neck, and Mackenzie and Clark ran him up through his body for good measure.

"All this passed in a second," Mackenzie said afterwards, "but the following sepoys became excited with anger."

The officers had never been entirely sure of their loyalty, and now the shouts of *"Maro! Maro!"* came from their own men.

"We all thought the end was approaching," one of them admitted. "However, nothing happened."

This was probably because they had already reached the

gaol, although too late to prevent the prisoners from being freed. As they sat on their panting, foam-flecked horses, while the white, powdery dust billowed about them in clouds, the prisoners stormed out of the gates, waving stakes and torches. Blacksmiths had anvils set up outside the gates and smashed off the shackles with hammers and chisels. Then the prisoners fled cheering into the darkness to add their quota to the general chaos and confusion of the night. There was nothing anyone could do now to stop them.

Mackenzie asked a sepoy of the Native Infantry, the regiment which had formed the gaol guard, who had opened the gates.

"They answered our questions by firing at us, fortunately without hitting any of us."

Mackenzie turned his little force and they set off back towards the cantonment. Although only minutes had passed since they had ridden out, it seemed that hardly any landmarks remained. Nearly every building was ablaze, and "if before we rode fast, now we flew."

Although still mystified as to the causes of the outbreak, the mutiny seemed so universal that they were powerless to do anything to stop it, and so Mackenzie decided to discover what had happened to his sister and to Craigie's wife. He raised his sword above his head as a rallying sign and shouted for any volunteers who would come and help him. About a dozen of the troopers agreed, and rode after him as he thundered through the burning shell of the garrison. The rest slunk off into the bazaar. He did not see them again.

Every house they passed was in flames, his own included. "My heart sank within me," Mackenzie admitted, but he gave no outward sign of his feelings. Oddly, Craigie's home was, indeed, the only one that had not been fired. It stood alone, a two-storeyed house in large grounds, surrounded by a high wall, and, since there seemed nowhere else to head for, Mackenzie turned his horse in at the compound gates. He was lucky; his sister and Craigie's wife were inside the house with an Indian carabineer of the 6th Dragoon Guards.

The two women had set out for church earlier in the evening, but their coachman became alarmed by the temper of the mob that was already gathering, and had turned back. As they passed the bazaar a carabineer rushed out of an alleyway in front of them with a crowd in pursuit eager to lynch him. The two ladies stopped their carriage and took him inside and then they all drove off at full speed. It was a very dangerous thing to do. All the anger of the crowd was at once turned on them and the mob pursued the carriage angrily. But at last the galloping horses left them behind. Even so, the carriage hood was slashed to shreds with their knives and *tulwars* as the infuriated crowd tried to reach the occupants.

The two women did not know where their menfolk might be, and they had no idea what was happening except that the fury of the mob seemed to be directed against Europeans. They thus resolved to make their own defence, and to defend themselves for as long as possible until help came. They looked out Craigie's three double-barrelled guns, and stood, backs against the wall of a downstairs room, with powder flasks and bullets and caps ready. For all this brave front, they would soon have been overpowered, for the guns were not loaded—neither of the women knew how to prime them—and the carabineer was in a state of nervous collapse and could neither give them help or advice.

Mackenzie realized that they were all in a most dangerous position. If the twelve troopers who still were with him decided to join the mutineers as well, then they would be murdered within seconds. He had to think of some way to hold their loyalty. Like most of the Europeans still alive in Meerut, he was sure that General Hewitt would soon have the British troops out to restore order from the chaos. He expected that this would be done very quickly, and felt that if he could hold out for a few hours then they would all be rescued.

He had nothing to offer the troopers but an appeal to their consciences; he was agreeably surprised at the result.

I brought the ladies down to the door of the house, and calling the troopers to me, commended their lives to their charge, [he explained later]. It is impossible to understand the swift torrents of feeling that flood the hearts of Orientals in periods of intense excitement. Like madmen, they threw themselves off their horses and prostrated themselves before the ladies, seizing their feet and placing them on their heads as they vowed with tears and sobs to protect their lives with their own.

As soon as he saw that his manoeuvre was successful, Mackenzie ordered the men out into the grounds on patrol, and took the two women upstairs and showed them how to load the guns. One gun he put a little apart from the other two. If all else failed, this could save them from an even worse death—a point which did not escape the ladies. "Long afterwards, in quiet England, my sister . . . told me that both she and Mrs. Craigie well understood the sacred use to which that gun was in the last resort to be devoted."

Mackenzie then walked out on to the veranda that ran along one part of the house to see if there was any sign of rescue. The smell of burning wood was sharp on the night air, and mingled with this was the terrible, sweet stench of burning human flesh. Blazing timbers crackled like rifle fire and great showers of sparks soared up on every side. Some of the natives saw him as he stood there, for the flames made the night nearly as bright as day.

"There is a *Feringhee!*" they cried. "Let us burn this big *kothi!* (house)." They began to run towards the wall, holding up their burning torches. Mackenzie raised his rifle and took aim at the nearest man. Some of those who hung back saw the action and shouted a warning to their comrades, who slowed and stopped and turned away. Mackenzie lowered the rifle again, and stood watching them. They drew back to the gate and prepared to charge a second time. Several times they attempted to fire the house, but the sight of the two chased barrels of his sporting gun, and the belief that, as a *sahib*, he was also a good shot, persuaded them to change their minds.

Even so, it was only a matter of time before they did succeed in rushing him, and there was still no sign of any British troops. At that moment of Mackenzie's indecision, his friend Craigie—for the second time that Sunday—arrived to help him. His face was blackened with smoke and his uniform torn and soiled. He reported no sign of British troops anywhere. They could not rely on anyone else to save them; they would have to save themselves, and quickly.

They gathered together what clothes they could find, running from room to room in the darkened house, afraid to use any lamps in case the light attracted the mob who were gathering for another charge. Their torches cast big, horrible shadows on the walls as the Europeans gathered up what small belongings they could find. In one room Mackenzie discovered the standards of the regiments and took them along as well.

They left the house by the back door and made for a small stone Hindu shrine which stood behind it, reached by a short flight of steps. It was really a room about ten feet square, with a narrow door at the front and slits in the thick walls like loopholes. The whole place smelt strongly of incense; there were petals on the floor from some offering of flowers. Here the Mackenzies and the Craigies crouched in the darkness, and every now and then one of the troopers, who still stayed loyal, would tap on the door and whisper what news they had gleaned. Their news was of arson and murder only, until, about midnight, one trooper reported that the whole body of mutineers, horse and foot, had marched away to Delhi.

Towards dawn, one of the troopers walked over to the house opposite, which had been the home of the Adjutant. It was just a charred, roofless shell; ashes lay thick on the floor, glowing as the wind blew through the open doorway and the empty, gaping windows.

The trooper found the body of the Adjutant's wife, who had been pregnant. She was terribly mutilated. The man pushed his way back over the hot ashes with the news of her death. Gloom descended on the four people inside the shrine. Mackenzie sent out other troopers to discover what was happening. Their stories only added to the general feeling of dismay and hopelessness.

One man replied that another Englishwoman had put on her *ayah's* clothes and attempted to escape thus disguised as an Indian, but she had been recognized and murdered.

Another young trooper, who had actually been in the same squad at the riding school as Mackenzie, warned him to be ware of his Havildar-Major—the equivalent of a sergeant-major—who was trying to incite the troopers to murder him. Shortly after Mackenzie received this depressing message, the Havildar-Major and two others rode out through the gate into the darkness and were seen no more.

Minutes afterwards, a Hindu bearer employed by Craigie hurried up to the shrine, tapped on the door and explained that "a crowd of *budmashes* was coming in at the gate." He begged for a gun, and they handed him one, primed and loaded.

"Almost immediately afterwards," said Mackenzie later, "we heard a report, followed by yells and groans. In a few moments the bearer returned, and gave us back the gun, saying that he had fired 'into the brown' of the advancing mob and brought one of them down, and the rest had fled."

So the night wore on slowly in hope and prayer and wakefulness. Some time after midnight, when the firing died down and even the shouts and cries from the bazaar seemed more intermittent and more distant, the Craigies and the Mackenzies decided to escape from their shrine. It was so oppressive in the scented darkness that they felt they were almost in a tomb already; better any attempt at freedom than this gloomy incarceration.

They opened the door, went down the steps and then ran

towards the stables. They could find no groom to help them harness Craigie's horses to his carriage, so they did the job themselves, working by feel, without lights, stroking the horses' trembling flanks, murmuring soothing words, for the beasts were terrified after the fearful noises of the night. At last they were ready to chance a dash for freedom.

Mackenzie put his sister and Mrs. Craigie inside with the carabineer and gave them a gun each. At that moment the little native boy, who usually rode postillion and had been too terrified to escape early on, turned up unexpectedly out of the darkness, and they put him on one of the horses and set off.

Craigie and the Colonel rode close in on either side of the carriage with drawn swords, ready to cut down anyone who attacked them.

As they came out of the compound into the road a knot of troopers, "evidently wavering in their intentions," blocked their route. The native boy hesitated and looked at the British officers appealingly for advice. "On our threatening to run him through the body if he did not at once gallop on, he took heart," Mackenzie said afterwards, and at breakneck speed, with the high, unwieldy carriage rocking from side to side on the rutted road, they charged the human road-block. The men scattered. Those who moved too slowly were trampled underfoot.

The carriage turned left where the road lay across a plain, now deserted and cool with the dust laid by the night dew. At the far end they suddenly saw a glimmer of subdued firelight. Mackenzie guessed that this must be a British outpost, and halted his carriage before they came too close, and then rode ahead with Craigie.

"Friend! Friend!" he shouted. "Is there anyone here?"

"Yes," came a voice in English from the darkness. "Who are you?" A man stood up, sword in his hand, the blade glittering like amber in the firelight. He was a British subaltern in command of a gun which was trained up the road towards them and which he admitted he was on the point of firing until he heard their shouts.

So they reached safety—or, rather, an outpost of safety, and their own people. The ladies were at once given shelter by the wife of an English sergeant, and for the rest of the night the officers discussed the ineptitude of the High Command that had done nothing to prevent the massacre or the mutineers leaving for Delhi.

An unexpected error in timing had handicapped the sepoys and saved many British lives. They had chosen to mutiny at six o'clock that evening because they knew the British troops would be in church wearing their side arms and without rifles. But they did not know that on this particular Sunday, because of the increasing heat and the lighter evenings, the parade had been set back half an hour. Thus, instead of having all the British troops unarmed and *inside* the church building, they were still being fallen into their ranks *outside* when the mutineers came galloping across the parade ground from their lines. Those thirty minutes undoubtedly saved the lives of hundreds, but, even so, the British troops had not been put to any use by their senior commanders.

The buglers of the 6oth Rifles had been drawn up at attention in front of their men outside the church, and as they heard the distant firing and saw the columns of black smoke rise from the native quarters and the dust of the racing horsemen, they sounded the "Alarm" and then the "Assembly" on their own initiative.

At once the church parade was cancelled, and the British troops dashed back to their barracks for their rifles and ammunition. The civilian congregation streamed out of the church, some to their homes and others—like Mrs. Rotton and her two children—to the protection of the nearest quarter-guard. She should not have been surprised, for only a quarter of an hour before she left for church, when their carriage was actually waiting at the door, a woman servant had given Mrs. Rotton a warning about those future events.

"Oh, *Mem,* don't go to church this afternoon," she pleaded.

"Why shouldn't we go to church?" Mrs. Rotton asked.

"Because there will be a fight."

"*Who* will fight?" asked the Chaplain.

"The sepoys," said the servant.

Rotton took no notice of the talk; he didn't believe it, anyway, but to appease his wife he said that the children could ride with them in the carriage, instead of staying at home. The woman servant also came along, to look after them during the service.

He laughed away any suggestion that he should take a weapon, but, as a compromise, agreed to carry his walking-stick, which he had bought when he was an undergraduate at Cambridge.

Even as they set out for the church, they heard the distant crackle of musketry and, beyond the palms and sugar cane, dark pillars of smoke rose from burning bungalows in the native lines.

The servant had been right, after all. Rotton sent his wife and children to the safety of the quarter-guard of the 60th Rifles—a Queen's regiment. None of them returned to their bungalow until the small hours, when Meerut seemed deserted and the moonlight on the gutted houses cast grotesque shadows in the soft pale dust.

"Our military authorities were paralysed," said Rotton bitterly. "No one knew what was best to do, and nothing was done. The rebels had it all their own way. . . ."

One of the young British second-lieutenants who was shocked by the events in Meerut on that Sunday was Fred Roberts, later to become famous as Field-Marshal Lord Roberts, V.C. For the rest of his life he believed that "no action, however prompt," on the part of the Meerut Commander could really have arrested the momentum of the mutiny. ("The sepoys had determined to throw off their allegiance to the British Government, and the when and the how were merely questions of time and opportunity.")

Not all the authorities supported this view. Sir John Lawrence, Chief Commissioner for the Punjab, where he resolutely stamped out all signs of revolt, was especially bitter
about the ineptitude of those in authority at Meerut.

Like James Rotton, he blamed the military. He believed
that "the evil caused by General Hewitt's incompetence, and
the delay in marching to Delhi, will be kept for the next fifty
years."

That night General Hewitt and Brigadier Wilson had the
time, the opportunity, and the men to have changed the
course of history. But instead of sending out patrols to find
the Indians and discover their intentions, they indulged in
what a Staff officer called a "lengthened discussion." The
noise and commotion from the native city convinced Hewitt
that sepoys were hiding there, and would eventually come out
and attack them. No one seemed to realize that the mutineers
had no longer any need or wish to do so. They had gained
their initial object of freeing their comrades and were already
miles away, marching towards Delhi, forty miles away.

Because of its 700 years of history as capital of the Moguls
and because an old Mogul King lived on in his palace
within the Red Fort—admittedly as a supposedly harmless
pensioner of the East India Company—Delhi was the natural
focus of their loyalties. Whoever commanded this walled city
could command the respect of all India; psychologically, geographically, and politically, it was the capital of the country.

Thus, while the British troops slept on the barrack square
at Meerut and the flames gradually died down as, one by one,
the bungalows burned themselves out, the mutineers streamed
towards their King and the capital, out across the desert.

In carts and buggies, on horseback, with camels and even
elephants they went; and at each village, people turned out
to cheer them on and to join them.

History was on the move; and up front, in positions of
honour, were the original eighty-five men whose treatment
had been the catalyst for such terrible events.

As they marched, so they shouted and sang; the future was wild with promise and freedom. Behind they had left their chains, a burned-out prison, and their British masters who had been so easily and hopelessly outmanoeuvred.

Ahead were new and greater conquests; and already in the first dawn sunshine of Monday morning, the spires and minarets of Delhi shimmered and shone on the horizon like some vast celestial city—a symbol of the triumphs that would be theirs.

CHAPTER II

Monday in Delhi

DELHI, FAR FROM being a heavenly city, was one where every thought was given to earthly pleasures; in a prim Victorian Empire it remained an anachronistic outpost of sensuality and wealth, the home of the last Mogul, Shah Mohammed Abu Zuphur Saraz-o-dain Mohammed Bahadur, descendant of the Emperor Shah Jehan who had built the Red Fort as his personal palace in the early seventeenth century. Glittering like a ruby, with its great red walls the colour of blood that has dried in the sun, with its turrets and domes and minarets, the Fort dominated Delhi; a city within itself, one of the wonders of the Eastern world.

Shah Jehan had moved his capital to Delhi from Agra, where the climate was too hot and dry for his taste, and the Red Fort, with walls a mile and a half in circumference and 110 feet high where they overlooked the River Jumna, had been built to satisfy the whim of a man whose turbulent character and love of great things are still his best memorials. Unnumbered slaves had toiled for ten years, at a cost of 10 million rupees, to make this fortified palace worthy of the Shah-in-Shah.

It had eight sides of uneven length. Two longer ones faced east and west; the six shorter walls were on the north and south. Round them slaves had dug a ditch 75 feet wide and

30 feet deep. No known engine of war could cross this great moat, for from thousands of loopholes high up on the walls such intrepid folly would be met with a withering fire of muskets; or, at close quarters, siege engines and such older specialties as cauldrons of boiling oil and rocks hurled from catapults would halt the progress of any invader.

The Fort contained royal dwelling places, council chambers, and halls of audience. Through the east wall of the Rang Mahal—the Colour Palace—five windows overlooked the river, and from these windows the Begum, with other princesses of the royal house and any favoured ladies of the harem, could watch the fights that were staged on the sandy ground beneath between elephants and other wild beasts for the amusement of the Shah and his court. The ladies could see without being seen, for to look on the faces of the Mogul women, even by accident, was to ask for disaster.

Like the man for whom it had been built, everything about the Red Fort was rather larger than life. When, in 1648, the great Shah arrived to hold his first Royal Court within its blood-red walls, his son had scattered showers of gold and silver coins over his father's head as a symbol of Mogul wealth and prodigality. The Fort itself was both a better and more abiding symbol of their greatness, for the courtyard was spread with gorgeous Persian carpets and silk curtains; the Emperor sat on a throne that had taken the best craftsmen in his kingdom seven years to build.

This was called the Peacock Throne because it was built round the figures of two peacocks of solid gold "so blended with sapphires, rubies, pearls, emeralds and other valuable stones of appropriate colours," a contemporary description noted with wonder, "that they almost correctly depicted living birds." Twelve emerald pillars supported a canopy of beaten gold studded with pearls. A parrot had been carved out of a single gigantic emerald to amuse the Shah and cause those who saw it to ponder on the wealth and substance of a man who could combine such riches with such taste.

The terrace of the great building that housed this throne was of white marble, its roof crowned with four white marble domes that could be seen from afar off, shimmering in the sunshine.

His palace contained sunken baths with fountains that sprayed rose water and lavender water. Outside the Shah's private apartments sat a Rhapsodist, whose sole job was to tell tales "in a loud voice." The Shah, or King, to use another title, lay on a scented couch behind a thin curtain, listening to his stories of love and bravery. At last the droning of the Rhapsodist's voice soothed him and, alone at the heart of his kingdom, ringed in with moat and walls and the sabres of his fighting men, sleep would come to the Shah-in-Shah.

Such wealth as was concentrated in this palace presented an irresistible invitation to plunderers; and in the 200 years between its building and 1857 there had not been lacking those with envious hearts and armed men who came to sack the riches of the Red Fort. In 1739 the Persian invader, Nadir Shah, carried off the Peacock Throne to Teheran, where the gold was melted down. Twenty years later, the Marathas sacked the palace of what the Persians had left. But still, after each vicissitude, the ruling Shah remained, poorer perhaps, but still a ruler by birth. Although his wealth was diminished, his name was still great and to be feared; and the memories of the glories of Shahs who had gone before were still spoken of, and old men told tales and shook their heads over past times, so that in their hearts it was as though the reigning Shah was still rich and still important. Steamships and trains, missionaries and telegraphs could come and diminish the frontiers of the world, but the Shahs stayed remote and beyond such things. They ruled in a country where time had no meaning; where the word for "yesterday" is the same as that for "tomorrow."

Then in 1803, after defeating the forces of Scindia—the Maratha leader who used French generals to command his men—General Lake entered Delhi and ran up the British flag.

Lord Wellesley, the Governor-General, issued a proclamation in which he described how Lake had found the Shah.

"General Lake was ushered into the royal presence," he announced, "and found the unfortunate and venerable Emperor oppressed by the accumulated calamities of old age and degraded authority, extreme poverty and loss of sight, seated under a small, tattered canopy, the remnant of his royal state, with every external appearance of the misery of his condition. . . ." Thus the sad reality after the years of make-believe.

Wellesley had the idea of supporting the old man, for he was held in immense esteem by both Moslems and Hindus, and he felt that this concession might also help to make English rule more acceptable to the conquered people.

This did not prove to be such a wise move as it had been thought, for the King retained authority within his tiny territory, and he saw to it that this authority did not dwindle.

The Company failed to realize that the more outward semblance of power the King possessed, the more powerful did he appear to be in the eyes of his people. To them he was not a figurehead, supported on sufferance, but a real King whose word was their law, the descendant of the Great Mogul. Thus, when riots occurred in Delhi, the Indians would look to him for protection from the British authorities. Even his coins were struck until 1835, when the Company's rupees superseded them.

At last the Board of Directors of the East India Company had compromised in an impossible stiuation by maintaining the King's royal position, but vesting the administration of revenue and Customs in the British Resident, so that although the King might sound important to his subjects, the British Resident really pulled the strings—and kept watch over the Royal expenditure and income. But officially the Resident could only advise on municipal matters and administration of the revenue.

In the fifty odd years of British rule, the Royal assets had benefited to such an extent that these revenues had risen from about £41,000 to £145,000, and with the rise of wealth there was also a rise of self-esteem on the part of the King.

Although instances of his arrogance were reported to the Company, they would not admit them, for, as Charles Metcalfe, son of a former Resident, Sir Thomas Metcalfe, described their policy, their traditional tendency was to follow "a middle course." This meant, in fact, "to tolerate a double executive authority in the city . . . lest the King's deposition should alarm the whole Mohammedan race in India."

The Kings of Delhi were as turbulent as the climate of their kingdom. Shah Akbar II kept insisting that he be given larger and larger allowances of money to keep him in the style to which his ancestors had been accustomed. Increases were granted—and then he claimed that he should have precedence over the Governor-General.

His successor, Shah Mohammed Abu Zuphur Saraz-o-dain Mohammed Bahadur, who reigned at the time of the Mutiny, was under the thumb of professional pleaders, who fomented litigation and played the law as others play the markets, sharing any profits they could make in the way of damages. They goaded the old King to ask for more money and privileges until many Europeans in Delhi urged that he be removed before he should regain too much power. They feared that he might become a rallying point, a figurehead to attract and weld together Indians of different religions—as, indeed, happened in the Mutiny.

In 1849 the old King's heir-apparent died, and the *Delhi Gazette* "sincerely trusted" that the Government would seize the opportunity to "disperse the family on the death of the King."

This possibility aroused the greatest alarm in the minds of Hindus and Moslems for the proposal was as repugnant to them as it was to the King. Indeed, when he succeeded to the throne in 1837, he had refused a British attempt to obtain his formal renunciation of all claims upon the East India Company. He knew why they wanted him to go, and he was determined they should not have their way; the wealth of his ancestors might not be as it had been, but their strength of will remained.

Inside the red walls of Delhi was a strange world, described as:

> a maze of houses, some of masonry, some of mats, some of mud. The larger houses contained underground rooms, intricate passages, enclosed courtyards, dark and mysterious holes and corners, secret doors and outlets, which communicated from house to house.
>
> Dirt and filth were everywhere . . . rich carpets and dirty mats were side by side on the floors; ivory and silver chairs were covered with filthy rags. . . . Hundreds of young men and women living without occupation and with little to amuse them; hundreds of worn-out old men and women, with nothing to look forward to but the grave. The young were given over to lust, the old to intrigue. . . .

Here was a changed morality, remote from Victorian reforms, a throw-back to the great days of old conquerors, to the ways of Tamburlaine and Genghis Khan.

> Incest, murderings, poisonings, torturings were daily occurrences. . . . Men and women skilled in the preparation of poisons, of drugs to cause unconsciousness, so as to facilitate robbery and incest, throve. . . .
>
> Wrestlers, jesters, dancing-girls who danced naked to inflame the passion of old age, musicians, forgers, swindlers, thieves, receivers of stolen property, distillers of spirits, compounders of sweetmeats and opium. . . . Criminals to escape punishment sought refuge there.
>
> Wives intrigued against wives, harlots against wives, mothers against sons; men and women scoured the country far and wide for beautiful girls to sell as slaves within the palace. . . . Assassinations were frequent and the silent river was close at hand. . . .

At nearly ninety, the last Mogul was past much active part
in these diversions; the fire in his blood had cooled. He was
white-bearded and spent much of his time sitting cross-legged
on his bed or writing couplets on the walls of his chamber on
topics that took his interest. When the Mutiny broke out, he
was moved to rhyme again. He composed what he called a
"Persian couplet," which was highly regarded by the members of his Court.

> *Kuchch Chil-i-Rum Nahin Kya, ya Shah-i-Rus Nahin*
> *Jo Kuchch Kya na sare se, so cartouche ne.*

A rough translation is:

> Not Czar of Russia nor Sultan made the conquest easy
> The only weapon was a cartridge greasy.

His youngest wife, and his favourite Begum Zeenat Mahal,
was worried lest her eighteen-year-old son would not succeed
to the Royal title. The Company, as the Begum knew, had
directed Lord Canning to tell Bahadur Shah that on his death
his family would have to leave Delhi and live a few miles
away, where their influence would be less. His son, however,
would succeed to everything, save that which his mother
wanted for him most of all—the Royal title.

And so, in this strange, scented atmosphere, both physically and psychologically remote from the world, she became
the centre for anti-British intrigue.

Above and below the King's Palace were the "civil lines,"
offices, bungalows, schools, a courthouse and the Darya Ganj,
a European suburb. To the west of the palace was the Bank,
and, north of this, St. James's Church. The north-east wall of
the palace overlooked the River Jumna, which was about
three-quarters of a mile wide, and spanned by a bridge of
boats lashed together, which led out on to the Meerut Road.
The walls round the city were pierced with two main gates,
the Lahore Gate and the Delhi Gate, both 41 feet high and
24 feet wide. Besides these there were six smaller gates.

The King was provided with a ceremonial force of artillery and infantry, under the command of a British officer, Captain Douglas, who was known as the Killadar, the Keeper of the Fort. He had rooms above the Lahore Gate. With Douglas on May 11 was the Chaplain at Delhi, the Rev. M. J. Jennings, and his daughter, with another girl of eighteen, Miss Clifford. Her brother was in the Bengal Civil Service, the Assistant Commissioner at Goorgaon, seventeen miles away.

Jennings had been appointed Chaplain to Delhi in 1852. Two years later he established a mission there, and with two European helpers he had held daily services for Indian Christians, and had even opened a small school for English and Anglo-Indian children. He faced strong opposition from the indigenous religions of Delhi, however; there were already 261 mosques in the city and nearly 200 temples.

The British Resident and Chief Commissioner, Simon Fraser, administered an area of about 800 square miles, with a population of half a million. He was in a most unenviable position because he had no British troops to back him up, should any of his decisions need reinforcing. Only sepoys were garrisoned within the city because it was feared that European troops would "wound the delicate sensibilities" of the King. The authorities felt that by having strong bodies of British troops and artillery at Meerut, only forty miles away, they could cope with any emergency.

Since the city's capture in 1803, Robert Napier, the great surveyor and military engineer of the day, had strengthened the walls prodigiously; it was reasonably believed that none could take the city from without. But there was one overriding weakness to this theory. No one had reckoned that Delhi might be captured from within.

Some time in the early Sunday afternoon, a carriage containing a number of sepoys from Meerut, in their ordinary Indian clothes, arrived in Delhi. Thus, by the Monday morn-

ing, it is likely that the sepoys in Delhi knew what their comrades in Meerut intended to do, and what their part in the
proceedings would be.

No word came to Delhi from General Hewitt regarding
the violence in Meerut on Sunday, but a civilian horseman
galloped on his own across the desert to warn Simon Fraser
of the outbreak.

He arrived exhausted in the late evening and demanded to
see the British Commissioner. Fraser's Indian servant took
the letter from him and went in with it to his master. But the
Commissioner had dined well that night; he was fast asleep
in his chair, head back, legs thrust out. The servant knew the
message was important; no one would ride alone from Meerut at such a time of night unless he had an urgent reason;
and he decided to wake Mr. Fraser so that he could read the
letter at once. But Fraser was a sound sleeper, and had to be
called several times; and then the sudden start into consciousness annoyed him. He was not at all pleased at having
his sleep disturbed with news that a letter awaited him to
read. What did it matter that it *had* been brought by a special messenger? He rebuffed his servant, and, taking the note
from his hand, mechanically put it into his pocket unread.
Straight away he fell asleep again.

His servants were afraid to wake the Commissioner a second time; he was known to have a sharp temper. Thus it
came about that Simon Fraser did not read the letter until
next morning, and although he then did everything he could
do, it was too late to save the city.

Other news had also arrived in Delhi of some unrest at
Meerut, but this was also disregarded. It had come by way
of a new invention that many thought was little more than
a toy and not to be taken too seriously—the electric telegraph.
In 1857, India had only 4,044 miles of telegraph; each mile
did tremendous service during the Mutiny. Telegraph lines
ran between various military stations, and Meerut was con-

nected by wire with the small wooden telegraph bungalow in Delhi.

It was the custom for all telegraph offices to shut on Sun-
days during the heat of the day, between nine in the morning
and four in the afternoon, and just before he closed down on
Sunday morning, William Brendish, the Delhi signaller, heard
that there had been some disturbance at Meerut regarding
the sentences passed on the men of the 3rd Cavalry.

"He was told that eighty men were to be blown away from
guns," a friend recalled afterwards. This was an absurd exag-
geration, of course, but Brendish was not to know, which
made his action in still shutting down his office so promptly
all the more surprising. Had he kept his telegraph office open
for even a little while longer, events might have taken a different course.

When he did open up again at four in the afternoon he
had to report that "communication with Meerut was found
to be interrupted." He assumed the line was broken—a very
frequent failure, for villagers cut it to make bangles for their
wives.

The wire was carried over the River Jumna by a cable, with
a small cable house on each bank, and there was nothing to
do but to follow it and see if he could find a fault or a break.
So Brendish and Pilkington, one of his assistants, a young
man with a withered leg that forced him to wear a surgical
boot, crossed to the far side of the river. They tested the line,
but found the break seemed to be much nearer Meerut. As it
was then evening, they returned, and Mr. Todd, their superior, arranged to go out next morning to find the break and
restore communication.

He set out at eight o'clock on Monday morning in a *gharry*
drawn by two ponies, and was never heard of again. It is possible that he met the first group of the mutineers on their
way to Delhi. Thus two very young men, one a cripple, were
left in charge of the telegraph office.

The local newspaper, the *Delhi Gazette,* used to have mes-

sengers waiting posted there in case news reports came through
from other parts of India, and from one of these men Brendish and Pilkington heard the first news of unrest in the city.
As they had no means of getting in touch with Meerut, they
telegraphed this news, on their own initiative to Amballa,
where there was a British garrison; the office forwarded it to
the Chief Commissioner at Lahore. No official telegraph message was sent by anyone in authority at Delhi all that morning, although the line to Amballa was in perfect order.

Later that morning, some cavalry mutineers from Meerut,
still wearing their best uniforms, with French grey jackets
and light dragoon shakos, rode over the bridge-of-boats and
up to the lower windows of the King's Palace, which overlooked the river.

This was the traditional place for people who had some
personal petition to present to the King, and so, in answer to
their shouts, the old man came to an unglazed window to see
what they wanted.

At the sight of their King, white-haired and frail as he
stood looking down on them, framed in the high window of
his Fort, the sowars raised a tremendous cheer. Their horses
reared up on their hind legs in salute and the cloud of dust
they raised blew past the old man. He wrinkled up his eyes
against it, wondering who these men might be. They did not
seem to be subjects imbued with a fit sense of his authority;
they had none of the meekness usual in men who sought a
boon from him. Something in their noise and strength disturbed him. In some alarm, he sent for Captain Douglas, the
English guard-commander.

News of the arrival of these men from Meerut reached
Brendish and Pilkington in their cable office. At once they
tapped it out along the line to Amballa. As they worked in
their tiny office, they became aware that far more people
seemed to be milling about outside than was usual on a Monday. There were shouts and cries, and steadily the clamour

grew, until it seemed that hundreds must be rushing past their door in a frenzy.

At noon, Brendish pushed his head out to discover the reason for all the activity. He was astonished to see local Indian shopkeepers and stall-holders padding past him with their families, and all carrying as much on their heads as they could balance. Some had *gharries* laden with their possessions and were thrashing the lathered ponies to force them through a mass of frightened, excited people. Everyone seemed to be escaping—but where, and from what?

Suddenly Brendish heard someone calling out to him in English. A British soldier was threading his way through the crowds to reach him. His uniform was half ripped off his body, stained with blood, and slashed in shreds. He seemed half crazed with pain and fear.

"For God's sake, get inside and close your doors!" he gasped. "Close your doors!" And then the pressure of the mob took him and he disappeared, whirled away like a cork on a driving tide.

Brendish and Pilkington realized that the state of affairs in Delhi was far more serious than they had understood; they were unarmed and wanted to abandon their office and reach the Cantonment, where they could be with their fellow countrymen and find out exactly what was happening.

Mrs. Todd, however, still believed that her husband would return, and could not be persuaded to leave until two o'clock. Then, tearfully, she agreed to go with them to seek refuge in the Flagstaff Tower, a four-storey building up near the Cantonment, which was a traditional meeting-place and lookout position for Europeans. Before they left, Brendish tapped out a message to Lahore:

We must leave office. All the bungalows are being burned down by the sepoys of Meerut. We are off. Mr. Todd is dead, we think. He went out this morning and is not yet returned. We learnt that nine Europeans were killed. Good-bye.

They reached the Flagstaff Tower safely and stayed there for the rest of the day. The two men helped the ladies and other non-combatants to load muskets in case the place was attacked. In the afternoon, Brigadier Graves, who commanded the troops on the Ridge near the Cantonment, gave Brendish an escort of sepoys to go back to his office and send a last message to the military authorities at Amballa:

> Cantonments in a state of siege. Mutineers from Meerut, 3rd Cavalry, numbers not known, said to be 150 men. Cut off communications with Meerut. Taken possession of bridge-of-boats. 54th N.I. sent against them, but would not act. Several officers killed or wounded. City in a state of considerable excitement. Troops sent down, but nothing known yet. Further infantry will be forwarded.

Brendish's previous telegram from Delhi reached Lahore early on Tuesday morning. The Chief Commissioner in the Punjab, Sir John Lawrence, was in Rawalpindi, 200 miles away, and so his deputy, Robert Montgomery, had to make his own plans for the emergency. He believed that all four Indian regiments in the cantonment, five miles out of Lahore, were ready to follow the example of the sepoys in Delhi. (*"Sahib,* they are up to *this* in it," a Brahmin clerk assured him, pointing to his own throat.)

Montgomery rode at once to the Brigadier who commanded them and urged that all the sepoys should be immediately forced to give np their gun caps and ammunition. He explained the reasons for this strange request, and the Brigadier agreed to go even further, and to make them surrender their arms as well. This would render them harmless as a military force.

A ball had been arranged for the officers of the European regiment in Lahore that evening and, since to cancel this would only arouse suspicion and rumour, Montgomery agreed that it should go on as arranged. Many officers who danced with their ladies under the punkahs went straight from the ballroom to the parade in the early hours, not even bothering to change. Only a few senior officers knew exactly how the sepoys would be handled, but speed was the essence of the Brigadier's plan.

He drew up the sepoys in front of the British regiment which was to disarm them. Twelve cannon were behind the British and the men stood so close together that they screened the guns from the sepoys.

An officer read out a message from the Brigadier. He praised the sepoys for their past brave conduct, but added that as "an evil spirit seemed to be abroad in the Indian army," it was thought expedient to save them from others—and possibly even from themselves—by taking away their arms.

Even as he spoke, the British marched back smartly between the guns, and the surprised sepoys found themselves staring down the huge black throats of the twelve cannon. British gunners stood by with the portfires already lit, and an officer gave the command: "Eighty-first, *load!*"

The sepoys stirred uneasily, but the ringing of the ramrods as the gunners forced home the charges helped them to decide in favour of obedience; within minutes they surrendered 2,000 muskets and 700 sabres.

That same morning the Indian garrison in the Fort at Lahore was also disarmed, and the capital of the Punjab was safe from mutiny. Not content with this, Montgomery sent messengers to small civil stations over the province urging them to distrust all Hindustani guards, and to stop sepoys' letters passing through the Post Office, in case they were carrying harmful messages. "Whilst acting vigorously and being alive to the great importance of the crisis," one of his orders ran, "I would honestly suggest calmness and quietude. There should be no signs of alarm or excitement. But be prepared to act. . . ."

Later he wrote with some satisfaction, and modestly ignoring his own contribution: "The electric telegraph has saved India."

It had certainly saved the Punjab, but nothing could save Delhi. There was no plan for a proper defence of the city, because everyone expected early British reinforcements from Meerut. Even when Brigadier Graves sent his message to Amballa, he still believed that they would arrive within a few hours, for one of the main reasons for having British troops in Meerut was to safeguard the Delhi magazine.

Graves and his officers kept riding among the Indians who still stayed loyal, trying to persuade them not to join the mutineers in the city. The British regiments would soon arrive, he explained, and then great would be the retribution on those who had deserted. But as the hours passed and the sun began to move down the sky, even Graves had to admit that his optimism was waning.

"It seemed strange, but it *was* possible, that the danger was not apprehended by General Hewitt," he said later. The only explanation he could think of to cover the fact that they had still not been relieved was that Hewitt had no idea of their danger. The sooner he got word to him, the sooner they would be safe.

Since he could not send a message to Meerut by the telegraph, he decided to send one by a personal messenger.

He wrote out a note describing the urgency of their position, and Dr. Batson, the surgeon of the 74th Regiment, who spoke Hindustani fairly well, volunteered to take it to Meerut. He would have no chance of success if he went in uniform on his horse, so he decided to disguise himself as an Indian *fakir* and go on foot. He borrowed a *dhoti*, a long white toga-like garment, blackened his face and hands, rubbed lamp-black into his hair and then, trusting that he was thus adequately disguised, he kissed his wife and children and set off for Meerut in his bare feet.

He had not gone very far before some sepoys saw through his disguise and chased him. ("The colour of his eyes had betrayed him," his Brigadier explained afterwards.) They fired on him and although he was not hit, villagers, seeing him

run, came out against him and robbed him. They stripped
the doctor, and then let him go to wander naked over the
desert, miles from anywhere.

Back in Delhi, however, the fact that Batson was clear of
the cantonment gave a great spurt of confidence to everyone
who had seen him go. They were sure the doctor would succeed in his mission. It would only be a matter of time before
they were saved, and then the mutineers would be taught a
lesson that would never be forgotten. The thought comforted
the Europeans as they huddled together in the Flagstaff Tower
while robbers and renegades from the bazaars joined mutinous sepoys in the welcome work of looting the European
houses in the cantonment.

The rooms of the Tower were not designed for crowds.
The heat was intense, and every now and then some woman
would break into hysterical tears, screaming for an absent
husband or brother. A Mr. Wagentreiber, a civil servant and
one of the survivors of this terrible Monday, afterwards described the Tower as it was when he arrived in the late afternoon:

> We found a large number of ladies and children collected
> in a round room some 18 feet in diameter. Servants, male
> and female, were huddled together with them; many ladies
> were in a fainting condition from extreme heat and nervous
> excitement, and all wore that expression of anxiety so near
> to despair.
> Here were widows mourning their husbands who were
> murdered, sisters weeping over the report of a brother's
> death, and some there were whose husbands were still on
> duty in the midst of disaffected sepoys of whose fate they
> were as yet ignorant. It was a Black Hole in miniature . . .
> and I was glad even to stand in the sun to catch a breath of
> fresh air. . . .

Meanwhile, the King of Delhi was experiencing an unpleasant feeling of alarm. Although the walls of the Red
Fort, where they overlooked the river, were 12 feet thick, he

felt uneasy as he looked out at the gathering mob of sepoys while he waited for Captain Douglas to arrive. About forty troopers were chanting in chorus, and every minute brought others to join them, so that the menacing volume of their voices grew and grew and the hot dust billowed up from the hooves of their restless horses.

"Help, O King!" they shouted. "We pray for assistance in our fight for the faith! Help, O King!"

Some of the leaders were already beating on the iron gates for admission, for the keeper had slammed them shut when he saw the men approaching, not knowing who they were or what they wanted.

As the tumult grew a *chobdar,* a Royal attendant who carried a silver-handled cane to wave before the King and keep the flies away, arrived at a great pace with Captain Douglas. The commotion amazed him and he was for going down among them right away to find out what they wanted and why they were making so much noise. He had heard rumours of unrest in Meerut, but he knew of no trouble in Delhi.

As the two men reached the steps that led up to the King's apartment a sentry *salaamed* and explained that one of the sowars from Meerut wished to speak personally to Captain Douglas.

"We have come from Meerut, where we have killed our officers because they insisted on our using cartridges smeared with the fat of cows and pigs," he explained bluntly. "An attempt has been made to destroy our caste. . . . We have come here as complainants seeking justice from the King. Please advise us what we shall do. . . ."

Douglas stalled for time, falling back on a threat.

"You have committed a great crime in killing your officers," he replied. "Unless you cease at once from bloodshed in the city, you all will be severely punished, as I have four companies of Gurkhas."

The *chobdar* was already showing his impatience, and begged Douglas to hurry; the King was waiting. On and up the stone stairs they rushed and into the presence of Shah Bahadur. He was alarmed for his own safety and that of his family. As a Government pensioner, he pointed out rather petulantly that he should have Government protection, and he wanted to know just what Captain Douglas meant to do about it.

Douglas had no idea, for he had no means of knowing the extent of the disturbance. He had no reason for believing it was anything more than a local religious riot, and he felt he could cope with that. He therefore assured the King blandly that the European troops would soon be following the mutineers and that the authorities had "already taken steps to dispose of these men."

As he spoke, the shouts of the mutineers came up even more loudly, and Douglas called a couple of senior subahdars over to him under the Palace windows and asked what the disturbance was about. They saluted.

"The English tried to make Christians of us, and gave us these cartridges for that object," one explained. "For this reason, we have come to the King for protection, as we have been attacked and some of us killed by the English soldiers."

This reason did not impress Douglas.

"This is under the zenana" (the private apartments of the King) he retorted. "This is not the place for you to make a disturbance. Encamp somewhere on the river-bed and the King will afterwards listen to your complaints."

The men moved off sullenly and Douglas, watching them go, suddenly decided to follow them and reason with them, and try to dissuade them from any further acts of folly.

He started for the stairs, but the old King seized his arm and dragged him back, begging him not to go. As Douglas paused, astonished by the look of terror in the old man's face, the Court Physician, Assan-ullah, added his entreaties to those of Shah Bahadur. For the Captain to go among the troops in the mood they were in would be fatal, he said. They would tear him in pieces.

Douglas looked out again at the growing crowd. Many were waving muskets and swords and clubs. He could hardly hear the King's voice for the shouts of the mob. Reluctantly, Captain Douglas agreed not to go to see the men, but he insisted on going out on to a small parapet, and leant over the edge and shouted down to the sepoys to go away.

"Stop disturbing His Majesty!" he bellowed. "If you've got a petition to make, then present it in the usual manner!"

The only result of this appeal was a great swelling roar of rage. One trooper aimed his musket at the Captain, and fired. A few chips of red granite flew out of the wall above his head. He came back into the King's room, and as he did so a voice shrilled out above all the rest. With a mixture of horror and astonishment Captain Douglas recognized the voice of the Begum, urging the sepoys against their European officers.

About this time, Munshi Jeewan Lal, the accountant of the various pensions that the British Government paid to the King and his family, and also a go-between much used both by Simon Fraser and the king, was preparing to go to Court as usual in his *palki* when his servant told him that some Indian clerks wished to see him.

They urged him on no account to leave the building, as he would never get through the streets in safety. Men had already been murdered, they said. The city gates were closed and the riff-raff of the bazaar were plundering on every side. Jeewan Lal was too experienced a courtier to show surprise at this, but he sent a servant to Captain Douglas in the Fort, asking if he had any orders for him in view of this disturbance. If any decisions had to be made, it was better that others should make them.

The servant soon returned with news that the road to the Palace was blocked by groups of sepoys on every corner. Already the *budmashes* had marked down the houses of the Europeans and the wealthier Indians for looting. The Bank had been broken into and the manager and many others were murdered. The man had heard such fearful screams and wails from others who were being slaughtered that he had fled back to Jeewan Lal, terrified.

"I, too, was terrified," admitted Jeewan Lal, "and my heart almost ceased to beat. I wept to feel how utterly powerless I was. . . ."

He wept with good cause, for even then armed men were advancing on his own house to kill and loot. Jeewan Lal locked every door, sent his family down into the cellars, and, with his servants, prepared to defend himself. But his house was as strong as a small fort—it dated from the time of the Emperor Ferozeshah—and the doors and shutters held firm against the onslaught of the *budmashes* who soon tired of beating on them and went off after easier conquests.

By now Simon Fraser had heard of the mutiny and was out in his buggy on his way to the King. Luckily, he met Captain Douglas, and together they peered through the Commissioner's telescope at burning bungalows in the Cantonment, a mile away, and at reinforcements arriving from the mutineers at Meerut.

As they stood with some other Europeans, five troopers galloped up, firing wildly into the air. One took aim at the little party. Douglas leaped into the ditch beneath the Palace wall, but was hit in the foot. His companions ran for cover towards the Law Courts. Fraser spotted a sentry box and leapt inside. The sentry was still standing there, not knowing which side to take, so Fraser kicked him out, seized his rifle and shot one of the troopers. The rest fled in alarm.

Fraser jumped into his buggy and, abandoning Douglas for the moment, ordered his driver to take him to the Palace. A hail of shots followed him from other sepoys, attracted by the firing, who had rushed up to help their comrades. The little buggy with its frightened, foaming horses cut through the crowds of angry sepoys like some Roman chariot, the driver's whip going up and down on the heads of all those who stood in their way.

At last Fraser reached the Calcutta Gate and summoned the King's agent and ordered him to send two *palkis* for Miss Jennings and Miss Clifford, who were with the Chaplain in Captain Douglas's quarters. Then he asked the King to turn out all his armed men, and the two ceremonial cannon the Palace possessed, to try to stem the revolt while there was yet hope.

The King was still afraid to come too close to his subjects, but from a distance he gave orders that what the Commissioner had said should be done. But, in fact, nothing was done.

Neither the King nor Fraser had the power to make the sepoys carry out the orders. They could do nothing to them if they refused—and the sepoys knew it. So they stood about insolently, enjoying their power, waiting to see what would happen.

Fraser, thinking that the insurrection would soon die now that the King had given orders for his troops to turn out, watched the crowd for any change in their attitude. The crowd also watched him. They saw that his horses were tired, and they closed in on him with sticks and swords and muskets. Too late Fraser saw his danger. He stood up and shouted to his Indian guards to close the gate and load, preparatory to firing. They refused. Streaming with sweat, he shouted at them in an agony of rage and vexation. They stood watching him silently, confident that they were beyond his power to harm. Fraser realized that he could expect nothing from them in their present mood and so drove on to the Lahore Gate. As he jumped from the buggy on to the steps that led up to Captain Douglas's quarters and steadied himself from the leap, two men rushed forward, swords above their heads, and cut him down.

One spiked his head on the end of his sword, and with a

tremendous roar of approval the crowd streamed away behind this bleeding token of a dead authority.

Douglas heard the commotion on the steps, but had no idea what it was. When Fraser had dashed off to the Palace he had not been entirely abandoned. Two orderlies had come to his aid and laid him on a rough litter of long sticks and carried him, hovering on the brink of consciousness from his wound, through the streets and up the stairs to his home. Someone poured out a drink of water for him, and he recovered enough to order that the door and all the windows should be closed.

Hardly had the bolts been shot than there was a tremendous beating on the panels. His servant opened them and let in the Chaplain and his daughter, with Miss Clifford. They had been out to see the cause of the shouting, and had thought it best to return.

At once they set to and bound up the Captain's ankle. He was in fearful pain, and all the while the mutineers outside kept beating on the door and chanting: *"Ja Allah! Ja Allah!"*

Suddenly Douglas realized that he was unarmed; he had dropped his sword at the bastion, and he sent an orderly off to recover it. The stairs down from his rooms were crowded with men, mostly sweetmeat sellers, shouting and spitting betel-nut juice on the walls. When they saw the Captain's Indian orderly they yelled that if he did not open the door for them at once they would kill him as well. The man drew back, but the Chaplain, thinking he could reason with the rabble, told the orderly to open the door again. At once the mutineers had overpowered him and were in the room. Douglas died within seconds. The girls hid in a mahogany wardrobe, but were dragged out and killed. Jennings broke free, seized a sword from someone and charged the mutineers himself, laying about him right and left until he was brought down on the landing with a dozen wounds.

Then the murderers were away, racing barefoot through the streets, glorying in their strength and the feeling that none could stand against them. All houses and shops were closed and bolted, and Indians and Europeans alike crouched in their darkened rooms terrified of the shouts of triumph and agony.

Everyone with a grudge or a desire for gain was making the most of his opportunity. Groups of people ran in different directions, all intent on grabbing what they could find of value, and destroying any symbols of British or Imperial interest while they had the chance.

A swarm of men broke into the Delhi Bank, attacked and massacred the staff, who, although unarmed, put up a brave fight with ledgers and sticks, and then they plundered the safes and vaults.

Mr. Beresford, the manager, took refuge with his wife and family on the roof of some outbuildings. He had grabbed a sword on his way up and his wife was armed with a spear. The looters came up the stairs after them, but the Beresfords had the advantage of height. They let them come as close as they could and struck them down from above. Soon the stairway was jammed with the dead and dying, and the rest retreated. For a moment the Beresfords thought that they had won the day, but their thankfulness was short-lived. The Indians clambered on to the roof of another higher building and from there leapt down with clubs, swords, knives and sticks, and soon, by sheer weight of numbers, overwhelmed the Beresfords and murdered them. Then they set the Bank ablaze.

The offices of the Delhi Press received similar treatment. The Christian compositors were actually setting up in type news of the general disturbance—and even the edition was stamped "*Delhi Gazette* EXTRA"—when they heard the shouts of the mob outside. "It was theirs to record in type that the hand of death was upon them," wrote Kaye and Malleson in their history of the Indian Mutiny. The mob rushed into the office, killed all the compositors they found, and then destroyed the equipment with clubs and poles.

St. James's church in Delhi was a special target for their fury. Men with hammers and axes smashed the monumental slabs on the walls and those that resisted their blows they tore down. Some seized the sacramental plate, and others rushed to the belfry, where they rang a peal in derision and cut the ropes so that the bells crashed on the stones below and splintered.

Everyone looted and destroyed as fast as they could— sacking a shop here, breaking into some locked stronghold there—as though they were working against time. In a sense they were, for they believed that British troops would soon arrive from Meerut, and then retribution would be swift and terrible.

In the Palace, too, this belief prevailed. The two subah-dars who had talked with Douglas now came and sought a private audience with the King. He would not see them, but his Palace Chamberlain did, and they asked for orders for their troops. He did not know how to reply, for he thought the insurrection would be what Jeewan Lal called "a passing thundercloud."

"You have been long accustomed to regular pay under the British rule," he pointed out carefully. "The King has no treasury. How *can* he pay you?"

The subahdars were old enough soldiers not to be put off by this.

"We'll bring the revenue of the whole Empire to your treasury," they assured him smoothly. Unconvinced, the Chamberlain ordered them to produce a return of all their men—which, at least, had the object of getting them out of the way for the time being.

The King thought it wise to show himself, but such was the chaos and the shouting that many urged him to do more than just make a routine appearance. They set him on the back of an elephant and he rode unwillingly through the streets, begging the people to keep quiet and stop their looting.

Angry troopers rode out to meet him on his way back to the Palace. They protested that mutineers in Delhi had seized the treasury for themselves and refused to share the loot with the sepoys from Meerut. Would their King redress this wrong? The old man shook his head. He was distracted, weary, almost ill with the noise and exertion; he could do nothing for anyone. He told his sons (now in charge of regiments) to do something about it and get the soldiery out of the ctiy as soon as they could.

That evening, the subahdars visited the Palace again and complained that there were no rations for their men. This time they saw the King. They claimed to represent thousands of armed mutineers; no one dared refuse them entry to the King's private apartments.

By now familiarity with Royalty was breeding contempt. The subahdars would interrupt the old man rudely as he tried to reason with them and explain that he had no food to feed their forces.

"I say, King," they began; or "I say, you old fellow."

As he turned away wearily, one caught him by the hand. "Listen to *me*," he said, and the other subahdar touched his beard to bring his attention round.

When at last they left him, the old man was almost demented. He had no one to trust, no one who cared what happened.

In desperation he appealed to his servants and asked them what he should do. They suggested he should ride round the city again and show himself to his subjects. And so, almost weeping with exhausiton, he was helped up again on to the back of his elephant and, behind trumpeters and drummers and a mob of sepoys, the old King who was not a King set out again around his tiny Kingdom.

All this while, Brigadier Graves on the Ridge was waiting with increasing impatience for the reinforcements from Meerut. He was sure that even if General Hewitt had not already sent men he would do so as soon as Dr. Batson arrived with his message. He had, of course, no means of knowing that Batson had been intercepted. And although all was now quiet in Meerut, General Hewitt had sent no troops at all to Delhi, preferring to ignore the whole shambles of the previous day, as though by ignoring it he could persuade himself that it had never happened.

Meanwhile, Graves had to control the situation as best he could, so he sent out all but two companies of the 54th Regiment under Colonel Ripley to defend the King's Palace. Behind Ripley came Captain de Tessier with the two other companies and a field battery of Indian gunners and drivers. Graves had no idea that the Palace was already in the hands of the mutineers, and the Colonel led his men down cheerfully to the Kashmir Gate with their band playing. Inside the Gate was a small grass plot, and at the far side a white wood fence with gates leading to St. James's Church in one direction and the treasury, the arsenal, and some bungalows in another.

The guards of the 38th Native Infantry, under Captain Wallace, presented arms as Ripley marched through. The grass and all around it was deserted, but suddenly a detachment of the mutinous 3rd Cavalry from Meerut rode out from the Palace and barred their progress.

The two detachments halted and faced each other, wondering what would happen next. Colonel Ripley ordered his men to load their muskets and fire upon the rebels. Not a man moved.

The mutineers saw their advantage and fired their pistols at the officers of the 54th, killing four with the first volley. At this, the sepoys of the 54th broke ranks and bayoneted their Colonel, who fell from his horse and was stabbed repeatedly as he lay writhing on the ground.

At this moment de Tessier entered the gate at the head of his men and saw the fearful scene with the smoke from the pistols still hanging in the hot noon air. The mutineers fled at the sight of the big guns, taking with them most of the 54th Regiment. Ripley managed to explain what had happened before he lost consciousness, and de Tessier placed his two guns at the main-guard while Wallace galloped back to Brigadier Graves on the Ridge to ask for reinforcements.

Lieutenant Edward Vibart, a nineteen-year-old subaltern with the 54th, ran into the main-guard and found all in confusion. A few mutineers still in their French grey uniforms were galloping back towards the Palace while a British artillery officer, Lieutenant Wilson, tried desperately to wheel a gun round to fire on them, but they disappeared before he could take aim.

No one knew what was happening or what was likely to happen. It was now nearly one o'clock, and the day was at its hottest, so that the ground shimmered with heat and the corpses of the murdered officers were already beginning to swell. Brigadier Graves sent down 150 more men and, to everyone's surprise, 200 men of the 54th who had fled with the mutineers now returned, bringing back the regimental colours.

They explained that the attack had taken them by surprise, and since their muskets were not loaded they could do nothing but flee. But although they were back with protestations of loyalty, they stood about in groups, whispering to each other. One sepoy refused to go on sentry duty when ordered to do so, and when anyone gave orders to the others they went on talking and pretended not to hear.

Someone suggested that the bodies of the dead officers should be sent back to the cantonment, and so they were loaded into a bullock cart, and draped with the only covering that could be found—some ladies' dresses taken from a looted house near the Gate—and sent on their way. By some mischance the cart was abandoned with its grisly load opposite the Flagstaff Tower, where most of the Europeans had gathered, and there it stayed, a fearful reminder of what might happen to them all.

Earlier that day Sir Theo Metcalfe, the joint magistrate, had asked two young officers, Lieutenants George Willoughby and George Forrest, to put two guns on the bridge-of-boats to prevent the mutineers from crossing into the city. They arrived too late, for the mutineers were already marching over in their thousands, headed by a cavalry detachment with pennants flying.

There was nothing anyone could do to stop this advance, and so the officers returned to the magazine, which was manned by Indian troops, closed and barricaded the gates, and prepared to defend themselves against what they were sure would be a fierce attack. Just inside the gate they had two six-pounder guns, double-charged with grape; and one 74-pound howitzer in front of their little office buildings.

The sepoys moved about sullenly and so the officers themselves laid a train to the powder magazine, which they could fire if need be. A British warrant officer near the gates would give the signal by raising his hat as soon as they were rushed, and all expected to die when the magazine went up.

There were no heroics about it; they believed this was their duty, and they meant to carry it out. Even as they discussed their plans, Palace guards were beating on the gates and demanding the magazine should be surrendered in the name of their King.

"To this," Forrest said afterwards, "no reply was made."

An Indian subahdar then announced that the King had promised the mutineers scaling ladders so that they could climb in over the walls, and indeed these arrived within minutes. But instead of the mutineers climbing in, the Indian magazine detachment used them to climb out, and left nine British officers and warrant officers in this huge arsenal on their own. Before they left, the deserting sepoys hid as many ammunition pouches as they could.

As soon as all the Indians were out, the mutineers started to fire on the defenders from the walls. In their excitement, they fired wide, and the nine men replied with every gun they had until they had no more ammunition for cannons or muskets. Forrest was struck in the left hand and the warrant officer, Buckley, in the right arm. It was only a matter of time, Willoughby knew, until they were overcome, and so he gave the order to fire the magazine. Conductor Scully volunteered to light the various powder trains, and in an instant, with an explosion that rocked the city and was heard in Meerut, forty odd miles away, Delhi's arsenal exploded. The great wall around it was blown flat and hundreds of mutineers were buried, but out of the reeking ruins, blackened, with hair singed and their uniforms almost blasted off their bodies, Willoughby and Forrest reached the safety of the Kashmir Gate together, and, after them, some of their comrades.

In the Kashmir Gate all was already confusion. Brigadier Graves had sent down two more guns and then recalled them, but on the way back to the Ridge the mutineers attacked the battery and overcame it and discharged a volley into a great group of officers and civilians who had gathered at the gate. Men were falling, horses rearing up, women screaming and no one knew who was friend or enemy, for every bayonet was bare and every man was for himself.

Suddenly Vibart realized with the horrible clarity that comes to men hard-pressed that within seconds he would be murdered if he stayed where he was, and in an extremity of fear he fled up the ramp that led from the courtyard of the Gate to the bastion above it.

"Everyone appeared to be doing the same," he said later. "Twice I was knocked over as we all frantically rushed up the slope, the bullets whistling past us like hail and flattening themselves against the parapet with a frightful hiss."

As they reached the embrasures of the bastion, they heard cries of "Help!" from some English women who had taken shelter in an officer's quarters up there. Mrs. Forrest, whose husband was even then arriving from the magazine, was with her two young daughters; she had been shot in the shoulder.

Vibart and the rest pulled them out and at once a gun down in the courtyard fired at them and a roundshot passed within feet of their heads, "expediting our movements in no small degree," as he dryly remarked afterwards.

The officers fastened their sword-belts together and used them as a rope to climb down into the ditch 25 feet below. Some stayed on top and handed down the women while others below caught them as they fell. One very stout old lady, Mrs. Forster, started to scream and refused to jump, but at that moment the gun in the courtyard fired again, covering them with splinters from the wall. Someone gave her a shove from behind and she fell headlong into the ditch.

Now they faced the ascent of the almost perpendicular counterscarp. This was a fearful task. Behind them, on the parapets, sepoys were potting at them for the fun of it. Time and again they reached the top, and then the earth crumbled under their hands and knees and they would roll all the way down to the bottom, but at last, bleeding and covered with dust, they staggered out and took shelter in a patch of thick shrubbery.

They wanted to wait until dusk, but already search-parties were out, and when they heard Indian voices, they decided to run for it. Mrs. Forster had been struck by a spent bullet, and she was also suffering from the effects of her jump into the ditch, and staggered about blindly from side to side. They tried to carry her, but her weight was so enormous and the belt of brushwood through which they were passing so thick, that eventually they could carry her no more, and abandoned her and fled on themselves. Vibart felt guilty about this, but assured himself that she would die anyway and was already long past human aid.

In the distance they could see the edge of the wonderful 1,000-acre park round Metcalfe's house, and decided to reach his house and shelter there. But to their horror they found that some sepoys were apparently tracking them and so they stumbled off again into the bushes, forcing themselves through the mango swamps and past the prickly jungle trees that lacerated them with thorns.

By this time the short Indian dusk was closing in, and quite unexpectedly they found that they were opposite the back door of Metcalfe's house; they must have been running in a circle.

Some Indians—a few servants who had not yet fled—led them down into a cellar, and by the light of candles they drank some bottles of beer and rested for three hours. Then the servants warned them that mutineers were on their way to plunder the house, and so wearily they roused themselves and staggered out again.

To their horror, they saw that the entire Cantonment was ablaze, and clear on the evening wind came hoarse shouts from the looters and the boom of cannon and the sharp rattle of musketry.

"It appeared to us to matter very little whether we remained or not," Vibart wrote afterwards. "Either way we were sure to be captured, and I don't suppose there was one amongst our little party who expected to live through that terrible night. . . ."

Before they left, they filled their pockets with bread and meat, and someone carried a water-bottle. A couple of miles away they halted and the sky flared up behind them; Metcalfe's house was already on fire. On through the swamps and the stubble-fields they trudged, blistered, scratched, fainting with exhaustion, but still determined not to give up.

Just before dawn they sank down wearily and tried to sleep, but someone spotted ten mutineers approaching them on ponies on their way to Delhi from Meerut, and so up they started again and fled out into the desert.

By noon next day they reached the banks of a wide tributary of the Jumna River and waded through it. On the far bank they rested and dried their scraps of bread and meat in the sun. Mrs. Forrest was in a terrible way; her husband had been injured from the recoil of a howitzer during the defence of a magazine as well as being wounded in the hand, and he begged them to leave him where he was, so that he could die in peace. Vibart and Salkeld, another young officer, refused, and they went on to a water-hole.

Wilson and Salkeld went off on a scouting expedition and returned at speed, pursued by a number of half-naked villagers, armed with spears and lathis. Despite their appearance, these men were not unfriendly and promised to provide some ponies for them. In return for this, all the Europeans surrendered their valuables and loose coinage, but no ponies appeared.

They realized that they had been tricked, and so set off again in the direction of Meerut. To their surprise, four Indians followed them and offered to guide them, but instead took the bedraggled party on a long detour on the pretext of avoiding robbers in the villages. Vibart soon realized that they were really hoping to lead them back to the mutineers and refused to go any farther with them. ("Seeing we were not to be taken in, they hastily fled.")

Farther on some other villagers gave them milk and *chapatties,* but would not let them stay within their boundaries in case the mutineers should find them.

Then, on the burning midday plain, blinded and suffocating with the scorching dust, they met the worst hazard of the journey: a gang of *goojurs*—roving robbers who lived on what they could steal. The men in the little party stood back to back to defend themselves, but were disarmed within seconds and robbed of studs, watches, and even the clothes off their backs. The *goojurs* let them go in their underwear and on again they trudged. Half a mile up the road another gang of *goojurs* attacked them. There was nothing left to steal, save the gilt buttons off a frock coat that one man had been allowed to keep.

But, when all seemed lost, a messenger arrived from a small village which had a German headman, a Mr. Cohen, who offered them hospitality. He had heard of their sufferings, and they reached his village at eight next morning; he gave them tea and clean clothes and a chance of a wash. He had gone quite native and could scarcely speak his old language, and was delighted to be able to help Europeans.

Cohen agreed to let them stay in his village while he sent a messenger to Meerut to ask for an escort. No one had a pen to write with, so one of the lieutenants, Gambier, made a rough nib from a piece of stick and wrote the letter in French in case it fell into the hands of the mutineers.

The letter reached Meerut safely. It was handed in to General Hewitt as he sat at dinner, but rather than be bothered with such a communication he threw it on the floor. Lieutenant Mackenzie, who had already had a narrow escape in Meerut, picked it up and read it, and on his own initiative set out with Hugh Gough in bullock-carts to bring in these weary survivors of a Monday in Delhi.

The Europeans who had stayed in Delhi fared much worse. Fifty were dragged from their houses and marched through the streets to the Palace, where they were huddled in a cellar without a window. For several days they were kept thus, and then the guards opened the door and assured them that they would be moved to "a better place." They staggered out into the hot sunshine and at once sepoys ran a long rope all round them so that they were held as in a giant lasso. A few of the troopers began to shoot at them with carbines and pistols, while a crowd gathered to watch this massacre of the Christians. One bullet, unfortunately, hit one of the King's retainers, and this angered everyone so much that the sepoys unsheathed their swords and killed forty-nine of the Europeans. One woman escaped—by calling out that she wished to become a Moslem. She kept her word.

By nightfall on Monday, when the expected reinforcements from Meerut had still not arrived, Brigadier Graves fell back with his men on the Flagstaff Tower, which provided a natural rallying point. It was an impossible position to defend, however, and soon the whole British force was in retreat. By carriage, bullock-cart, on horseback, and on foot, they moved off sadly towards Kurnaul and Amballa and Meerut.

A previous Governor-General of India, Lord Amherst— who died in the year of the Mutiny—had instituted the custom of escape from the sweating heat of Calcutta in the hot season, and spent this time in the hills of Simla. Subsequent Governor-Generals and Commanders-in-Chief had followed his example.

In 1857, General Anson, the Commander-in-Chief, with the Adjutant-General and their whole headquarters staff, had left for Simla by leisurely stages in March, inspecting units on the way. Thus, at the time of the Mutiny, Lord Canning, the Governor-General, who was still in Calcutta, was separated by 900 miles from his military commander. From this stemmed some of the worst disasters.

The situation was made more serious because the telegraph line had not been laid to Simla, and the nearest telegraph office was at Amballa, fifty miles away. General Sir Henry Barnard, who had come to India from the Crimea, commanded a division which had its headquarters in this town. His son, a Captain, was with him as an A.D.C., and to give the young man something to do he would send him out on horseback to the telegraph office every morning to see whether there were any messages for him.

On Wednesday there were two: the telegrams Brendish had flashed from Delhi on Monday before he left his office for the safety of the Flagstaff Tower. Sir Henry read them, and the news was of such urgency that at once he sent his son galloping to Simla to inform General Anson. On his way, the young man called on the Commanding Officer of the British 75th Foot at Kasauli and ordered him to be ready to march at short notice.

This initiative was lost in Simla, for Anson was entertaining some friends to dinner, and did not wish to be disturbed by Army matters. His wife was in England and the wife of one of the senior officers in Simla was acting as *burra mem,* or official hostess. Anson was half-way through dinner with about twenty-five guests when the telegrams arrived. Out of deference to his guests, he did not read them, but put the envelope under his plate, and then, when the party was over and he was alone in the wide, candle-lit room, the Hon. George Anson opened the envelope. Thus, pleasantly full of wine and memories of good table-talk, the Commander-in-Chief of the Bengal Army learned the terrible news that his army had mutinied and marched on Delhi.

Anson was a great authority on whist and horses and a considerable lion in London society—so much so, indeed, that his acceptance of the Meerut Division four years earlier had surprised his friends. India was not considered a very fashionable place for service. For two of his four years in India he had been C.-in-C. and, with forty-three years in the Army, he liked to tell people how he had been an ensign at the Battle of Waterloo. He did not usually add that he had seen no active service since that date.

As with many officers of the time, he had no experience of dealing with emergencies; and, of course, no one anticipated action occurring within the Indian borders. The whole defence of the country, such as it was, had been based on the possibility of attacks on her frontiers, and so ammunition and ordnance depots were hundreds of miles away in the north-west.

Although work on a railway system had begun, by the outbreak in May only a few hundred miles of line had been laid and the main means of moving military stores was still by river or in a convoy af carts, called a "train."

Troops marched or went in boats or by bullock-carts. Heavy guns were drawn by elephants; officers were allowed two camels each to carry their kit. The distances were enormous, measured by "marches"—the distance a regiment could march in a night, for the day was considered too hot for travel.

Anson's first need was for transport to take men and munitions down to Delhi, and here he faced the greatest obstacle to any urgent undertaking in the East: the Oriental outlook. It was almost impossible to impress upon Indians that speed could ever be essential.

A few years before the Mutiny, an Army scheme for proper Transport Establishments to move troops and equipment in just such an emergency had been abandoned for economy. In place of this efficient organization, the old Mogul system of having a native bazaar to supply the Army was brought back. When a commander wished to move his troops, he would order the quartermaster to call in local Indian contractors. In their turn, they would round up as much grain, or meat, or as many bullock-carts or elephants as might be needed.

This arrangement had the great advantage of cheapness in Governmental eyes. It had the equally great disadvantage of being almost unworkable.

To move a division required several thousand bullocks, which had to be fed, watered, and looked after. If they died on the march, others had to be seized from villages; and if the villagers wisely concealed their beasts, knowing they were irreplaceable, then the troops had to pull the guns themselves. (This happened when the Naval Brigade marched to Cawnpore.) The needs of the camp followers—grooms, *khitmutgars, bhisties* (water-carriers), sweepers, and the like —had also to be considered. These men travelled with the Army and brought along their families and all their relations, so that a force of 1,000 British fighting men would always have at least as many hangers-on, who had to be fed, clothed, paid, sheltered, and cared for if they fell sick.

This unwieldy column of march was often more than a mile long, and in camp covered an enormous area which was difficult to defend from snipers or guerrillas.

Then the carts that Anson needed were in daily use around Amballa for carrying grain or vegetables, and their owners were understandably unwilling to see them go. Many were dismantled or hidden, or even buried, rather than have them removed to help the Army. Anson's efforts in organizing transport were further impeded because it was the custom for the cavalry to help with this task before a march. But since most of the cavalry regiments were on the side of the mutineers, either actively or in spirit, they could not be trusted.

All these problems weighed on Anson's mind, and behind him, spurring him on by letters and telegraphs from Rawalpindi, was Sir John Lawrence, the Chief Commissioner in the Punjab, who, better than almost any other European, knew the immense importance of coping with the emergency with speed and decision.

On 15 May, the day that Anson reached Amballa from Simla, Lawrence wrote to the Chairman of the Board of Directors in London his own assessment of the situation:

> This seems to me the greatest crisis which has as yet occurred in India, and it will require great good management to weather the storm.
>
> I must strongly urge that a large body of European infantry be despatched to India as soon as may be possible. After what has occurred, it would be the extreme of fatuity not to strengthen ourselves in this way. . . .

Two days later, Anson wrote to Lawrence: "The whole of the army (native) may be said to be in a state of mutiny. None are to be depended upon. . . . It was, and is, impossible to move for want of tents, etc."

In Amballa, General Barnard was much put out because the 75th Foot and both regiments of the Bengal Fusiliers had arrived with at most twenty rounds a man, and nothing in reserve. They had no tents, and many of the gun limbers were empty of ammunition; others had no beasts to draw them. Both Anson and Barnard knew the importance of marching to Delhi, but they agreed that their forces were just not strong enough to capture it. Nevertheless, they decided to march, and Hewitt, in Meerut, was ordered to send troops to join them.

Anson, irritated by Lawrence's insistence on speed, telegraphed him that the only guns at Amballa were 6- or 9-pounders; that they could not get transport in less than sixteen to twenty days, and that they could not depend on any of the three native regiments in Amballa.

Lawrence suffered dreadfully from neuralgia, and this news irritated him intensely, for he was already in considerable physical pain and under great mental stress with his own difficulties in the Punjab.

> Your Excellency remarks that we must "carefully collect our resources" [he replied bitingly]. But what *are* these resources but our European soldiers, our guns, and our material? These are all ready to hand, and only require to be handled wisely and vigorously to produce great results. . . .
>
> Pray only reflect on the whole history of India. Where have we failed when we acted vigorously? Where have we succeeded when guided by timid counsels? Clive with twelve hundred men fought at Plassey, in opposition to the advice of his leading officers, beat forty thousand men and conquered Bengal. . . .
>
> I cannot comprehend what the Commissariat can mean by requiring from sixteen to twenty days to procure provisions! I am persuaded that all you can require to take with you must be procurable in two or three! . . .

It was one thing to talk, however, and another thing to deal with the problems as they were. No sooner were the British assembled than all the bullocks and camels that had brought them down from the hills had to return there to carry their baggage.

In the middle of his worries, Anson sent for a young officer, William Stephen Raikes Hodson, appointed him

Assistant Quartermaster-General on his personal staff, and
ordered him to raise and command an entire new regiment
of irregular horse to march on Delhi. The move was sound,
for Hodson was of all irregulars the most irregular, and of
all officers in the Mutiny he was to become the most controversial and the most discussed.

He was a tall man, in his mid-thirties, with very pale blond
hair. He had been at Rugby—where he was a contemporary
of Thomas Hughes—and at Cambridge; and was now married to a widow rather older than himself who had a son by
her previous marriage.

Hodson was a man of Lawrence's stamp—although he did
not like Lawrence. He worshipped action and was given to
quick decisions which often offended others. Once, in the
mess, he noticed that another officer had a bottle of French
liqueur on the table and asked to see it. The officer handed
it over and Hodson calmly called a servant and told him to
take it away and empty the bottle outside.

"I can't allow you to drink such unwholesome stuff," he
told the frenzied owner quietly.

Then he was notoriously careless about money, and confused his own accounts with those of the regiment. One day
a brother officer returned from leave unexpectedly and asked
for his own back pay. Hodson exclaimed casually that he had
spent it himself.

He acted as he saw fit, without reference to his superiors.
For instance, he took a sudden and irrational dislike to
Pathans and discharged many of them from his regiment
without even giving them their arrears of pay. Another time,
when his regiment was short of a baker, Hodson arranged
for an Indian baker to be kidnapped—and the poor man
stayed with that regiment for some years!

Eventually, Hodson faced a court martial owing to irregu-
larity in a regimental account, and he was suspended from
commanding his regiment, the Guides, while further charges
of ill-treating an Indian were investigated.

He was cleared in February 1856, but thirteen months later—in March of the Mutiny year—he discovered that this vindication had never been forwarded to the C.-in-C. or to anyone else. It had been filed away in some desk and quietly forgotten.

His annoyance was increased when he was refused a request to join the expeditionary force in Persia, on the grounds of his previous conduct. On the spur of the injustice, he went to Simla and personally explained things to the C.-in-C.

"There were clearly three courses open to me," he wrote to his wife. "First, suicide. Second, to resign the service in disgust and join the enemy. Third, to make the Governor-General eat his words and apologize. I chose the last. The first was too melodramatic and foreign. The second would have been a triumph of my foes in the Punjab; besides, the enemy might have been beaten. . . .!"

He told Anson of his intention to see Lord Canning in Calcutta, and Anson approved, and liked this enthusiastic officer who had such a strong and vigorous personality. Less than a week later, the Mutiny broke out in Meerut, and Hodson found his chance and seized it. Within a few months, his new regiment was famous as Hodson's Horse, a name by which it is still proud to be remembered.

On 24 May Anson set out on his first day's march; it was also his last. Next morning he fell ill. Sir Henry Barnard rode into Kurnaul, where the column had halted, at midnight, and reached Anson's tent just in time to hear him whisper: "Barnard, I leave you commanding. You know how anxious I was to do my duty. I cannot recover. May success attend you. God bless you. Good-bye."

Anson died of cholera, but the unkind persisted in saying that what had really killed him was "an attack of John Lawrence."

Barnard set off at once for Delhi, and by 5 June he had reached Alipore, twelve miles from the city. Here he halted

while a siege train from the arsenal at Phillour and Brigadier
Wilson's forces from Meerut joined him. Hewitt would not
come. He did not like to leave Meerut, where, although the
danger was really past, all the ladies were shut up in one
barracks, while their husbands slept in another and rarely
went out beyond the sentries they had posted outside.

Barnard's march to Delhi had been a tremendous achievement. The nights were close and sultry and the hot, dry
wind of the plains lifted the dust and blew it in their faces.
Heads down against this driving grit, the leading company
would sing as they marched, and the others would take up
the tune behind them. Every hour they halted for five minutes and threw themselves down on the warm sand and at
once were asleep.

Then, footsore, with faces cracked with dried sweat, they
set off again, up to their ankles in sand, but never breaking
ranks. Many fell asleep as they marched and lumbered against
others, so that sometimes they appeared like an army of
zombies, marching out of darkness into darkness. And behind them, miles away, the baggage trains came on more
slowly, catching up with them when they halted, and then
losing them as they began to march.

Years later, one officer recalled that journey and, in remembering it, was back with the marching men:

> The stars were bright in the dark deep sky and the fire-
> flies flashed from bush to bush [he wrote].
> Along the road came the heavy roll of the guns, mixed
> with the jangling of bits and the clanking of the steel scab-
> bards of the cavalry; the infantry marched behind with a
> deep, dull tread; camels and bullock-carts, with innumer-
> able *sutlers* and camp servants, toiled along for miles in the
> rear; while gigantic elephants stalked over bush and stone by
> the side of the road. . . .

On 7 June Brigadier Wilson's men met and routed a large
force of mutineers at Budli-ka-Serai, a suburb about seven

miles out of Delhi. From then on the column had no serious
resistance until they reached the Ridge.

It was a strange sensation to be so near Delhi at last, and
yet to be so far away.

They were so close to the walls of the Red Fort that they
could see the dark, stripped bodies of the mutineer gunners,
shining with sweat as they sponged and fired their guns.

They were still so far away from their intention of captur-
ing the city that four months would pass and nearly two-
thirds of their number die before it could be accomplished.

CHAPTER III

Reasons for Unrest

ONE OF THE PECULIARITIES of the English national character that perplexes foreigners—and occasionally enrages them—is an initial inability to believe that bad news from overseas can possibly affect them in any way. Then, belatedly, they demand the fiercest action, regardless of whether such a course is wise or even possible. This trait was much in evidence in England during the Indian Mutiny.

On 23 June, when the Mutiny was already nearly seven weeks old, when thousands on both sides had been killed, and the whole foundations of the Empire in India were shaken, a group of "noblemen and gentlemen" met at Willis's Rooms, St. James's Street, London—now the site of Government offices—to honour the memory of Clive, as "the Founder of the British Empire in the East." The day was the centenary of one of his greatest victories, the Battle of Plassey, which had won Bengal for the British East India Company in the space of a single afternoon, and at a cost of only twenty-three killed and nineteen wounded. They drew comparisons between the genius of Clive and the present administration in India. One gentleman, Mr. Campbell Robertson, was reported by *The Times* as stating "that the late defection in the Indian Army was caused by a departure from the principles laid down by Lord Clive, which was to treat the sepoys, not with severity, but with kindness."

This statement crystallized two misconceptions that were widely held in England at that time. The first was that the Mutiny was an unimportant affair that had already been dealt with; "a late defection." But even as Mr. Robertson was speaking, thousands of mutineers in Delhi were marking the centenary of Plassey in their own way, by opening a ferocious attack on the British and loyal Indian troops who faced them.

The second misconception, equally widely believed in Victorian England, was that Clive—and most of the other British officers associated with India—were kind to those under their command and popular with them. With some honourable exceptions, these men used their years in India to enrich themselves at the expense of that country, a short-sighted policy of plunder which, between then and now, has proved most expensive to Britain and the British reputation abroad.

Only eight years after Plassey, Clive himself declared sadly: "Alas, how is the English name sunk! I could not avoid paying the tribute of a few tears to the departed and lost fame of the British nation, irrevocably so, I fear!" Nine years later, afflicted with sleeplessness and weary in body and mind, he killed himself by cutting his throat with a penknife.

The English had lost their good name in India largely through their greed, and the tremendous temptations to which they succumbed. They were so far removed from home authority that almost any act of plunder could go unpunished, and during the 200 years preceding the Mutiny men of the highest calibre in England's cool climate acted with undisguised self-interest and avarice in India.

The British colonizers and traders in India were in much the same position geographically and politically as colonizers now might be on the moon. They were separated by an immense gulf of time and distance from London; they were out on their own, forced to make their own decisions and trust their own judgment. Advice or aid could be asked for from England, but took weeks to arrive, and so was scarcely worth seeking. By the time it came, the crisis had resolved itself. The prizes were great, but so were the risks.

The "defection" in 1857 was the first clash on a national scale in a battle that has run on ever since, spreading across oceans from India to Africa, to America, and then back East again: the growing rift of hatred between white and coloured peoples. Although the Mutiny was essentially a military uprising, it was the first tentative stirring of hidden, gigantic forces, not yet quite sure of themselves, but feeling for the first time their strength and a sense of unalterable destiny and the numbering of days. The seeds of a last discord were being planted, and would not be uprooted.

During the first few weeks of this outbreak, however, little more interest was shown in it in England generally than had been expressed by Mr. Robertson. Even in India its significance was not fully realized. Only a few weeks before it began, for instance, a Bombay newspaper had congratulated itself that India was quiet "throughout."

And in the autumn, when the Mutiny was five months old and nearing its end in a welter of slaughter and bitterness, a district officer in Kumaon wrote to the North-West Provinces Government complaining that he had no reply to a letter sent in May. He suggested that this dilatoriness might be due to "the late disturbance in the plains."

London, being further divided by time, distance, and interest from the scene of events, was even less concerned. And although a few evenings after the meeting in Willis's Rooms there was some casual, desultory discussion in Parliament about the "doubtful news" from India, it was all very far away, and no one appeared greatly troubled.

Things would resolve themselves; so much else of more interest was happening nearer at hand. The transportation of convicts to Australia was ending; the Princess Royal was about to marry Prince Frederick William of Prussia; the great new liner, *Leviathan,* was to be launched; and runaway

Above, the Delhi Gate, and, *below,* the Lahore Gate—two of the main gates that led into the Red Fort, home of the aged King of Delhi, and a natural, geographical and psychological rallying-point for the mutineers.

The face of a famous soldier: Fred Roberts, as a subaltern in his early twenties. He served at Meerut, then at Delhi; later was warded the V.C.; died a Field Marshall.

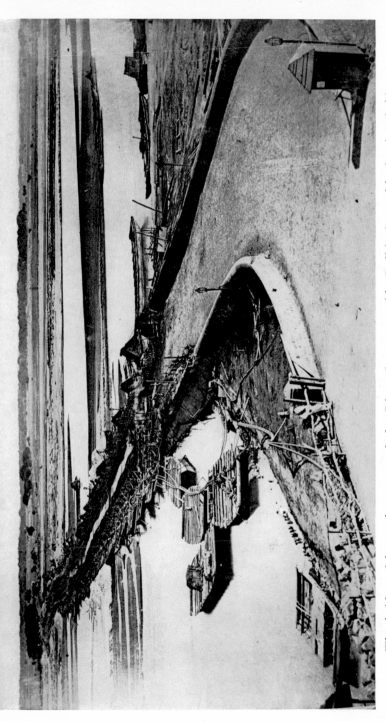

The bridge of boats that spanned the River Jumna outside Delhi. Over this floating bridge the mutineers poured from all parts of India, watched through telescopes by the besieging Delhi Force.

Beneath this tree in the courtyard of the Red Fort, many captured European civilians were slaughtered. One woman saved her life by becoming a Moslem. See page 84. *Below:* The Delhi Bank after the mob had fired the building. The manager and his wife put up a great defence until they were overpowered. See page 74.

Two contemporary sketches show: *above:* the Subzi Mundi, the vegetable market—a suburb of Delhi and scene of some of the fiercest fighting of the Siege; and *below:* a panoramic view of part of the Red Fort and the domes of the Jumma Musjid, the greatest mosque in Delhi, as seen from the Flagstaff Tower. See page 138.

Above: British gunners prepare to march off, watched by idlers on the walls. Behind them is the Jumma Musjid mosque. *Below:* A mosque near the Custom House battery, showing damage done by artillery fire.

Above: After the Siege. Metcalfe's House, for long a landmark, and famous for its library, was only a burned-out shell. *Below:* In this alley British troops fell back under a withering fire from the defenders of Delhi. Brigadier Nicholson rallied them, but fell fatally wounded.

Two of the strongest personalities in India at the time. *Above:* Major William Hodson, whose precipitate killing of the sons of the old King of Delhi raised a storm of controversy. *Below:* Brigadier John Nicholson, stern, implacable, unwearying, who was mortally wounded in the assault on Delhi.

marriages on the blacksmith's anvil at Gretna Green had
been stopped by law. Everywhere, so politicians were sure,
Britain's standing and good name and prosperity were on
the increase; it was going to be a wonderful summer.

Talk of mutiny by distant native levies was something
no one wished to credit or even consider. The world was
still a big place; this matter could be put on one side until
a more convenient time.

Then reports of atrocities began to arrive and were printed
in the newspapers. There were stories of children being
tossed in the air and caught upon bayonets, of slices of flesh
being cut from the bodies of babies and forced into the
mothers' mouths; of English mothers and wives driven naked
through the streets.

Slowly the shadow of distant blood darkened that brilliant London Season. Dowagers, débutantes and their escorts
had some strange facts to consider at their soirées in the big
houses along the Bayswater Road. A brief hiatus of disbelief
greeted such reports, and then, with alarming and unexpected
suddenness, the pendulum of public opinion swung to its
other extreme, and the call was for vengeance, instant, swift,
and red, on all Indians; for troops to avenge the white population; for savage reprisals.

Towards the end of the Mutiny, Lord Canning, the
Governor-General, wrote to Queen Victoria about the "rabid
and indiscriminate vindictiveness" of the Europeans in India.

". . . Not one man in ten seems to think that the hanging
and shooting of 40,000 or 50,000 men can be otherwise than
practicable and right," he reported in amazement, for his
own hatred of such violence earned him the nickname of
"Clemency" Canning.

Queen Victoria agreed with him: ". . . Lord Canning will
easily believe how entirely the Queen shares his feelings of
sorrow and indignation at the un-Christian spirit shown also
to a great extent here by the public towards India in
general. . . ."

It was noticed that those Europeans in the safest places and least exposed to Indians of any kind—those up in the hill stations and in towns with British garrisons—were loudest in their denunciations of atrocities by mutinous sepoys.

But the feeling was infectious. Even Robert Montgomery, the Lieutenant-Governor of the Punjab, and a cool and usually detached administrator, could write to Major Hodson after the capture of Delhi: "All honour to you (and to your "Horse") for catching the King and slaying his sons. I hope you will bag many more!" Sir Robert was a leading advocate of the propagation of Christianity in India; he had been nicknamed "Pickwick" because of his benevolence.

William Russell, the correspondent for *The Times,* noted in his diary how British forces had burned Indian villages with all their inhabitants, in revenge for earlier Indian atrocities. As a more refined torture, Mohammedans—who abhor the pig—were even sewn up in pig-skins and daubed with pork lard before they were killed.

This sudden synthetic hate, even worse in Britain than in India, was aroused in vain, for although there was much bloodshed and bitterness in the Mutiny, with even more fear and folly, no records remain of calculated Indian atrocities, such as were so freely talked about at the time. Indeed, after the Mutiny, Sir William Muir, head of the Intelligence Department of the Government of the North-West Provinces, submitted a memorandum to Lord Canning on an enquiry that had been made about the tales of horror that caused such feelings in England. He reported that "the stories of dishonour done to European females are generally false. . . . The colour . . . is repugnant to the Oriental taste. . . . Dishonour was done not to gratify passion, but to inflict shame and degradation upon the English name." There was, however, "cold and heartless bloodthirstiness at the farthest remove from the lust of desire."

But since stories of such happenings would probably be referred to by the average Englishman of the day as "too horrible to mention"—a description that frequently occurs in the contemporary accounts—the Victorian mind would leap unfailingly to one conclusion.

Mr. C. B. Thornhill, the Officiating Secretary to the Government, submitted further reasons for disbelieving some of the wilder tales of rape and complicated sexual assaults.

"We all know that Hindoos would regard connection with a Christian as involving loss of caste," he wrote. "The feelings of Mohammedans would lead them to veil such an act with closest secrecy. . . ."

Most of these tales of horror were hearsay, built on rumour; falsehoods carried on the winds of fear. But they had one good result; they made the British public aware that all was not well in the distant land ruled by the Honourable East India Company.

And as soon as the seriousness of the Mutiny was appreciated, reasons for the outbreak were sought. There were many causes, but at the time the public was in no mood to find them. They wanted a quick answer to the question: Why did it happen?

The Mutiny was no hasty thing touched off spontaneously by the celebrated incident of issuing cartridges to sepoys who believed that they were greased with cow's fat and pig's lard. This was a link in the chain of events, but certainly not the most important. It caught the imagination of the public of the day, however, and by its acceptance they were relieved of any obligation to dig deeper for the roots of the trouble. The roots of unrest in India were deep indeed, and could be traced back over the years to 1600, when the East India Company was formed.

"The causes and motives for sedition," so Bacon had decided, "are innovations in religion, taxes, alterations of laws and customs, breaking of privileges, general oppression, advancement of unworthy persons, strangers, deaths, disbanded soldiers, factions grown desperate, and whatsoever in offending people joineth and knitteth them in a common cause."

Not all these basic impulses to mutiny were strong in India, but certainly many were, and to an extent quite unrealized in England.

Two acts above all others probably precipitated the vast unease. The first was the abolition of *suttee,* a custom that had called for a Hindu widow to throw herself on her dead husband's funeral pyre and die in the flames. The second was Lord Dalhousie's annexation of Oudh, a kingdom roughly the size of Scotland, between Nepal and Central India. Both deeds were done with the best motives; both had unexpected results.

Instances of *suttee* had been recorded by the historians of Alexander's Indian campaign. For some centuries thereafter it was not very common, but in 1817 seven hundred cases were recorded in Bengal. This showed that it was a growing evil, and twelve years later *suttee* was abolished by law in British India. It was still practised furtively in lonely places, rather as cockfights were arranged in England long after they were declared illegal—as much to show a certain basic independence of unwanted laws as for any deeper reason. But the fact that it had been forbidden rankled as an example of British interference with a Hindu religious custom.

Oudh had been a flourishing province under the Moguls, but in the year before the Mutiny Lord Dalhousie deposed its ruler "for continued misgovernment." His territory was incorporated in what were named the North-Western Provinces.

The King of Oudh had lived an aimless, sybaritic life, and had brought his own deposition on himself, but this did not soften the blow of alien rule. He had been an unusual monarch, happy to compose small rhymes or to march through the streets with a big drum tied round his neck, making as much noise as he could. According to one traveller, he was surrounded by "fiddlers, dancers, singing men and eunuchs . . ." who helped him to "usurp the Government and to absorb the revenues."

Sunk thus "in the uttermost abyss of unfeeling debauchery," the King pushed aside such business of government as he felt himself incapable of transacting, and went daily in search of new pleasure. While he had thus passed his time in a world of make-believe, urged on by courtiers and others, the sinews of his kingdom were weakened to the point of ruin. There was no Government worth the name. The British Resident in Oudh, Sir Richard Sleeman, reported with some alarm that

> powerful families, waxing gross on outrage and rapine, built forts, collected followers, pillaged, tortured, and murdered in every direction.
>
> No road, town, village or hamlet was secure from their merciless attacks [he declared]. Robbery and murder became their diversion, their sport, and they think no more of taking the lives of men, women and children who never offend them, than those of deer and wild hogs. . . .
>
> They seize all the respectable men whom they find in villages which they attack and plunder, keep them in prison and inflict all manner of tortures upon them till they have paid . . . all that they have. . . .
>
> If they refuse to pay . . . they murder them.

The King of Oudh was the last remaining independent Mohammedan ruler in India, and hence the centre of Moslem regard. Deposing him so precipitately, and at such a time, excited the resentment of cavalry regiments which had been recruited almost entirely from his kingdom, and disturbed other regiments, too.

Thousands of Hindu and Mohammedan sepoys transmitted all their savings to Oudh, and when they left service in British provinces they returned there to buy land, a form of investment that has always been popular in India.

When Oudh was annexed, two-thirds of the King's army was disbanded, and no other work could be found for them. The King was kept a State prisoner in Calcutta, but with 1,000 armed retainers and access to large sums of money.

Dalhousie argued that he was forced to take over the corrupt kingdom, and certainly he had a strong defence for his action, but similar reasons could also be given for the annexation of the Punjab, of Jhansi, and Nagpur. The sum total of such seizures remained one of growing alarm in the Indian mind. They saw no end to this gradual encroachment on ancient kingdoms and princely states, and in their forebodings they were quite right. No attempt was made to explain why these annexations were being made. It was long before the days of even semi-literacy in the land, and the opinions of subject peoples were not sought by colonizers.

Lord Dalhousie, the Governor-General who directed these wholesale annexations of states as large as European countries, was a brilliant administrator. He built roads and railways and brought cheap postage to India. Within eighteen months of his arrival in India an electric telegraph system was working from Bombay to Agra and on to Calcutta. He had schemes for more education and for irrigation, but great as his planning abilities were, he lacked the last essential quality of brilliance: imagination. He arrived a young man in his prime, and left a cripple, worn out by the extent of his labours. But he could not notice that, in the Indian mind, all these good deeds were found wanting against the policy of acquisition which he pursued so relentlessly.

Dalhousie believed that a change of rule would be welcomed, if only because it would bring a better and more stable form of government than any of the seized states had previously known. But, as others have also found, he discovered that alien populations are not always immediately grateful to foreigners who uproot indigenous rulers and replace them with their own. However much more efficient such a new rule may be, it is at best a foreign yoke and one that has been forced, unasked, upon them.

Cobden had written truly of India: "Its people will prefer to be ruled badly—according to our notions—by its own colour, kith, and kin, than to submit to the humiliation of being better governed by a succession of transient intruders from the Antipodes. . . ."

The fact that the sepoys had been used to depose their own King also rankled, and was remembered.

Then there was the case of the Nana Sahib, the adopted son of a former *peshwa* of the Marathas, Baji Rao. He had a grievance against the British Government because they did not continue giving him the pension of 800,000 rupees (about £61,500) which had been promised to Baji Rao in the early nineteenth century. This pension was a life grant to the *peshwa*, and was intended to be handed on to his legitimate heirs. Nana Sahib was only his adopted son, but, nevertheless, he felt he had been cheated out of his rightful money, and many agreed with him.

He appealed to the Company and then to Queen Victoria, and actually sent an envoy to London to plead his case, but without success.

Nana Sahib represented to the Brahmins a symbol of British duplicity; and the case of the King of Oudh presented a similar example to the Moslems.

There were other contributory causes. The Indians, like all the other Eastern races, respected power and strength successfully used. Their whole background was a tapestry of violence. War they understood, and the necessity of victory. Thus the disasters to British armies in the Crimea and, in India, at Chillianwalla during the Sikh war, had been viewed with surprise.

To the mind of the world, the chaos of Crimea might overshadow the comparatively minor fiasco at Chillianwalla, eighty-five miles north-west of Lahore. In India, both were of high importance.

Chillianwalla had been a sharp battle. By some misunderstanding of orders or purpose, the front rank of the British cavalry, instead of charging the Sikhs, had retreated. They turned round into the ranks behind them, which were still advancing, overturning their own guns in the confusion.

Three British regiments lost their colours, and 2,800 men. But, more than all this, the British Raj lost caste. No longer was it invincible as of right.

Then many Indians also believed that the English were working to a calculated plan to eradicate their castes and force them to become Christians. The thought alarmed them and could not be driven from their minds.

They pointed to English missionaries, who taught a religion that undermined the teachings of both Hindu and Moslem. Other English people began to lay railway lines along which engines would travel; and might it not happen that in one of these carriages the high-caste Brahmin would be polluted by the nearness of an untouchable?

When it was announced that convicts in gaols would be issued with drinking cups—instead of having to bring their own with them—this was construed as another stage of the plan to ruin the caste system.

There had been other signs and portents of change and unrest. The Hindu prophecy that the power of the Company would be destroyed in 1857—the centenary of the Battle of Plassey, which had brought Bengal under British rule—was repeated and believed.

In February 1856 Lord Canning succeeded Dalhousie as Governor-General. A colonel who watched the ceremony in Calcutta wrote:

How wretched and miserable he looked as he ascended the great outer steps of Government House. He looked as if overwhelmed and bowed down with the sense of responsibility.

On his way up he stumbled and nearly fell. There was a visible shudder amongst the vast throng of superstitious natives assembled, and the words "a bad omen" were repeated by more than one European. . . .

Lord Canning was the thirteenth—and last—Governor-General.

Then, during the early part of 1857, *chapatties* were made

and passed, four at a time, from one village to another with the words, "From the north to the south, from the east to the west." The watchman in one village would pass them on to a watchman in the next. Many people had no idea why they did this. Some thought they were being passed on the orders of the British, again, in some unexplained way, as a means of breaking their caste. But the general feeling was that the *chapatties* had some sinister significance. The view of many was summed up by Mainodin, a *thanadar* (head police officer) of a small village outside Delhi, who said: "I thought it was the sign of a time of trouble. . . ."

The sepoys were especially susceptible to such rumours, for their pay and privileges had been steadily whittled down, and at the same time more was being asked of them.

In July 1856, for instance, a general enlistment order had been passed—because of a British war with Persia—and the Hindu sepoys feared that they might lose their caste by crossing the sea. Previously, men had enlisted with the Bengal Army on the clear understanding that they would not be asked to serve outside that province.

Sir William Temple, who had served with Lawrence in the Punjab, had a simple answer to all who sought reason for the Mutiny. "The short and plain truth," he declared afterwards in a book on his career, "is that the great Mutiny of 1857 arose because the British Government in India had for a long time maintained a native army much too large and the British force much too small."

There were at that date only 34,000 British troops in India, compared with 257,000 Indian sepoys.

The East India Company paid little heed to such warnings, or to the signs of unrest. Their policy was to make as much money as quickly as possible, and in almost any way. Many of the Company's officers used their authority under its charter to do business on their own account. They forced the Indians to sell their cloth and other goods as cheaply as possible, so that they could be sold at the highest price in England with a larger profit to themselves.

Nothing was done to plough back a proper proportion of the profits that were made at such a rate.

"They forced the natives to buy dear and sell cheap," Macaulay * wrote in his Essay on Clive. "Enormous fortunes were thus rapidly accumulated at Calcutta, while thirty million human beings were reduced to the last extremity of wretchedness. . . . They had been accustomed to live under tyranny, but never under tyranny like this. . . ."

The Portuguese were the first European people to explore the fabled riches of the East (and fittingly are now the last European power to maintain a colony—Goa—on Indian soil).

Both Drake and Raleigh had intercepted Portuguese ships returning home with Indian cargoes, and one of these vessels was actually brought into Dartmouth. The sight of their sumptuous cargoes of spice and gold and ebony impressed the British merchant-adventurers. Some made attempts to send their own ships to India; others, less adventurous but no less enterprising, engaged pirates who could plunder Portuguese ships returning with Indian cargoes, but it was not until 1599 that the East India Company was formed. It received a charter in the following year, which granted the Company a monopoly of Indian trade—a state of affairs that lasted for more than 250 years.

Their ships sailed from Torbay to Sumatra and Java and returned with a considerable profit to their Company. But India was held to be the fountain of riches, and so permission of the Mogul Emperor was sought to establish trading ports—called "factories"—at Ahmadabad, and at the three great ports of Madras, Bombay, and Calcutta.

* But while Lord Macaulay was shocked at the greed of others, he had not done too badly himself out of India. He travelled East when his father failed in business, and in a letter home to his sister he told her that it was his intention to "live in splendour" on £5,000 a year "and return to England at only 39 years of age, in full vigour of life, with a fortune of £30,000."

Thus from such tiny footholds did an Empire start and grow.

"Scarcely any man," wrote Macaulay, "however sagacious, would have thought it possible that a trading Company, separated from England by 15,000 miles of sea, and possessing only a few acres for the purpose of commerce, would in less than a hundred years spread its Empire from Cape Comorin to the eternal snows of the Himalayas. . . ."

With vast sums to spend, the Company bought favour at Court, and power elsewhere. Many officials of "John Company" made enough money in a few years to retire from all business, and live the life of country gentlemen in England with vast estates, and a mansion built to their order. Others felt disposed to enter Parliament, where they felt they could exert some power on wider affairs. They bought up "rotten boroughs" as they became available, just as they had bought reams of cloth or bags of pearls when they were in more orthodox trade.

Lord Chesterfield, for instance, wanted to buy a seat in Parliament for his son in 1767, but was willing to spend only £2,500. Just before Christmas of that year, he wrote rather irritably to the young man to say that "there was no such thing as a borough to be had now, for the rich East and West Indians had secured them all at the rate of £3,000 at least, but many at £4,000 and two or three . . . at £5,000. . . ."

As the private fortunes of the Directors of the Company and many of their employees increased prodigiously, so the conditions of the Indians worsened. An unusual means of prompting speedy work was employed in some weaving sheds, for instance, where, if a weaver was slow, according to the evidence of Sir Thomas Munro, the Governor of Madras, a *peon*—a low-class labourer, was empowered to beat him with a cane until his pace increased. The irony was that the wretched weaver had also to pay the wages of the *peon!*

The Company expanded in India by a brilliant and ruthless adherence to the old imperial policy of divide and rule.

One local leader was backed against another, and then a third was brought in against the first. The policy succeeded because the rulers did not trust each other; and because they were also greedy and wanted to believe the promises they were given.

Such a background of intrigue and deception meant that the Battle of Plassey was really won before it was ever fought.

After the battle, Clive was taken into the great treasure-house of the Nawab whom his forces had installed and invited to take what he fancied. Coins of every currency were stacked all round; rubies, diamonds, emeralds glittered with a wealth beyond assessing. Clive took as his part the equivalent of £250,000 sterling.

Years later, when the ethics of this transaction were questioned in Parliament, he retorted indignantly: "By God, at this moment do I stand astonished at my own moderation!"

The East India Company had from their very early years enrolled *peons* to act as guards on their various factories and warehouses. Gradually these men were decked out in uniforms—at first, as much to satisfy the vanity of Company officials as for any other reason. Then they were drilled and trained for more serious forays than guarding the Company caravans and storehouses.

French traders in India were doing the same thing, but with less success, for there was between British and Indians some curious affinity that neither race shares so fully with any other. Their qualities seemed to be complementary; they understood each other.

The sepoys fought well and doggedly under British officers —far better than when they fought for the French. Indeed, French Commanders complained that their sepoys would not fight against sepoys with British officers, although the East India Company troops would willingly take on a white French army—and rout them!

By the mid-seventeenth century the Company bought land at Madras on which to build a fort. A few years later, when

Catherine of Braganza married King Charles II, part of her
dowry included Bombay, which the Portuguese had held for
more than 100 years. By 1668, when the Company was leas-
ing Bombay from the English Crown at a rent of £10 a year,
the town had a small garrison of twenty commissioned officers
and N.C.O.s; 124 European private soldiers, and fifty-four
half-castes. France, by this time, had also formed an East India
Company, so that now three nations—England, France, and
Portugal—maintained trading posts in India. Portugal was
already a waning world power, France and England were
more evenly matched; and as they both began to build up
armies in India they were not above continuing on Indian
soil wars that started in Europe.

These wars with the French in India had led to the sepoy
armies being modelled, both in dress and formation, on the
British armies which had come out to fight in India. They
fought as the British had fought at Balaclava, in scarlet jackets, white belts, black trousers, and shako-like headdresses.
In 1857, the Bengal Horse Artillery wore the uniform of the
Dragoons and Horse Artillery at Waterloo.

As the Company's Indian Army grew, more and more British officers joined them. By the early nineteenth century
there were three armies—one in Madras, another in Bombay,
and the third in Bengal—and it was already noticeable that
men for the Bengal Army of the Company were being recruited more and more from among the sons of landowners
and farmers, and from the yeoman class. Previously they had
come from lower castes; others were out-of-works who had
been anxious to enrol as mercenaries.

In particular, the Brahmins from Oudh were highly regarded because, in addition to being good soldiers, they looked
the part. "Their active frame and curled beards and whiskers gave them a distinctly attractive martial appearance,"
one of their British officers noted with approval.

Now the fact that Brahmins, the highest caste, were in the
army as sepoys, the lowest rank, was disturbing to other Hin-

dus who might be their senior in rank, but who were certainly beneath them in caste. It was an inversion of all they
believed in. It became no uncommon thing for a *havildar*
(an Indian sergeant) to abase himself in the dust and kiss the
feet of some Brahmin sepoy he felt he might have offended.

One officer who served under Sir Charles Napier (who admitted himself that he had "no great confidence" in the loyalty of the Bengal Army) put the problem thus:

> If a low-caste Hindu happened to fill the responsible posi-
> tion of subahdar [an Indian commissioned officer] and . . .
> were a mutiny hatching in the lines, he would not dare to
> divulge it, for the fear of a penalty more dreadful than even
> death—excommunication.
>
> By means of this pernicious system of caste, the men of a
> Bengal regiment, though nominally subject to the British
> Crown, are really under the orders and control of a Brah-
> minical clique formed in each regiment, constantly corres-
> ponding with one another and acting without any sense of
> responsibility whatsoever.

This was indeed a curious form of military trades union,
and a most dangerous means of undermining the authority
of both officers and N.C.O.s.

The three Company armies, in Bengal, at Madras, and in
Bombay, had different rules for promotion.

In Madras and Bombay, merit was allowed to influence the
selection of officers and men to a higher rank, but, in Bengal,
seniority and age were the qualities that decided promotion.

Thus, the *subahdars* and *jemadars* there were not young
and keen men, but often so old and weary that they could not
keep up with their troops on the march, but had to be carried.

Promotion by age was not limited to the Bengal army of
the East India Company. The Queen's Army in India also
suffered from this fault. Lieutenant Charles Griffiths of Her
Majesty's 61st Foot, who marched from Ferozepore to Delhi
during the Mutiny, had some caustic things to say about their

own senior Captain, a man of thirty-five years' service and "the greatest oddity for a soldier that our army has ever seen."

According to Griffiths, this officer was "five feet two inches in height, with an enormous head, short, hunchbacked body, long arms and thin, shrivelled legs. Marching, he was unable to keep step with the men, and on horseback he presented the most ludicrous appearance, being quite unable to ride and looking more like a monkey than a human being . . . vainly endeavouring to make his horse go faster and kicking him every now and then on his flank with his sword. . . ."

Since in England it would have been impossible for such a person to obtain the Queen's Commission, he was forced to serve perpetually abroad. When the regiment to which he was attached was posted home to England, he would have to transfer to another regiment, in his desperate efforts to keep his rank.

The Indian troops in Bengal had several other grievances, in addition to complaints about promotion. They were promised pensions at the end of their service, but as the time for retirement drew near, various reasons were put forward to make them soldier on.

Colonel Keith Young, who joined the Bengal Army in 1824 and became Judge Advocate-General—a position he held up to his death in 1862—was convinced that this was one of the main reasons for the manifest discontent:

> To my mind, the one great cause of complaint is the difficulty there now is for a man, Native Officer or Sepoy, getting on the Pension Establishment [he wrote to a friend in London].
>
> There is no chance whatever of his being granted a pension as long as he can put one foot before another; so a commanding officer of a regiment, do what he will, cannot get rid of useless, worn-out men, who are sent back to him by the invaliding committees to become a source of discontent in the camps.

Norman, our Assistant Adjutant-General [Lieutenant H.

W. Norman, later General Sir Henry W. Norman] who is a
very smart young officer, told me of an instance . . . of every
man who was sent before an invaliding committee of a
certain regiment having been rejected, excluding one, and
that poor fellow died before his papers could be made out
for pension.

At Bombay, where the Army has also been in a more contented state than here, the invaliding rules are quite different, and men are admitted to pensions there . . . who would
be kept on the strength of the Army for years longer in
Bengal. . . .

By the standards of the time, the sepoys were well paid,
with 7 rupees—about 11s. a month. But many were heavily in
debt. The curious *silledar* system, under which the Indian
cavalryman provided his own horse and its provender for his
monthly wage, meant that many sowars were in debt to the
moneylenders for years. Any means of ending this servitude
was very welcome, and in the Mutiny the *banyas,* or local
moneylenders, were often among the first to be struck down.

The sepoys knew little about England. Many imagined
that the entire British Army was in India and that the total
population of Great Britain was only about 100,000 people.
Even the Sikhs, who were our allies during the Mutiny, believed, in the words of G. O. Trevelyan, the historian, that
Colin Campbell paraded his men "like the stage manager at
Astley's Theatre," by marching them in at one end of the
town and out of the other, and then brought them back, so
that they would appear to be more than they really were.

When the Highlanders in kilts first appeared, some mutineers "wept with joy that the men of England had been exhausted and that the Company had been reduced to calling
out the women. . . ."

For months before the Mutiny, the pride of the sepoys in
their turnout had been diminishing. As soon as they were
dismissed from a parade, or when they came from guard duty,

they would rip off their uniforms and go about in linen drawers.

In some regiments they even took off their uniforms when they were on guard. On marches, they straggled along in a slovenly way, smoking or creeping up on baggage carts when they thought no one was looking. Then they would fall asleep with their uniforms undone. Old soldiers blamed these slacknesses on a loosening in general discipline, which they claimed had come about since Lord William Bentinck had abolished corporal punishment for the Indian Army twenty years before.

An old sepoy cynically summed up the position thus: "Ah, *sahib*," he said, "the army has ceased to fear. . . ."

Certainly they had little to fear from the wrath of their commanders. Too many senior officers had served in comfortable stations for too long; many had never seen any active service at all.

Lieutenant William Hodson, one of the few great figures thrown up by the Mutiny and proof, in the words of a brother officer, that "the discipline of a public school and subsequent university training are no disqualification for hazardous warfare," was loud in his contempt for the senior officers of the day.

At the age at which officers became colonels and majors, not one in fifty is able to stand the wear and tear of Indian service [he wrote home bitterly some time before the Mutiny].

They become still more worn in mind than in body. All elasticity is gone; all energy and enterprise worn out; they become, after a fortnight's campaign, a burden to themselves, an annoyance to those under them, and a terror to everyone but the enemy. . . .

Hodson had indeed been unfortunate in his superiors, and his experiences had coloured his impressions and shortened his patience.

One officer he knew was so old and obese that he could not mount his horse "without the assistance of two men." And a Brigadier of infantry was so senile and had such bad eyesight that, when he came to inspect Hodson's men, Hodson had to lead his horse by the bridle "until his nose touched the bayonets."

Then the Brigadier asked faintly, "Pray, *which way are the men facing*, Mr. Hodson?"

In 1851, Lord Dalhousie had grumbled that "Commanding Officers are inefficient. Brigadiers are no better. Divisional Officers are worse than either because old and more dull; and at the top of all they send Commanding Officers seventy years old. . . ."

Fred Roberts, who was a Lieutenant at the time of the Mutiny, and who later rose to be Field-Marshal Lord Roberts, V.C., came of a family old in the Indian military tradition. His father, General Roberts, had commanded a division on the Frontier; and his superiors prided themselves on "the youth and activity of their choice." He was then sixty-nine.

Such elderly officers were still in command because, so long as they behaved themselves, there was no means of getting rid of them until they chose to retire. They were like clerics in the Anglican Church; in the job until death relieved them, or they chose to retire.

The fact that many were quite unsuited for their posts, and some even without any proper military training, was not at all surprising because many had bought their commissions.

This system of buying commissions went on until 1871, despite the terrible examples of the Crimea and the Indian Mutiny, which showed the folly of entrusting professional armies to officers of little training or talent.

Set prices were laid down by the Government for the various ranks. A cavalry captain could buy his regiment for £6,000; a captain in the Foot Guards would pay £4,800 for his company.

In the majority of cases, however, incumbents already holding these commissions would sell them to friends or relations at considerably above the official figures, and so unusual situ-

ations arose, because not every officer had the money necessary to buy promotion from the lowest commissioned rank.

In one Indian regiment at the time of the Mutiny, for instance, a Lieutenant who could not afford to buy promotion
to a higher rank had seen more service than any other officer
in his battalion. In another, there was a Captain serving who
had fought at Waterloo. He had been soldiering before any
of his brother officers—including his own Colonel—had been
born!

In his *Recollections,* Sir John Adye mentions the case of a
Captain who had stayed in this same rank for twenty-three
years—simply because whenever a vacancy for promotion occurred, it was sold to some officer who could make a higher
offer than he could afford.

The system of buying commissions was not new. As long
ago as 1794 the British Adjutant-General in Flanders had
written home bitterly about the state of affairs in the Army
at that time:

> . . . We are the most undisciplined and the most ignorant
> army that ever took the field [he declared]. There is not a
> young officer that cares a brass farthing whether his com-
> manding officer, his brigadier, or even the commander-in-
> chief, approves his conduct or not.
>
> His promotion depends not on their smiles or frowns—his
> friends can give him a thousand pounds, with which he goes
> to the auction room in Charles Street, and in a fortnight he
> becomes a Captain. . . .

Shortly before the Mutiny, a Royal Commission on Purchase reported that "an officer who keeps a sum of money
available to purchase his promotion as opportunities offer
may look forward to the attainment of high military rank."

His contemporary "who had not such a sum of money"
found that knowledge of "military science and attention to
duty do not avail him unless he is able to buy the rank to
which his qualifications entitle him."

This state of affairs was held by many to be a very good

thing, because, in their view, so long as the Army was officered by men of means, then it would be a far better bulwark
against revolution than if it were merely led by professional
mercenaries.

Indeed, Lord Palmerston told the Commission on Purchase
that he thought "it was very desirable to connect the higher
classes of Society with the Army."

The best method of connecting them was "by allowing
members of high families who held commissions to get on
with more rapidity than they would by seniority. . . ."

Once a man had bought his commission, he had no need
to serve with that regiment. He could go on half-pay in his
rank the day after he joined. When a vacancy in the next
senior rank occurred in some other more congenial regiment,
then he could buy this, too, for, though all had to go through
the motions of promotion from rank to rank, Falstaff's service of a single day in any one rank was as good as the service
of years.

By going on half-pay when a draft was announced, or even
exchanging his position in a regiment due to go abroad with
some fellow officer less well endowed, many rich officers
avoided overseas service altogether. Although on paper it
might appear that they had many years of Army service, they
need, in fact, only have been with their troops for a few
weeks or even a few days throughout their entire career.

"When a fashionable regiment had to do a turn of duty in
India," wrote Cecil Woodham Smith in *The Reason Why*,
her brilliant book on the Crimean campaign, "it was notori-
ous that a different set of officers went out from those who
had been on duty at St. James's Palace or the Brighton Pa-
vilion. When the regiment returned, the Indian duty officers
dropped out and a smarter set took their place. . . ."

Such methods of securing commissions and promotion did
not make for happiness among those officers who lacked
money and who, for this reason, had to take their regimental
duties seriously. They might be condemned to ten or twenty

years of service in India. Indeed, General Roberts, a professional soldier entirely dependent on his salary, had actually served for nearly thirty years in India before he was granted home leave! Because of his own experience in the Army, he did not wish his son to follow him in his career.

Such obviously unfair dealing made for a latent discontent among British professional officers which was reflected in a vague feeling of unease among the British civilians.

They all lived well, with retinues of servants, but this could not entirely shield them from the deepening feeling that somehow their strange, exotic life was unreal and could not last. They were living in a world of false values and inflated ideas, and some realized it and were afraid of the deep forces they could sense stirring against them.

The Editor of the *Delhi Gazette* remarked to a friend one day that he doubted the wisdom of the annexation of Oudh.

"Oh, the thing will last our time, and so we need not care," his friend replied, expressing thus the belief and hope of many among the English civilian population.

Here there was also discontent, for, as in the Army, influence counted for much more than ability.

"There was, of course, no pretence that the Directors went about looking for the best young men," admitted Sir George Campbell, who was one of the senior members of the Company at that time.

"They nominated their sons and nephews and friends. . . . Still," he pointed out in fairness, "the qualifying exam. not only threw out a few of the worst, but frightened away a good many more. . . . A considerable number were sifted out at Haileybury. . . . The fashion was to send into the cavalry a young man too idle or too stupid to go through Haileybury. . . ."

Prophets of doom were not lacking; the system of Army purchase was too pernicious not to be heavily criticized.

Sir Charles Napier, the General who had conquered Scinde, and thereby acquired a place in the quotation books by alleg-

edly sending the signal, *Peccavi*—"I have sinned" (= Scinde)
—was strong in his criticisms of the Indian Army.

> The general framework of this army is bad [he grumbled].
> The present European is a youngster who makes curry,
> drinks champagne and avoids the sun; in ten or twelve
> years, if he has brains and health, he acquires some knowl-
> edge, and is put on the Staff; thus the regiments are con-
> stantly commanded by Lieutenants. At this moment a
> troop of Horse Artillery here is commanded by a cadet of
> 15 . . . whom I puzzled by asking him what the dispart of
> a gun was . . . The natives, ever at their posts, are the real
> officers, and very good ones too! . . .
>
> No one seems to foresee that your young and inexperi-
> enced wild cadet will some day find the Indian Army taken
> out of his hands by the Subahdars who are men of high
> caste and very daring. . . .
>
> If we continue to imitate the Eastern style [i.e., of show
> and decadence] our officers will deteriorate and the native
> officers will take the Empire from us. A radical reform of
> the Indian Army and an increase of European officers is
> absolutely necessary. Some years hence—for they will not
> increase the officers—my words will prove prophetic. The
> sepoy now has no European officers to look to—no Captain,
> I mean; he is devoted to us as yet, but we take no pains to
> preserve his attachment.
>
> It is no concern of mine, I shall be dead before what I
> foresee will take place, but it will take place.

Napier was right; Lord Ellenborough, a previous Governor-General, also had voiced the opinion on many occasions
that a general mutiny of the sepoys was the only real danger
threatening the British Empire in India.

Then, four years before the Mutiny, General John Jacob
of the Bombay Army declared that the "normal state" of the
Bengal Army was "a state of mutiny."

In a letter to *The Times,* he said: "There is more danger
to our Indian Empire from the state of the Bengal Army,
from the feeling which there exists between the native and

the European, and thence spreads throughout the length and breadth of the land, than from all other causes combined. Let the government look to this: it is a serious and most important truth."

An officer who served with Sir Charles Napier, describing general conditions in the Indian Army, noted that "Twenty-six officers make up the complement of a native regiment, but of these nearly half were generally absent, and there were seldom more than fifteen present at headquarters."

For the most part, the officers lived in thatched houses or bungalows near their regimental lines, but they were too far away to have any direct control over their men during the hours of daylight.

For eight months of every year the weather was considered too warm for them to ride out, save in the early morning and the early evening. As a form of liaison, two European sergeants lived in the lines with the sepoys, and they reported daily to the Adjutant.

The officers could see no reason for exerting themselves. Their pay was poor—the initial salary was roughly £120 a year. Sir Thomas Munro, who joined the Madras Army of the Company in 1780 as a Lieutenant, and later rose to be Governor of Madras, described his own wretched financial state with wry amusement: "My dress grows tattered in one quarter, whilst I am establishing funds to repair it in another. And my coat is in danger of losing the sleeves while I am pulling it off to try a new waistcoat."

As well as being badly paid, the British officers in India led very dull lives. Letters took a month or more to come out from England, and as long again to follow them from Bombay to their station. (Missionaries in Calcutta complained that letters from Agra, only 800 miles away, took forty days to reach them.) Books were few, and any English newspapers that arrived were hopelessly out of date. Thus the English officer was a physical and cultural exile from England until he retired or went on furlough after years of Indian service.

The Indian sun was thought to be harmful, and any un-
due exposure to it might be fatal—a belief that persisted up
to the 1930s. Thus, European officers were forced to spend
most of their time in their bungalows, save for early morning
or evening rides, or games of racquets.

A few used their time more profitably, and learned the lan-
guages of the country; others studied music or painted. Many
just drank or gambled their time away, grateful for a temporary escape from the wearying heat, the boredom, the sense
of frustration that service in India could mean. But claret
and brandy and sherry were expensive. In that climate, and
in the quantities most officers drank, they were also dangerous. Tempers sharpened, duels were common, and sudden
deaths or suicides not infrequent.

British officers had little contact with women of their own
race; there were very few out there, in any case. In 1810 one
officer, a Captain Thomas Williamson, wrote a guidebook for
young men who sought service with the Honourable East
India Company, and he noted that while only about 250
European women lived in Bengal, "the European male inhabitants of respectability, including military officers, may be
taken at 4,000."

Thus the Indian "housekeeper" became an institution and
the accepted easy answer to a problem the Victorians considered unspeakable. (The children of such unions would form
a special problem years later, but no one seemed to think of
this; it was, in any case, a problem for another generation,
not for them.)

The latent discontent of many officers was reflected in the
shoddiness of their work. Lord Dalhousie wrote despairingly
to the President of the Board of Control that "the discipline
of the army, from top to bottom, officers and men alike, is
scandalous." After the fiasco to British troops in the Afghan
War, this deterioration of discipline became much more
marked.

During that unfortunate campaign, the British garrison at

Kabul—4,500 men, with nearly three times this number of camp followers—perished in retreat along the road to Jellalabad. There were only a few survivors. One was Dr. Brydon, whose escape was the subject of a famous painting by Lady Butler, "The Remnant of an Army." This shook the sepoy's faith in the legend of Britain's invincibility—which was also undermined by the fiascos of the Crimea and Chillianwalla.

Added to this, Hindu troops had been compelled to eat food and drink water which they regarded as impure; and on their return to India they had to pay for re-admission to the castes which they had lost. The Moslems were equally uneasy; they had not liked fighting an enemy of their own faith.

Because the Governor-General ruled from Calcutta, he naturally chose subordinates for civil officers from officers of the army nearest to him—the Bengal Army. Thus many of its best brains were seconded to civilian posts—men like John Nicholson, James Outram, and Henry Lawrence. Their departure left the Bengal Army short of experienced officers at a time when it needed them most.

Sometimes the latent discontent which officers and sepoys felt with their pay and conditions showed itself in openly mutinous behaviour. In 1758, for instance, nine captains of the Bengal European Regiment could no longer contain their resentment that officers of the Madras and Bombay detachments, which were incorporated with their regiment, were promoted over their heads. They all resigned their commissions.

Clive accepted six resignations at once, but allowed the other three to retain their commissions—with a loss of seniority—when they had further thoughts and pleaded with him not to take them at their word.

Then, in 1806, sepoys in the Madras Army were ordered to shave off their beards, and to wear shakos instead of their turbans; and it was announced that neither caste-marks or ear-rings would be worn on parade.

They regarded these instructions as a direct attack on their religion. At once the garrison of Vellore murdered their British officers and hoisted flags of rebellion. British troops acted quickly and without mercy, but 400 sepoys died before the insurrection was quelled.

In the thirteen years before the Mutiny there had been four such sudden outbursts against orders, but none of them had the same character as the insurrection of 1857. The previous outbreaks had been local, isolated affairs; the great Mutiny was a wide infection that tainted garrisons 1,000 miles apart—at the same time and in the same way. Every mutineer seemed to believe that his religious beliefs were being violated, or that ancient privileges were being withdrawn.

At Meerut, the sepoys claimed that flour for their food was being mixed with bones of unclean beasts—a definite attempt to undermine the caste system.

In Lucknow, the surgeon of one regiment was said to have tasted a bottle of medicine before he gave it to a Brahmin soldier. This, said the sepoys, was a further attempt to break down their caste. They revenged themselves by burning down the doctor's bungalow.

Elsewhere, there was resentment that the privilege sepoys enjoyed of being able to send letters free under the frank of their commanding officers should disappear under a reorganization of the Post Office. Sepoys from Oudh had lost another right—of being able to lay any complaint about conditions in Oudh before their own commanding officer. He would pass on their charges to the Government in Calcutta, who ordered the British Resident in Lucknow to make inquiries about the matter. This meant that the families of sepoys were treated with more respect in Oudh than were any other subjects in the kingdom. But when Oudh became just another part of British India, this right disappeared with its independence.

Every setback, every odd occurrence—the passing of *chapatties* from village to village; the lotus flowers; the blazing arrows in the darkness—all these were signs and symbols of a dying authority.

There was another factor that contributed to the Mutiny, and which allowed it to spread, and this was the attitude of the English in authority in India. They could not believe that any lasting setback could come to their tremendous possession. Thus they did not think it seemly to take such precautions as having the magazine in Delhi outside the city, where British troops could guard it. Prophecies and portents they felt strong enough to dismiss as the foolish mouthings of a heathen and subject people. And even when the Mutiny was at its height many British officers refused to believe that *their* sepoys could rebel against them—an attitude that cost many their lives.

Gradually, this festering discontent, tinctured with old resentments on the part of the sepoys, and with too many officers resolutely refusing to believe that such grievances had any importance, came to a head. One day in January 1857, in the artillery station at Dum Dum, outside Calcutta, a *classie* —a workman of low caste—asked a high-caste sepoy in the 2nd Native Grenadier Regiment to give him a drink of water from his *lotah,* a brass drinking vessel. The Brahmin refused because of his superior caste: the *lotah* would be defiled if such a low-caste man touched it.

This explanation annoyed the *classie.*

"You are very particular about your caste today," he retorted angrily ,"but you don't mind biting cartridges that are made up of animal fat!"

The taunt struck home, and was repeated. Sepoys of high caste feared that if they were defiled in this way their friends and families would have nothing to do with them in this world; and they would have no place in the scheme of things in the next. Their alarm became so widespread that all Indian troops in the station were paraded and asked if they had any complaints to make.

All the N.C.O.s in the regiment, and about two-thirds of

the men, stepped forward and spoke of this business of the cartridges. They suggested that wax and oil should be used instead of the grease. This was at once agreed to, but too late; the harm was done, and the feeling of discontent spread. At Barrackpore, another station near to Calcutta, there were three cases of arson in four days; one fire destroyed the electric telegraph bungalow.

On 6 February a special court of enquiry took evidence from some of the regiment at Barrackpore about their objections to the use of this wax paper.

Subahdar Kladu Buksh said that he had "no objection to the cartridge itself, but there is a general report that the paper is made up with fat."

Jemadar Gholal Khan, another Indian officer, reported: "There is grease in it, I feel assured, as it differs from the paper which has heretofore been always used for cartridges. . . ."

Four days later a jemadar of the 34th at Barrackpore told his superiors that on the day before this court of inquiry he had been ordered on to the parade ground by a force of 300 men of the different regiments in the station. He was amazed to see that their faces were bound up with cloth, so that only their eyes were exposed. They told him that they were determined to die for their religion. "If they could make an arrangement that evening," he said, "the next night they would plunder a station and kill the Europeans and then they could go where they liked. . . ."

The unrest spread quickly. At Berhampore, a station in close touch with Barrackpore, the men refused to take percussion caps for loading their rifles. Colonel Mitchell, their commanding officer, went on parade, and, as he reported later, found the men "armed, in undress, in line, shouting." He ordered them to lay down their arms. They refused to do so until all artillery and cavalry were withdrawn, lest they should be attacked. This was agreed to, and then they obeyed.

Nothing was done about the incident, but it was remembered in Barrackpore that insolence towards Europeans had been evident in the previous autumn. Three boats which were taking troops to the station by sea were severely damaged in a gale. There was danger of some boats, which contained officers, being swamped; but although the sepoys watched their distress, they made no effort to help the officers.

Later, some men were arrested for using insubordinate language, but Colonel Wheeler, the commanding officer, a man of seventy and old for his age, ordered that no notice should be taken of such conduct on the grounds that if he punished them, he would "for the same reason, have to put half the regiment in confinement."

On 24 February a small guard of the 34th Regiment arrived at Berhampore, and they discussed their imagined grievances with the men of the 19th who were already there. Their attitude became so alarming that Colonel Mitchell, knowing the weakness of his own position, for he was not supported by European troops, "begged them to desist." A report of the temper of both regiments was sent to the Government in Calcutta, but they had no suggestions for improving the state of affairs either, and so did nothing at all, hoping that with time the grievances would right themselves. Time, however, was on the side of the rebels, and on the morning of 29 March this became evident to all, when a sepoy named Mangal Pandy rushed out on to the parade ground, rifle in hand, shouting at the top of his voice.

"Come out, men! Come out, men!" he yelled. "Come out for your religion!" The Indian officer in charge of the guard stood watching him; he made no attempt to restrain him. An English N.C.O., Sergeant-Major Hewson, asked the officer to turn out the guard and seize the man, who seemed to be demented. Pandy raised his rifle and shot at the Sergeant-Major, who fell to the ground, wounded. The officer looked the other way. He gave no orders. The guard stayed in their guardhouse.

The sound of the shouting and the shot brought the British Adjutant of the 34th, Lieutenant Baugh, out of his office.

He took one look at the sepoy with his smoking rifle, then strapped on two pistols in holsters, rushed to his horse and galloped out on to the parade ground after him. Pandy saw him coming and darted behind a cannon which stood in front of the quarter-guard for the purpose of firing ceremonial salutes. As the Adjutant neared him, Pandy fired and wounded his horse in the flank. The beast threw his rider, but Baugh freed himself from the stirrups and drew a pistol and advanced on the sepoy.

Pandy had no time to reload and so threw away his musket and drew his sword. Baugh fired at him but, in the excitement, missed altogether. The sepoy leapt at him and bore him to the ground.

It would have gone badly with Baugh if Hewson had not staggered up, wounded as he was, with his sword drawn. He could do little to help, though, for he was at once struck down from behind by an Indian who hit him with a musket. (When this sepoy returned to his quarters with his uniform reddened by Hewson's blood, his Indian officer asked no questions, but simply told him "to change his pantaloons.")

By now other sepoys were running from the quarter-guard. They beat down Hewson, and when some tried to seize Mangal Pandy, the Indian officer forbade them.

"If you kill the man you will be hanged!" he promised them, and they hung back.

Someone had run to fetch the Colonel, and he arrived and ordered out the guard. After a few paces towards the scene, they returned to the guard-house again and refused to move. The Indian officer explained that none of them could go to arrest Mangal Pandy, as he was a Brahmin and they were men of lower caste.

Wheeler, very conscious of his age and lack of authority, rode away back to his own quarters and tried to explain his inaction in a report to his Brigadier, General Hearsey. "I felt it was quite useless going on with the matter," he wrote.

"Considering it quite useless and a sacrifice of life to order a European officer with the guard to seize him, I left. . . ."

General Hearsey was also seventy; but his outlook was of a much younger, more vigorous man. He spoke the sepoy's language, and understood their minds. He shouted for his horse and, with his two sons and his A.D.C., galloped to the spot.

Nothing had changed. Mangal Pandy was still by the ceremonial cannon. The sergeant-major was writhing on the ground, and the guards were looking on. Pandy had used the time well. As Hearsey rode straight up to the quarter-guard, an English officer ran out shouting: "His musket's loaded."

"Damn his musket!" roared the General, and spurred his horse at the mutineer.

Mangal Pandy raised his musket. The General called over his shoulder to his son, "If I fall, John, rush him and put him to death!"

At this Pandy spun the rifle round, pushed his bare toe inside the trigger-guard and pressed the trigger. Apparently he meant to kill himself, but, in the act of firing, the musket jerked away, and although he fell, he was only slightly wounded.

The General left him there and, drawing his own pistol, wheeled round towards the guard-house. He ordered everyone back to their posts, threatening to shoot with his own hand the first man who showed any sign of disaffection. The men fled precipitately.

So the moment was saved. The jemadar of the guard, Issuree Pandy, who had watched Mangal Pandy fire at the Adjutant, was court martialled. He was charged with refusing to allow men to interfere at the time of Mangal Pandy's attack; with spreading sedition by telling the sepoys that if any of them brought him one of the new cartridges "he would cut his head off," and with warning them to prepare for general revolt. Both he and Mangal Pandy were hanged. As the Indian officer stood on the gallows with two European regi-

ments fully armed on either side lest there should be further
disturbances, he gave a dramatic speech to the sepoys.

"Listen to me," he said. "I have been a traitor to a good
Government. I am about to be punished for my great sins; I
am about to be hanged and I deserve my punishment. Sepoys,
obey your officers, for they are your rightful and just rulers,
or else you will, like me, be brought to the gallows. I listened
to evil advisers, and you see what I am come to. I call upon
God to bless the Governor-General and all the great gentlemen, the General and all the *sahib logue* (people) here
present."

So they died, but their names lived on through the Mutiny
and beyond, for, to the British troops, all rebellious sepoys
became known as "Pandies."

Issuree and Mangal Pandy were hanged ten days after their
court martial, but the sepoys who had struck Sergeant-Major
Hewson and Lieutenant Baugh were not punished for five
weeks.

The Governor-General was afraid that swift punishment
might inflame the temper of the other troops, and so he spent
days discussing the matter with his Council. And when General Anson, the Commander-in-Chief, urged him to come to
some decision quickly, he still spent four more days trying
to find extenuating circumstances for their conduct.

Meanwhile, the 19th Regiment was disbanded at Barrackpore, and such was General Hearsey's personal popularity
that they cheered him as they marched off parade for the last
time!

Colonel Wheeler's supine behaviour came in for some
heavy criticism from the Governor-General. Wheeler admitted that for twenty years he had tried personally to convert "natives of all classes," including his own sepoys, to
Christianity. His view was that every converted Christian
"ought to be a missionary to convert the heathen. And that is
the principle thing he ought to think about." He agreed that
he expected to "suffer persecution" for this outlook, but he

said proudly and simply that he rejoiced in this kind of martyrdom.

The Governor-General said afterwards: "I could come to no [opinion] more favourable to Colonel Wheeler than that he is entirely unfit to be entrusted with the command of a regiment. But the occasion is so grave and as the conduct of Colonel Wheeler bears, *prima facie,* so serious an aspect that . . . I therefore propose that the Commander-in-Chief be requested to submit the conduct of Colonel Wheeler on the 29th March to an investigation by court martial. . . ."

So two officers, seventy years old, played decisive parts in the first most serious outbreak of unrest in the Bengal Army. One lost the situation, and the other saved it.

But although the Marquess of Tweeddale, a great admirer of Lord Dalhousie, insisted that his hero "would have stopped the Mutiny," the fact was that no one could have stopped it.

Years before there was any discontent in India, Sir Thomas Munro wrote that "the spirit of independence will spring up in this army long before it is ever thought of among the people. . . . All that is necessary is that they (the sepoys) shall have lost their present high respect for their officers and the European character; and whenever this happens they will rise against us, not for the sake of asserting the liberty of their country, but of obtaining power and plunder."

Some time in the afternoon of 10 May 1857, these conditions obtained and, like a spring tide, the stirrings of unrest and disaffection swept through India to their terrible climax.

CHAPTER IV

The Waiting Game

By THE SECOND WEEK in June the British Field Force, which contained British troops and also Indian regiments that had stayed loyal—a combined total of 2,300 infantry, with 600 cavalry and twenty-two field guns—was in position outside Delhi.

The Cantonment was a shambles of ruined and blackened bungalows which, even if they had been inhabitable, were not well sited from the point of view of an assault. The city of Delhi, ringed in with high walls, contained at least 40,000 mutineers all excited by their easy victories in garrisons throughout India, and eager to annihilate the saucy little force that had come out against them.

But despite the disparity in numbers, the little Field Force was, in the British way, supremely confident that the last battle would belong to them, although every day brought news of further mutinous outbreaks all over north India.

Sir William Muir, then head of the Intelligence Department, might complain gloomily that all was "one sea of anarchy to the foot of the Himalayas," but regarding Delhi, even he felt that "in two or three days by God's blessing we may confidently look to its being ours. . . ."

If Sir William, in his position, could feel such unreasonable optimism, then the junior officers and the rank and file, knowing little or nothing about the wide canvas of events, were even more optimistic.

Each day they delayed outside Delhi, however, made their task of subduing the city more difficult. The great city wall, seven miles round, bristled with cannon, and each day saw new pieces of ordnance in position pointing outwards to meet any attack that might come from any direction. And every day more mutineers arrived in the best Company uniforms of red jackets, with white blanco and brass buckles gleaming. They marched in by fours behind bands that went out to meet them, playing British regimental marches. One of the favourites was "Cheer, boys, cheer" and when the British troops heard it—as they did nearly every day—they would bellow out the words defiantly, thoroughly relishing the incongruity of the performance.

Nearly everyone in the Field Force felt sure that they would speedily overpower the mutineers. Young Wilberforce Greathed, a Lieutenant in the Engineers, whose elder brother had escaped death at Meerut, and others like him, lost no time in pressing home this idea of an early attack to his superiors.

No one was really quite sure *how* the city would be taken, although all agreed that their assault would be successful. As they cleared the old Cantonment parade ground behind the burnt-out lines, and pitched their little cone-shaped tents, everyone was in high spirits, and full of sound and fury against the rebels. They installed their guns upon the Ridge near the house of a Mahratta chief, Hindu Rao, who had died some time before the outbreak. It became known as "Hindu Rao's," as though the old warrior were still in fact controlling the fire-power from some Valhalla of his own.

He had been strongly Anglophile, a generous host and, unusually, a keen gardener. His house boasted a little garden, and so barren and rocky was the whole area that all its earth had been laboriously brought up from the plains. This garden now formed a convenient post for two field guns, a battalion of the Gurkhas, and two companies of the 60th Rifles. The Gurkhas regarded it as a point of honour never to leave their post, and even those who were sick used to beg their friends to help them conceal their disability lest they should be ordered to the rear.

Farther over, near the Flagstaff Tower, the returning troops found a reminder of less buoyant days: the bullock-cart which had been driven there on 11 May, loaded with the bodies of dead officers, covered with tattered dresses. They were given a proper burial.

A handful of British soldiers, out after what they could find, entered an old Pathan mosque near the Tower, and discovered an old Indian woman holding the body of a young man who had been a victim of the advance party's guns; his hands were still warm.

One of the troops put up his musket to shoot her, swearing that the women were worse than the men, but Colonel Keith Young prevented him.

"Do not disgrace yourself and us by killing a defenceless old woman," he said sharply. "Don't imitate the butchers of Delhi and Meerut." The soldier lowered his rifle and moved away sulkily, grumbling to himself. Colonel Young spoke for some time with the old woman, and explained that she would not be harmed. She told the Colonel that the dead young man was her only son.

For Young, up from Meerut, where his wife still remained, the whole area was full of sad memories. When he had last visited Hindu Rao's house with his wife, only a few weeks previously, tame deer and tigers were kept in the grounds for the wonder and amusement of visitors, and a swing had been rigged up on the veranda. But now the animals had fled back to the wilds again, and the swing was gone. The house was nothing but a reference on the Colonel's military map.

Under the Staff arrangements of the time, the Engineers controlled all siege operations, and so instead of being merely advisers, they were virtually a General Staff on their own who could say what would be done and when. Since, according to Army custom, no one could interfere with them where their own work was concerned, they were in a most powerful position—and one that could cause great irritation to the Gunners, who held that the assault was to be, in Colonel Young's words, "altogether an Artillery affair." But because the field-guns had to be dug in on the Ridge and elsewhere, a task which continued at a great pace for the next few weeks, the entire siege was one in which Engineer officers played a disproportionately important part. Young subalterns received unusually rapid promotion, largely because of the unusual responsibility which was thrust on them, and the lack of competition for it.

The Chief Engineer, Major Laughton ("a man of the Hewitt type" a colleague described him contemptuously), was quite without experience of war, and at an age when he turned to others for their advice in emergencies. Also, his mind was involved with personal problems not of a military nature. Since no order existed preventing wives being outside Delhi with their husbands, he had brought along his wife, a passionate Persian girl, with whom he spent much time. She was a demanding woman, and when she was not in his tent, she was in his thoughts. The Major's preoccupation with her caused some head-shaking from envious and lonely officers. Since her husband controlled the Engineers, and she controlled him, she had brought all her belongings with her on Army camels. Between twenty and thirty of these beasts and half as many carts were needed to bear the burden of her clothes, her camping equipment, and her personal maids. Most officers had one or two camels each to carry their kit, but since no proper arrangements were made for feeding or caring for the vast numbers of these beasts, many just starved to death.

The ground was so hard that graves could not easily be dug for their gigantic corpses, which were thus left heaped on each other, huge pyramids of decay, and breeding grounds for flies. They lay thus under the terrible heat of the sun

until the gas generated within their rotting bodies burst
them and the smell of their terrible putrefaction hung over
everything like a fog.

The troops were pestered by plagues of flies, which descended in thousands, darkening the air as they settled on
everything in sight. These visitors were the more hateful because everyone knew where they bred.

"Foul and loathsome," wrote Charles Griffiths afterwards,
they "fattened on the putrid corpses . . . which lay rotting
and unburied in every direction. The air was tainted with
corruption, and the heat was intense. . . ."

Temperature in the tents was often 112° F., and only the
prospect of the rains, which were due to start in about a
fortnight, could make the heat and smells tolerable.

Round Hindu Rao's house, into which it was decided to
bring any wounded men, the sappers—with no help from
Major Laughton—built the first battery that evening. Next
morning, the sight of these guns incited the enemy to heavy
firing.

At the end of the Ridge was a suburb known as Subzi-
Mundi—the "vegetable market"—and beyond this two others,
Kishengunge and Paharipore, where a southern continuation
of the Ridge began again.

The first task was the adequate defence of the position
against any possible attack by the rebels, and the Ridge could
scarcely be less adapted for the construction of artificial defences. Its entire face was bare and craggy except where, with
infinite toil, cart-loads of earth had been brought up to support a few small shrubs, as had happened around Hindu
Rao's villa. There was not a spadeful of spare earth anywhere, and so fatigue parties were set to scrape at the crumbling fragments of rock that had collected in some of the
hollows. Apart from these scrapings, all materials for the defensive works had to be carried from less arid parts beyond
the Cantonment.

Because of the angle at which the Ridge extended, the

left of the besieging army's position was almost out of range. Where Sir Theo Metcalfe's house, now stripped and gutted, stood surrounded by its 1,000 acres of parkland and ruined orange groves, a game of tennis could still be enjoyed by the strenuous—with the additional zest of a possible stray hit from a shell splinter to liven up the set.

All that remained of Sir Theo's celebrated library was a mound of feathery, filmy ash. Occasionally the wind would blow charred fragments of paper over the men as they sweated at the gun emplacements.

The area between the Ridge, the Jumna River, and the city formed a roughly triangular plain of baked brown earth, cracked by ravines, or *nullahs,* and dry stream-beds choked with brushwood. Here and there rough, unsurfaced roads, bordered with trees, stretched away amid abandoned houses and burned-out bungalows.

Nearer the city, a mass of buildings, gardens, mosques, tombs, and huts clustered amid clumps of trees and mangoes. The most advanced enemy post, Ludlow Castle, the home of Simon Fraser, the Commissioner of Delhi, who had been murdered, stood on a slight crest, nearly half a mile in advance of the Kashmir Gate. A dry drainage channel ran below this, stretching from the river near Kudsia Bagh to the Ridge, and so giving some protection to British troops adventurous enough to attempt an attack on the Castle.

The Kudsia Bagh, about 300 yards from the walls, had been an imperial summer palace in the days of the Moguls, but was now no more than a hollow shell. Outside, some of its ancient glory still remained in the gateways, cloisters, and arcades, framed with orange, lime, and rose trees, whose petals made a burst of colour against the brownish yellow dust all round.

Between the Kudsia Bagh and Ludlow Castle, 100 yards from the city, stood the modern, European-style Custom House, surrounded by trees and shrubs that had been lovingly planted to make the scene more English. The other houses in the district—only a month earlier the cheerful homes of English civilians and their families—were now ugly, charred shells, overgrown with jungle creeper, roofless, and blackened by flame.

Delhi stood in a plain, covered on two sides with buildings, ruins, thick undergrowth, and gardens. On the north-west, beyond the Jhil Canal that bounded the Cantonment, lay vast stretches of morass, green with bamboo beds and jungle, and then further ruins and native huts.

The Jhil Canal had been built to prevent flooding from the shallow hollow which extended for nearly thirty miles to the north-west of Delhi and was usually only a dry drainage channel. This year, however, because of abnormally heavy rains during the previous summer, the canal still contained drinkable water. This was fortunate, for all the Cantonment wells were stuffed with corpses and the Jumna water was too foul to drink.

The chief roads lay on the camp side of the city. The first, the Grank Trunk Road, by-passed the military station on the right, through dense gardens and old buildings to the Kabul Gate. From then it was in enemy hands, passing up the Chandni Chauk, below the Red Fort and out through the Calcutta Gate over the Bridge of Boats towards Meerut. The second road, the Cantonment Road, was much smaller. It crossed the Ridge and then led down to the Kashmir Gate.

The British tents were pitched below the Ridge's north-west slopes, behind the ruined Cantonment, with the native tents a little nearer the river. The Engineers were lucky. They found a house that still possessed a roof, and commandeered it for their mess, building their tents round it.

The encampment sloped down towards the canal, so that some tents were in a hollow. These were occupied by the most junior officers, for, of all stations for troops in the North-West Provinces, past experience had proved that this part of Delhi was easily the most unhealthy. The weary months that followed, were, according to the Rev. James

Rotton, "without exception, the very worst period of the year for life in tents anywhere in the plains of India."

The British key position was Hindu Rao's. This was the only position that actually faced the enemy, and it bore the brunt of every attack. Barely a week after it was occupied, for instance, a 32-pound shot came crashing into the portico one afternoon, killing an Ensign, a Havildar, four Gurkhas, two orderlies of the Carabineers, and a driver, and wounding several others.

"Nine killed and four wounded by *one* round-shot," exclaimed Major Charles Reid with fierce incredulity. *"And the regimental colours cut in two!"*

Three other forward posts were all close to Hindu Rao's. One stood near a small Hindu shrine known as "the Sammy-house" (from *swami*, meaning an idol); a precipitous crag known as the Crow's Nest, which became a favourite place for riflemen to gather; and, of course, the Subzi-Mundi, the lowest point of the British position overlooking the shallow gorge in which the Grand Trunk Road and the Western Jumna Canal ran towards the Kabul Gate. Hindu Rao's was on the extreme right flank of the British line, and the most advanced post. But even this was at least 1,500 yards away from the enemy.

The post behind Hindu Rao's house, and 180 yards to its left, was a dismal and dank structure built long ago as an observatory by a Rajput astronomer. It was a column of masonry, about 60 feet high, containing several small rooms, and with a narrow outside stairway, which led to an open upper platform only 5 or 6 feet across, without a parapet. This was easily the most exposed spot on the Ridge, and, like the other main posts, the Observatory was the site of two field-guns, and kept permanently occupied. Still further left, 650 yards away, was the massive Pathan mosque where Colonel Young had found the dead young man in his mother's arms. This became an infantry picket.

From here the road, surfaced wiht the red gravel of the

Ridge, led to the incongruously gothic Flagstaff Tower, nearly a mile away. This was a round, two-storeyed look-out, 150 feet high, which had been intended for nothing more sinister than to provide a fine view of the city, but which sheltered so many women and civilians on Monday, 11 May. Now, because of its sheltered position, the Tower became a favourite rendezvous for the sick and for officers off duty, who climbed up to the parapet to have a smoke in the cooler air, to survey the enemy's position, and discuss the day's events. It became the custom for every new officer, on the first possible opportunity after his arrival in camp, to climb its winding stairs and take stock of the situation which they had come to save.

From the top of the Flagstaff Tower, the view was indeed magnificent. The city lay open to them, over the walls, topped by eight-foot parapets and flanking bastions and mar-tello towers, and enclosing the cupolas and minarets of the Jumma Musjid Mosque and the delicate and intricate pierced screens and dome of the Red Fort, which held about 7,000 people during the siege.

The river bed was nearly a mile wide; in places a con-fusion of channels and sandbanks and shallow lagoons, sometimes bordered by jungle and malarial swamp, and sometimes by cultivated terraces and orange-groves. The panorama was fantastic; a delicate, ethereal city of domes and towers, framed in a deep green surround of swamps, gardens, and trees. But there was in the beauty something evil; and of those who admired the view less than a third would live to see what the city was like from the inside, looking out. Most of the shrubs and the smaller trees that had adorned the Cantonment had been torn down in a fury by the looting mutineers or eaten by the elephants and camels of the Field Force. The roadways were strewn with the remains of dinner sets and musical boxes, with European clothes and pictures. Officers of the former garrison who joined the Force would all visit their old bungalows to see what remained of their possessions. When young Vibart arrived late in July, he was disappointed to find nothing left to salvage from his quarters. The roof had fallen in and the whole interior was choked with rubbish; only the bare, calcined walls remained.

Between the camp and Ridge was a short-cut which was, however, terribly exposed to the enemy guns, and this became known as the "Valley of the Shadow of Death" from the numbers of men and beasts who were killed there. Before long it was filled with the carcasses of dead camels, horses, and bullocks, which were not dragged away for burial like the human victims, and so the stench of their decay was added to the smells from the other unburied animals that had died of starvation in the camp.

Up and down this valley, past the bloated corpses and the vultures and the black swarms of flies, the table servants or *khitmutgars* would toil bravely with the meals for their officers on duty balanced on their heads. They had begun to use this short cut before it became dangerous, and, being creatures of strict habit, they did not like to change their ways, but ran on, in and out of the bursting shells, covered with dust and flies, and occasionally with chips knocked out of the crockery by shell splinters.

Gradually, without leadership or official recognition, the initial brave enthusiasm for assault began to flag, but everyone was delighted when the Guides arrived, under the command of Captain Henry Daly of the 1st Bombay Fusiliers.

Daly, like so many of the officers who earned fame during the Mutiny, was of an Irish military family. He had served with the Company's Army since 1840 and was not at all the usual type of professional soldier. Though he never attempted to make a proper scheme of study, which in after years he often regretted, he was a tremendous reader, particularly of biography; he kept a daily diary and spoke Hindustani—a triumph not shared by all his contemporaries. A few years earlier Daly had been appointed to raise a new cavalry regiment, and had been so successful with his "wild horsemen" from the hills that the great Sir Charles Napier had written of him and Captain John Coke—who had recently done wonders with the 1st Punjab Infantry—that he was "more pleased with these two young commanders than he could well express." Although he was now only thirty-four, Daly's hair, probably as a result of the continued wearing of his tight cap, had receded far up his brow. His early career had been dogged by illness. At one time, indeed, he had contemplated giving up soldiering altogether; but since February 1856, when he had been appointed to assist in raising an irregular force in the newly annexed province of Oudh, he had done very well, with the quietly voiced ambition: "I mean it to be the finest irregular cavalry in India, and so it will be."

In March 1857, during the absence of the Corps Commander, Major Lumsden, Daly had been appointed to command the Guides, Hodson's old regiment, and, on the outbreak of the Mutiny, Herbert Edwardes, the assistant commissioner in the Punjab, had proposed to Lawrence that a movable column of two regiments, the Guides and some irregular cavalry, should be formed. So it came about that, in the middle of May, Daly and the Guides set off to join the Delhi Force.

It had taken them only three weeks to march 600 odd miles to Delhi—about thirty miles a day—and a Staff officer rode out from camp to meet them. Galloping up to Daly, he introduced himself, and then asked, "How soon can you be ready to go into action?"

Daly looked at him for a moment.

"In half an hour," he said briefly, and marched his men on. As the camp watched them move in—fierce Afghans, tall, powerful and swarthy, and the Gurkhas, short and muscular, with olive complexions, in their unusual uniforms, which as nearly as possible resembled their own ordinary clothes:

loose shorts, wide "pijamah" trousers, and turbans, plus as few accoutrements as possible—the word of their tremendous march went round. Even General Barnard pointed out on daily orders that none could recall a parallel feat.

"It was the talk of the border," wrote Herbert Edwardes exuberantly to Daly, and added: "I hope the men will fill their pockets in the sack of Delhi. . . . Bring back some standards from the Palace—especially Bahadur Shah's trousers."

The Guides swung into camp in perfect order and ready for the immediate duty to which they were called. That same afternoon, only three hours later, the enemy launched an attack on Hindu Rao's. It was the first of many they repulsed, and always with heavy casualties. During the Siege of Delhi, 320 of the original 400 Guides, who had marched in so bravely, died from wounds or disease.

Hodson, like the rest, watched their arrival, and no sooner did they catch sight of him (he wrote afterwards to his wife) than they crowded round him as he sat on horseback, shouting and cheering, *"Burra-lerai-wallah* (Great fighter)."

Hodson was exultant. They seemed frantic with joy, seizing his bridle, uniform, hands, and feet, actually throwing themselves down before his horse, tears streaming down their faces in their excitement. Hodson noticed with pleasure that all the Staff officers were witnesses to this remarkable scene— indeed, many of them hardly knew what to think and even imagined that he was being mobbed. He had little leisure, however, to chew over it, for at two o'clock in the afternoon the sudden attack put him and many others on horseback for the rest of the day. The enemy turned out in great numbers, and to repulse them the whole camp had to be up in arms.

The conduct of the Guides in the afternoon's fighting at Hindu Rao's, where the enemy had hoped to capture the guns, earned them still more admiration; but not without the wounding of all their officers. Daly was shot in the leg, though not seriously, and his horse was killed under him.

Their Adjutant, a young Lieutenant, Quintin Battye of the 56th Bengal Native Infantry, was mortally wounded.

It was Battye's first time in action, and he had no fear. Always he was at the front of his men, with Daly shouting excitedly: "Gallant Battye! Well done, brave Battye!" A mutineer shot him in the stomach at about point-blank range, and he lingered on in fearful pain till next day. His body was buried in that cemetery which he and the rest of the Guides had marched past so light-heartedly on the previous day.

An odd, ironic quirk of fate attended his deathbed, and a private joke of the Guides Corps became the admiration of the Army. Some time previously, at the Guides' headquarters at Hoti Mardan, Battye, who was a keen amateur artist, drew a spirited caricature of a charge of the Guides Cavalry on the white wall of the billiard-room and added the motto, *"Dulce et decorum est pro patria mori."*

His friends recognized themselves in the sketch, and were delighted, but objected to the motto as being "too tall."

Eventually it became a friendly joke at Battye's expense, for whenever he received a dull or unpleasant assignment he was sure to be reminded that it was "sweet and fitting."

The joke and the laughter of his friends meant much to him, and as he lay sweating in agony on a rope *charpoy,* waiting for death, he managed a faint smile to Daly, who sat sadly beside him and whispered, "Ah well, old fellow. *Dulce et decorum est pro patria mori.* That's how it is. . . ."

Not the irony, but the unintentional patriotism became the legend. Hardly a soldier who recorded the incident in later years but remarked upon its distinguished sentiments, and the Rev. James Rotton, who had attended Battye the night before he died, exclaimed in admiration: "His devotion to his country shone very conspicuously and brilliantly, even in anticipation of death." And, ever the Cambridge pedant, he added: "He seems to have been fond of classic quotation; and perchance, from frequent familiarity with the authors

of Greece and Rome in his boyhood and school-days, he im-
bibed the first inspirations of that noble military spirit which
afterwards so pre-eminently distinguished him." But poor
Battye was smiling at something more double-edged than the
kindly Mr. Rotton ever suspected.

The enemy were many times as strong as the British, and,
as Hodson admitted to his wife, "Their numbers tell when
we come near them, despite their want of discipline." The
mutineers also had some fine artillerymen who also told on
the British force alarmingly. The British guns were having
little effect while their casualties were serious. By next day,
however, a new mortar battery was ready to subdue the enemy's firing, and the other batteries—all called after different
Engineer officers—were also set up. Nevertheless, the sepoys'
firing was recklessly heavy, because they had unlimited reserves of ammunition, for, despite the blowing up of the
magazine, masses of explosives fell into their hands while,
on the British side, even the disabling of a single large-calibre
piece could be serious.

This state of affairs lasted throughout the siege, and indeed grew worse, for the pattern of the siege had begun and
from then on fights occurred almost every day and sometimes
three or four times a day. The favourite point of attack remained Hindu Rao's, which was the weakest point of the
British defences. And while the sepoys were always driven
back, the enemy was being daily reinforced by fresh bands of
mutineers from all over north-west India, while the British
suffered losses that were, in proportion, much greater.

Despite this, and although attack followed attack day after
day, no one made any attempt at organizing a rota for defence
and other duties. When there was an attack, the entire force
would get under arms and sally out to repel the intruders,
but without any plan or co-ordination of their efforts. They
fought under anyone who would lead them, and in the outlying positions this led to chaos and confusion, since in the

dust the cavalry kicked up it was often difficult to discover who were attacking and who defending.

"We came to besiege Delhi," James Rotton wrote home in disillusion, "but we very soon learnt that in reality *we* were the besieged and the mutineers the besiegers. . . . It was literally nothing but fighting by day and watching and expecting to renew the conflict by night, and in the discharge of both duties you could not fail to recognize the same hands everlastingly employed in the same work. . . ."

There was little chance of sleep for anyone, and whether or not there was an attack, even the normal pickets required enormous numbers to maintain, and the guards had no reliefs. Everyone had to remain under arms all night. Some men were on duty for sixty hours at a stretch.

Cholera appeared almost at once. There had been a few cases on the march, but less than twenty-four hours after the camp had been occupied more fell ill. To make matters worse, both the surgeons of the 75th Foot went down with it together, and though the assistant, a muscular Irishman, Surgeon Coghlan, survived, he had only just recovered from a serious attack, and throwing himself again into his work too soon, he collapsed and died within twelve hours.

At that time there were no other cases in camp, but Captain Octavius Anson of Her Majesty's 9th Lancers viewed the future with a certain amount of gloom. His regiment's tents were down close to the canal, and from his twenty years' service in India, he knew that when the rains came sickness of some kind would be almost universal.

His own regiment were comfortably enough clad in light uniforms, but others, such as the Carabineers, were in their heavy blue uniforms and overalls.

Temperatures in the tents were so high that officers and men would lie sweltering underneath their beds to try to get extra protection from the terrible heat. The Staff were best off, since the General's tents were made of finer material, and so were much cooler.

Colonel Young, not a very imaginative man, reassured his wife in Simla that they "didn't find it *particularly* hot in tents," and that nights and early mornings were "quite cool." But he had thirty-three years' service behind him, and as a former Civil Judge-Advocate in Simla he received more privileges than most of his comrades in arms.

On 10 June, General Reed arrived from the Hills to take command of the Delhi Force. He was the senior military officer in the Punjab, and as such his age and length of service entitled him to command. Sir John Lawrence approved the appointment, but Young was not at all impressed by the new Commander. "He is a poor, infirm old man, and seems as if a puff of wind would carry him away," he wrote disgustedly to his wife. "It was a terrible trip he had down here, and he was sick when he started; I almost wonder at his surviving it."

General Reed took to his bed the moment he arrived, and was so overcome by the heat, the strange surroundings, and the equally strange responsibility of commanding an army in action that he stayed there. What feeble strength he had failed him at the thought of the decisions he should make, and he lay, eyes closed, in his darkened tent while his aides tiptoed about anxious to know what to do for the best.

General Reed's senility had an adverse effect on General Barnard who, until his arrival, had been in command. He was also in his seventies. Although generally liked in the negative way that soldiers feel for a commander about whom they know almost nothing, but who has not yet done them any actual ill, Barnard was far too old for his position. He had served in the Crimea, and only recently arrived in India: the Mutiny was his first emergency there, and he had no real plan to cope with it.

He felt that the arrival of General Reed was in some way a slur on his capabilities as a general, and the thought preyed on his mind to such an extent that soon he could neither eat nor sleep, but, like Reed, lay inert on his bed, eyes closed, retreating from his unthinkable responsibility.

The combination of a strange country, the proximity of a senior officer, and the urgent need for a plan of action wore him down. Young felt kindly towards the poor old fellow, but thought that "though a very nice kind-hearted and brave old man, he was no more fit for his present post than he was to be Pope of Rome."

The hot-tempered and impatient Hodson was less charitable in his opinions—although he was the recipient of some coals of fire when he caught a heavy feverish cold and General Barnard exerted himself particularly on his account. Barnard was glad of any distraction to take his thoughts off the problems of command, and insisted on taking Hodson into his own, more commodious tent and nursing him like his own son.

"I woke in the night," Hodson wrote a little shamefacedly afterwards, "and found the kind old man by my bedside, covering me carefully up from the draught. . . ."

Major Laughton, as the senior Engineer officer, should have been working out a plan to breach the walls of Delhi with high explosive—for if the city were ever to be captured, a hole must be made in the walls to allow the troops to enter. But he had no ideas for such a plan, and no interest in it, either. He was fully occupied with his Persian wife, and glad to pass on his responsibility to juniors, or indeed to anyone who might be interested in looking after his men. He stayed in his tent with his wife, who was beginning to complain about the lack of comforts in the camp.

General Barnard, a stranger both to country and to the situation, received no help from his Chief Engineer and little from Brigadier Archdale Wilson, his Chief of Artillery, who earnestly dissuaded him from attempting any active operations.

"The actual course of events," a staff officer wrote later, "was therefore determined rather by the conduct of the besieged than by the councils of the besiegers."

But if this was the case with the senior officers, most of

the younger element thought that it was clearly up to them to convince their superiors that an immediate assault was imperative.

Young Wilberforce Greathed of the Engineers was the most vociferous of those demanding action, and so, possibly as much to quieten criticism as for any other reason, General Barnard entrusted to him, with Hodson, George Chesney, the Brigade Major, and Frank Maunsell, another Engineer, the task of working out some plan of attack.

Hodson felt that he personally had been asked by the General because he was well known to advocate vigorous measures. ("I do not urge others to do what I would not be the first to do myself.") But even so, he felt that the task was an unusual one.

"Times must be changed," he reflected, "when four subalterns are called upon to suggest a means of carrying out so vital an enterprise as this—one on which the safety of the Empire depends!"

The plan they drew up, headed "Project of Attack on the City of Delhi, prepared for Submission to Major-General Sir H. Barnard, K.C.B., Camp Delhi Cantonment, 11th June, 1857," was warmly approved by the General. Now that something was actually committed to paper, he felt relieved, and full of euphoric enthusiasm for the project, without any real conception of what was needed to carry it through successfully.

The plan depended on complete surprise. First, the gates would be blown in and storming parties would charge through into the city while others scaled the walls on bamboo ladders. It bristled with risks, but Hodson was keen on attempting such an assault, "or," as he said, "we may be many weeks before Delhi, instead of within it."

The assault was ordered for daybreak on 13 June, and the troops were to assemble at a rendezvous "by arrangement." But everyone was so excited at the strange, unexpected prospect of action that no one had remembered to explain the plan to the senior officers. Thus it came about that when a young subaltern raced up to Brigadier Graves, who was Officer of the Day, and asked him to withdraw the hundreds of men on pickets on the Ridge—and so leave it virtually un-guarded—he thought the man was having delusions.

The subaltern persisted, and explained that the men were needed to form the assaulting column, but the Brigadier had no idea what he was talking about, and decided to ride down to the General's tent to see what was happening.

Meanwhile, the rest of the troops in camp fidgeted and waited about, for though their officers knew an attempt on Delhi was planned no one seemed available or willing to lead them, or even to give the word to march.

The Rifles, however, actually advanced to within 300 yards of the walls, where they meant to blow up one of the gates and so take the enemy by surprise. But they were the ones who received the surprise, for by the time Brigadier Graves had satisfied himself as to the authenticity of his unusual orders, it was too near daybreak for the rest of the men to be assembled, and the affair fizzled out in fiasco. This plan was a bold one, for none but a handful of cavalry and non-combatants would have remained to defend the camp, and there were no reserves to be spared from the small force. Nevertheless, the chagrined Hodson was convinced that the affair would have succeeded. ("The rebels were cowed, and perfectly ignorant of any intention of so bold a stroke," he said that night. "The surprise would have done every-thing. . . .")

The first result of this needless setback was that everyone heaped the blame on Brigadier Graves. For a long time the officers ostracized him, as though he had deliberately ob-structed them in their attempt. Only General Barnard, glad to have a further distraction from the business of serious warfare, remained friendly, and did his best to make him feel that at least he did not hold him responsible.

Graves endured the insults and snubs of his comrades for

about a month, and then, on what Hodson called "a strong hint," he put in for a four months' sick leave and left Delhi altogether.

The day after this abortive assault, Barnard wrote to his friend George Barnes, the Commissioner in the Punjab, to tell him of his difficulties. There was, he wrote, "nothing left for it but to attempt a *coup de main,* not easy on these bright nights." The old man heaved a sigh as he thought of the few guns he could muster, "and these all served by raw hands." Matters were not helped for him by the continued misunderstandings which were the subjects of letters and dispatches coming in from other parts of India and, later, from England. Nobody seemed able to estimate the real strength of the mutineers in Delhi.

"Twenty-four-pounders mounted throughout their bastions with about seven thousand men behind them is not so easily walked into," he wrote sourly.

The General was inclined to think that the failure of the plan had been providential, for success would have been as fatal as failure. An attacking force of under 2,000 bayonets spread over a city the size of Delhi would have been useless, "and with the treachery that surrounds us, what would have become of my material?"

He felt that it was ridiculous to suppose their small force could hope to capture and hold the city "bristling with cannon and garrisoned with men who, however contemptible in the open, have sagacity behind stone walls and some knowledge of the use of heavy ordnance."

Only a few months earlier, feeling he was being by-passed for greater things, General Barnard had written to Lord Canning, the Governor-General, asking for a chance to show his mettle. "Cannot you find some tough job for me?" he pleaded. He had it now.

Inside Delhi all was confusion that verged on anarchy. The old King was not accustomed to being responsible for either the well-being or the safety of his subjects, and because of his age his assertions of authority were rare. Troops were arriving daily in droves from outer mutinous centres, and for months Delhi became the grand rallying-point of the mutineers of the north-west.

Rumour and lying report held the day, and his Palace was a magnet for every new arrival. Soldiers came to tell him how they had driven back the English, when the opposite was always the case. Private citizens arrived to lay false charges against their personal enemies; while stories of the death of some senior English officers were passed around without any confirmation of their truth. News arrived of the Lucknow mutiny, of the Agra mutiny, of the Jaggar mutiny. The tide of violence was sweeping inexorably across the land and was only stopped at Budli-ka-Serai when Brigadier Wilson's men from Meerut had routed the mutineers. All the city bastions were manned on that day, and citizens climbed fearfully to the roofs to watch the distant firing, which went on until far in the afternoon.

Finally, to the disgust of the watchers from the towers, the mutinous began to straggle in, defeated. First came the cavalry, (who stood their ground the shortest time), and, at last, the infantry, sweaty and beaten, all receiving showers of abuse and accusations of cowardice from those who had stayed at home. Had the English pressed their advantage, they would have found the gates open and the panic-stricken soldiery in too much confusion to drive them back. No one could understand why they did not attack, and only after waiting in terror for their expected onslaught did the townsfolk dare to voice their astonishment and relief.

The King tried to restore order to the troops by appointing a Commander-in-Chief, "General" Summud Khan, who had been a jemadar in the Company's Army. He issued a proclamation to the Army urging them to muster and advance under his command, "when victory would be their reward."

And so the sorties on the British camp began—sorties which always ended in retreats, but which could be covered by powerful artillery fire from the bastions. An ex-Gunner, Kuli Khan, distinguished himself with the accuracy of his fire and seriously hampered the building of the English batteries over against the Kashmir Gate.

Men were betrayed and threatened with death because they were suspected to be in league with the English, as indeed many were, for Hodson soon organized a spy service, and these people came to and fro in the darkness selling information for cash on the spot.

They had some unusual stories to tell. The King issued special orders to the traders to open their shops which had closed the day the outbreak started. On the day they reopened, confusion and terror were caused by the falling of shells within the walls, so they closed again.

Demonstrations and the murders of pro-English Indians took place nearly every day, and everyone detested the sepoys for their undisciplined behaviour and their oppression of the townspeople.

The King had no authority over anyone any more. He was reduced to threatening to poison himself if the Commander did not enforce better discipline. The Commander promised him that he would try, but he did not seem confident about the outcome.

The last Mogul had very little peace. He held councils almost daily, and so many people laid petitions and complaints before him that he had to push through crowds that became insulting if he did not at once give them what they wanted. They would stick their sweating faces into his, and some even pulled his beard.

He tried to drive the mutineers out to fight the English, threatening to leave the city himself if they did not justify themselves. Jeewan Lal, who acted as a spy for Hodson's intelligence service, kept a daily diary in which he noted without fail that the troops were got out to fight "under pres-

sure" and returned "in disorder." But even so they could still
go out in thousands.

One day they returned early from a foray complaining that
"the air did not agree with them." The King, in a fury at
this excuse, ordered that, since they had failed to drive away
the English, they must leave the city and go elsewhere. They
moved out of one of the gates farthest from the Ridge and
pitched their own camp outside the city walls.

No house was safe from the sepoys' plundering hands.
Before long all trade was at a standstill, nothing could be
done without a bribe, and looting was so serious that it led
to depopulation in some quarters.

The King's subjects were continually complaining to him
of the miseries and dangers from which they suffered, and,
fearful lest an English shell should accidentally blow up the
magazine, traders petitioned him against the position of the
powder factory, which might at any moment blow them into
eternity. Eventually, they succeeded in getting this moved.

Some treasure was brought in by the newcomers, and several batteries were built against the English, while the sepoys
began repairs on one or two of the fortifications that had
been damaged by firing. Now and then raiding parties intercepted carts of provisions intended for the English camp and
brought them into the city, but the besieged, like the besiegers, had no long-term plan; they lived for each day as it
came.

The English, meanwhile, with the unquenchable optimism
that is a national characteristic, were looking for reinforcements. General Havelock was expected; Sir Hugh Wheeler
was expected; reinforcements "from below" were *certain* to
come soon, and then the city would fall and the Delhi Force
be released to mop up the mutineers over the country. In
fact, reinforcements *must* be arriving soon, because there had
been a good omen in the camp—a birth.

By an oversight of a kind not entirely surprising in view
of the general state of preparation of the army before Delhi,

a young officer, Captain Tytler, had brought along his wife, who was too far pregnant to be left alone. She gave birth to a son; he was christened Stanley Delhi Force. Tytler over-heard a soldier saying with certainty: "Now we *shall* get our reinforcements. This camp was formed to avenge the blood of innocents, and the first reinforcement sent to us is a new-born infant. . . ."

When the annoyance over the fiasco of the first assault had died, General Barnard asked Colonel Young for advice on a second attempt. He had received news of the departure of about 4,000 troops from Jullundur to join the British force at Delhi, and he wanted to ask Young whether he thought they should wait until these reinforcements arrived or attack at once. Young did not know what to say. He suggested that Greathed and General Reed should be asked for their opin-ions. In the end, the easy way out was taken; they would wait until the reinforcements arrived in about ten days' time, and then decide what to do.

"The truth is," Young wrote to his wife—adding hastily, "You must not say a word about it to anyone—poor General Barnard has been so badgered by Greathed and one or two others about him to move on with his present force, that against his own conviction he had determined to do so, and in all human probability the attack, though a rather desper-ate one considering our limited numbers, would have been successful; but it *might* have failed for some unlooked-for accident, and then good-bye not only to our little force but to India itself. . . .

"It is not very pleasant," he added. "The prospect of being in tents for another ten days or so." Most of the letters by the officers and men contained some reference to the expected attack: "Another few days" . . . "We shall soon get the devils out" . . . "Not very long now" . . . "The next letter will probably be dated within the walls."

Although life in camp was in some ways hard and uncertain, the commissariat lacked very little, at least for the officers, for practically anything could be sent up from Amballa by bullock train. Captain Anson was made President of his own mess, and worried over his stocks of beer and brandy, which were probably the most important item in the menu. To the anxieties of the siege were added those of the continual run on the drinks. The officers drank so much soda-water that Anson wrote in despair to his wife, explaining the demand for it at Amballa, "that in eight or ten days the machinery for making it will be worn out, and no more can be made. Very pleasant news. . . ."

At the same time there was "no brandy to be had," despite the vast orders he had just sent. By the end of June he was finding it impossible to get either saltpetre or potatoes; and one evening, when he was entertaining his cousin to dinner, his servant came in to tell him that "all the claret was out." This was bad news indeed. "We shall soon be reduced to Commissariat rum," he told his cousin bitterly. Such was the feeling over this that his cousin could find nothing at all to say.

Colonel Young, however, was delighted with his culinary arrangements. "The pastry at the mess is about the best I have come across in India," he assured his wife. "It seems that the Artillery Mess cook or confectioner is famous for his skill. . . . You would be surprised to see how comfortable we are—with *tatties* (grass screens) and punkah. As to our living, we could not dine more luxuriously than we do if we were quietly located at Simla. . . ."

Hodson did not share this view.

"We are not very well off *quant à la cuisine*," he noted in a letter. "I never had so much trouble in getting anything fit to eat, except when I dine with the General. . . ."

On 16 June the senior officers held a meeting to decide what could be done. The Generals felt that a joint decision would be an easier way out of a difficult situation than for them to give a lead themselves. Colonel Young reported that the feeling of the meeting was "to wait in our present position for reinforcements, and Brigadier Wilson . . . was quite of opinion that this is the right thing to do. . . . Young Greathed . . . was the great advocate for a forward move at once, but his talk was too fiery and wild for anyone to listen to. Here therefore we remain for the next eight or ten days, and in that time it will be surprising if the dissensions among the mutineers do not increase. . . ."

All the assumptions in camp as to the actions and reactions of the mutineers were based on the reports of spies in the city. At the moment their news was encouraging:

> . . . The mutineers who first came to Delhi have grown heavy on account of their being laden with plunder, and are no longer fit for action, and on being ordered to fight set forth excuses. . . .
> The king said: "If you do not go out, I will blow up the powder-magazine and die." On this some of the troops went out to fight, and on their return at night, when it was found they also were dispirited and that defeat was only delayed on account of the protection afforded by the gates and walls, the force were still more dispirited. . . .

The messages the mutineers sent to other districts asking rulers and people to join them were said to be having small effect.

> Gwalior says: "When you are *really* King, I will come to your assistance." Dholpur was first going to kill the messenger, but let him go; and Bhurtpore said he was always disloyal to Delhi, and would remain so. . . .

Gratifying though these reports were to the British who read them over claret or brandy, some of the statements were exaggerated. The spies were paid by results and naturally hoped to bring news the British would want to read. Against this bias, however, must be set the fact that all the rebel attacks were repulsed with great loss to them, and little to the

European side; sometimes as many as 300 to 400 mutineers were killed, to half a dozen of the defenders.

During a temporary lull, a party of wounded were able to be taken off to Meerut, and Mrs. Laughton, the wife of the Chief Engineer, went with them.

A dejected company of homeless British civilians, who had been living the lives of refugees in camp, also took the chance to move to Meerut. They included Customs officers and deputy collectors, with their wives and children, of mixed ages, colours and races. The chaplain, Mr. Rotton, had visited them often, and was distressed to see the hardships they had suffered.

A few lived in tents, "some of which," he pointed out, "had been supplied at considerable inconvenience to the department by the Q.M.G. of the Army." In other cases, as many as seven or eight adults, "married and unmarried," he noted with some feeling of shock, were huddled together "in the greatest state of confusion and discomfort."

They would hardly have been able to find even bread to eat, had not the Army, in the person of British private soldiers, shared their own food with them with their customary kindness. There was no suggestion, apparently, that the commissariat should make itself officially responsible for their welfare. They were regarded as a nuisance, and some actually died while in the British camp.

When they had gone, General Barnard found that the enemy had started to build two new batteries just south of Kishengunge, and so he sent out two young majors, Charles Reid and Henry Tombs, with small columns and four field-guns, to destroy them. Had an enemy footing been achieved permanently in that area, the Ridge guns would become fatally vulnerable.

Reid destroyed both batteries and burned the village and all the timber that was stacked to make the magazines, and the gates of two *serais* or walled enclosures, which would have afforded enemy cover.

He lost only two men, with three or four more wounded, while he counted at least forty enemy killed, and captured the one gun which the enemy had so far brought out.

Major Tombs also showed characteristic verve and brilliance, and had two horses shot beneath him.

Despite such sudden sharp bursts of excitement, there were many occasions when not a gun could be heard firing on either side, a welcome change from the usual boom of the guns that reverberated for miles around, and on a clear day could be heard in Meerut.

Officers on their way to Delhi by mailcart—the usual means of transport—would hear their angry thunder from a distance and hasten on with even more enthusiasm, supposing that an attack was due, and that they were missing the excitement. To many young British officers all over India, the sole fear was that Delhi might fall before they could arrive to help with its capture.

Many of them belonged to native regiments which had mutinied, and they were left without any troops to command —a most unsatisfactory state of affairs that caused them to be known around camp as "refugees." They were attached to other regiments for the duration of the upheaval, postings accepted without much enthusiasm on either side.

The enemy, having failed to repulse the Europeans, had lost a great deal of their initial zeal. Since the chief lack among the mutineers was discipline, it became the habit to insist that new arrivals to their ranks must first go into battle before they could join their comrades in the Mogul city. Before any newcomers were allowed inside the walls of Delhi —no matter if they had marched a month to reach it—they were first sent up to attack the British from the Lahore Gate. And so, time after time, well-armed mutineers, newcomers all, would fling themselves unavailingly against the camp, unaware that, only days before, the last draft in had done exactly the same thing.

On 19 June the Nussereebad Regiments arrived, with a

native field battery and some cavalry. They came out in their hundreds during the late afternoon to attack the British and so win the right to enter Delhi. Those already safe within the walls would watch the progress of each "blooding" from safe vantage-points. Those too far away to see clearly used telescopes and spy-glasses. These new arrivals attacked vigorously with a violent artillery fire, and so large an area was threatened that only a small answering fire could be spared to reply.

When the alarm bugle sounded, the Rifles rushed to the expected point of attack—Hindu Rao's—but soon discovered that this was not to be the centre of the fighting after all. They doubled back to the General's Mound—a hummock over an old limekiln where General Barnard liked to stand with his staff and view operations, much as an owner might watch the progress of a favourite racehorse; not personally involved in the struggle, but intensely interested in its outcome.

While the main force was kept busy in front, the enemy began moving quietly round towards the rear, under cover of the thick foliage, and very nearly brought disaster to the small numbers of defenders on that side.

Colonel Hope Grant, who was leading out the 9th Lancers and Guides with four guns, decided to divide up his men in Subzi Mundi, as the ground was so broken and clustered with gardens and trees. He sent Daly off to the left with the Guides, together with a Major Yule and a troop of the 9th Lancers, and a Gunner officer, Lieutenant Hills, with two of Tombs's guns. This small party soon found itself faced by a large force of cavalry and infantry with six or eight guns across the canal, and as there was nothing to be gained by falling back, Daly told Hills to get his guns into action at once. Leaving a handful of Guides with him, he took off the rest to engage the enemy cavalry, which was threatening on the left.

Meanwhile, on the other side, Grant's small force was in the thick of fighting, Grant leading the main body of cavalry with his customary energy—"never better than when he has lots to do," said Anson later. At one point he was surrounded by mutineers and only saved himself from almost certain death by seizing the tail of his orderly's horse and letting the beast drag him out of danger. Tombs, with the other two guns, suddenly found that the enemy were picking off his gunners at close range, and were so close, under cover of the gardens and high mudbanks, that it was almost impossible for his gunners to shoot them. Men were falling like flies. If something were not done quickly, there would soon be no guns to serve, and Tombs dared not fall back, lest he should compromise the rest, who were still presumably advancing through an enclosure known as the Ochterlony Garden.

"I cannot describe the confusion in the dark," wrote Captain Anson later. "One could see the flash of every matchlock." During the turmoil a tumbril of ammunition blew up, and, in the words of one, it all seemed "a dreadful scrape." Some even began to imagine that the camp was being stormed and sacked by the enemy in their absence. Men and horses raced about in the darkness, and every now and then an exploding shell lit up the chaos with an orange glare.

In desperation, Tombs rode up to Daly, who was the only European officer out with the Guides.

"I fear I must ask you to charge to save my guns!" he shouted, a bit embarrassed at the request. Daly and his Guides charged on through the thickening dusk, and actually came within sight of enemy guns, recognizing them by their markings as being stolen by the mutineers from a British Artillery troop.

A bullet cut through Daly's left shoulder, mercifully on the right side of danger, but he fell to the ground and lay there in agony unable to move, and not able to shout for help lest his cries should give his position away to the mutineers.

Even though he kept silent, he was spotted by a young man who, rather against his will, was fighting with the rebels.

Before the Mutiny, this young fellow had been quite a pro-
tégé of Daly's, who had taken him into the Oudh Irregular
Cavalry as a cornet of horse. He was a prince, the grandson
of a king, "a handsome, elegant boy, pale and delicate, with
beautiful eyes." But, despite his royal lineage, he was in dire
poverty and only too thankful to be offered the rank of a
jemadar in the cavalry at £40 a year.

He saw Daly lying on the ground, wounded, and hastened
to point out his benefactor to Daly's own men, who picked
him up and carried him back to safety, where Tombs, seeing
his condition, was convinced that his action had saved the
day. It had indeed been a "very nasty position," as Hills said
with Victorian understatement, and Hope Grant, who recommended Daly for a V.C. later on, thought that at no other
time during the siege had their force been so nearly annihilated. Even the General visited Daly, whose wound had permanently crippled that arm. He said he was sorry Hills was
of the Company's Army and so not eligible for the Victoria
Cross, as he thought him worthy of one. The princeling rode
away again with the mutineers. His good deed did not save
him when the city finally fell. He was hanged with the rest.

Shots had been falling steadily in camp, and suddenly a
tremendous clatter of earthenware and metal pots and dishes
aroused the Rev. Rotton, who ran out of the mess-tent to see
what had happened. An enemy roundshot had landed right
in the General's kitchen-tent.

When more shots followed, there was a tremendous upheaval among the camel men and servants, who fled away
screaming, falling over guy-ropes and each other in their
eagerness to be elsewhere. The clergyman was amused at their
"unusual activity." Providence, he wrote in his diary, should
send more "playful, not destructive, round shot rolling into
camp . . . to stir up the dying energy of human character in
the East."

This engagement brought the British two captured guns
and some ammunition wagons, on one of which a few

wounded enemy gunners waited to be carried back into the city. They did not make their journey, for no quarter was expected or given. Only a very few prisoners of war were captured during the entire campaign.

Captain Anson attended the burial service which Rotton conducted for the fallen, and noted that the clergyman had not even brought his prayer book with him—a grim reminder that he could not fail to know the service by heart. The corpses were all tied up in their Guthries, and he thought distressfully that they "looked so snug and comfortable in their little graves, which were, however, hardly deep enough"—an opinion that the appallingly hot days proved quite right.

"It was the hottest day yet"—so everyone decided, as they mopped their streaming brows, and lay panting under their beds, or were prostrated by sunstroke with wet towels round their heads. The heat was really not exceptional, but everyone was quite unaccustomed to such unpleasant activity in it.

There was still no sign of the rains, and those camping in the hollow began to be anxious about the drainage of the ground. The mounds of dead elephants and camels were generating the most fearful smells, and men on picket duty near the scene of the last action were already vomiting from the stench of the bodies in their shallow graves. The air was thick with germs and decay.

Another Sunday came round, and this time Rotton preached —"such a long, sleepy sermon," yawned Young—at his service held in H.Q. at five-thirty in the morning. At eleven, he held one for the Rifle Brigade, and then one for the cavalry at six in the evening. This was his regular Sunday programme. On weekdays he held daily services for the hospitals, and, he recalled sadly afterwards, "Not a morning or evening passed without burials."

Most people still confidently supposed that only a short time would pass before they penetrated the city, and wishful thinkers were not lacking who could see without a doubt that already the rebels were "beginning to show signs of losing heart." News had come of the massacre at Bareilly, however, and communication with Calcutta and "all that side" was still quite cut off, although the road to Meerut was clear.

The arrival of a Major Olpherts on 23 June, with about 400 European infantry plus a Sikh corps of 500, with cavalry and six guns and a large convoy of ammunition and stores, cheered everyone up. The mutineers tried to intercept the train, and this caused a lively morning for Captain Anson. A Lancer officer saw three sepoys slipping away along a wall, and captured them as spies. "When the pistols were presented at their heads, they made a clean bolt for it, for their lives," he reported. "It was their only chance, and a poor one, too, for they were pursued and shot down and lanced."

A few days more, people thought, would see the end of "this business at Delhi," so that at least some of their force could move on towards Allygurh to reopen communications and restore order. Some relief was felt when the apathetic Chief Engineer, Major Laughton, was posted elsewhere, and it was announced that he would be succeeded by the energetic Colonel Baird Smith, who had come from Roorkee, where he had been Superintendent of Canals in the North-West Provinces. General Reed had at last been prevailed upon to get rid of Laughton. The General could not bring himself to do such a thing; he had heard that Laughton had "influence," but with whom he did not know. So, to be on the safe side, he sent a telegram to Sir John Lawrence, asking him to recall the officer. Lawrence did so at once.

Hodson still hoped that some batteries might now be made and the city assaulted, but he stuck to his opinion that the attack should have been made when first planned, before the enemy had time to prepare for it. "The city is so overflowing that the rascals are encamped outside the gates under cover of their formidable batteries, and in the glacis." Hodson's spies did not tell him that this was done on the orders of the worried old King, to keep the troublemaking sepoys outside the city walls.

The twenty-third of June had been awaited with dread by the Europeans, and with equal jubilation by the mutineers, for it was the centenary of the Battle of Plassey. The prophecy was that 100 years after Plassey the rule of the Company would end—and what better date to end it on than the hundredth anniversary of the battle?

Hindu and Moslem alike had listened with enthusiasm to the harangues of their leaders on this theme, and by five o'clock in the morning they were streaming out of the city wearing their red coats and all their British medals, filling Subzi Mundi, spreading behind the low banks and walls, to the rear and right of Hindu Rao's, to attack the British. The fight went on until evening in the liquid heat of the sun. "A wretchedly anxious day," said Young drily. "Not much generalship, I fear." Then the mutineers withdrew to the safety of their city.

The enemy artillery had done the most damage, and their training under the British helped them immensely. The officers of the besieging force were well aware that their own gunners were neither so accurate nor so quick in firing, and, besides, their guns were far fewer and of smaller calibre. The ordnance with which the British started the siege consisted of only two 24-pounders, with ten 18-pounders and as many howitzers.

On the 24th Brigadier Neville Chamberlain arrived by the springless *dak*-cart. He had been eagerly awaited for several days, ever since the news that he had been appointed Adjutant-General in succession to Colonel Chester.

Chamberlain had been in the innermost councils of Lawrence at Rawalpindi on the outbreak of the Mutiny. Captain Daly, who had met him there, had been much struck, as indeed were most people, with his business-like outlook, and the day he arrived he set about producing some order and method from the general policy of drift and vague optimism.

The whole of this month of June before Delhi had proved extremely costly in the lives and health of officers and men.

Lives were continually being thrown away because of the inadequate defences and the unplanned turnouts during enemy attacks, added to complete lack of foresight or resolution
of those in command.

Neville Chamberlain, looking back soon after the siege,
decided that when he arrived at the camp on 24 June "affairs
looked as unprosperous as ever they did." He meant the previous day's fight, the attack on the rear a few days earlier, and
a growing, unhealthy depression that was beginning to be
felt all through the camp. There was no plan, no order, no
aim. Cannon-balls fell daily within the perimeter, and every
day deaths from wounds and cholera increased so that already the original force that had set up camp in such optimism a few weeks previously was only a fraction of its former
size.

Everyone lived from day to day, and although some of the
bolder spirits talked continually of the assault on Delhi, their
talk was not translated into action. Most people seemed to
think that the mutineers would "come to their senses," and
that, in the end, as always, the British would somehow win
the last battle. But no one had any worthwhile or practical
suggestion to accelerate this desirable end.

Beneath their veneer of optimism, the British had much to
worry them: constant fears for the supply line, the dubious
loyalties of the Hindustanis, both soldiers and camp-followers; doubt about the future behaviour of Sikhs and Pathans;
and an irritation about the straggling length of the British
lines and their inadequate protection against enemy fire—all
the worse when compared with the secure cover available to
the enemy and their almost ludicrous advantage in numbers.
Yet, Chamberlain said, later, there was never a doubt of success, despite the temporary anxieties. ("The officers were as
cheerful as if quietly in cantonments, and never had I been
in a camp where there were fewer croakers.")

Chamberlain went over the whole position with the General, and since it was clear that the means of the Force were

quite insufficient for assault, he had no hesitation in telling Barnard so. The General did not thank him for this view and complained afterwards to a colleague that Chamberlain "did not give him much consolation."

The new Adjutant-General, however, was of the opinion that the failure to start on the plan of assault was a blessing in disguise, and that there "was no course but to remain where we were or to retire." Indeed, he found there was hardly a soul but was resolved to hold on and so "conquer or let our bones bleach on the hillside." Not for the first time, the British Army confused the qualities of fortitude with those of victory.

The general opinion on Chamberlain's arrival, however, was one of increased optimism. Young "hoped there would be some generalship now." Hodson "hoped much from him." General Barnard was no less pleased, for he found himself almost sinking under the burdens of command. Since the responsibilities of decision weighed on him, he asked advice of anyone rather than trust his own judgment. And then, when a joint decision had been made, he lacked the character to insist that it should be carried out.

Chamberlain was also well known as one who did not act without thinking; but having thought, he acted with resolution.

His arrival put new heart into many officers, including those who were facing strange and unusual responsibilities. One of these was Alex Taylor, in temporary command of the Engineers until the arrival of Baird Smith. He was a young man of courage, energy, and resource, a fine football player, a keen fisherman, a champion at jumping, and for some reason known in the Brigade as "Musha." He had been largely responsible for the building of the Grand Trunk Road, which is still his memorial. Although only thirty-one, he was senior in years in the Engineer Brigade, which consisted almost entirely of young and untried subalterns.

By the time Baird Smith arrived on 3 July, the Engineers'

mess numbered twenty-two officers, and they centred round
an ex-officer's bungalow of three rooms which had been one
of the few to survive the holocaust of 11 May. It contained
a large, high, central room which ran the length of the building, and two smaller rooms opening off it, with a wide veranda. Round it were tents and, beyond, the "Engineers'
Park" for their stores.

Some officers had found a large mahogany billiard table in
a ruined house, and, with the resource of their calling, they
had sawn off the edges to make a dining table which would
accommodate twenty, and which could even serve as a bed
for some, while others, whose tents had not arrived, slept on
the veranda.

Once they had got a punkah going it was comfortable
enough, apart from the incessant noise arising from a score of
young, high-spirited officers packed together in a small space.
When off duty they would cram together at the table under
the punkah with their books or letters or cheerful talk, "as
if," wrote Alex Taylor, "we were engaged on the most com-
monplace, ordinary business."

As far as anyone could be said to derive amusement from
the siege, the Engineers did so. They regarded themselves as
the crack brigade of the Company's Army, for it was only the
highest of the cadets of Addiscombe—the Company's training
school—who passed into this coveted service. And, despite
the lack of tents, privacy, comfort, and servants—most of
whom straggled into camp weeks behind their masters—despite the heat and the fatigue, nearly everyone, unless actually prostrated with cholera or a wound or dysentery as a
result of careless drinking of impure water, wrote jubilantly
home that they were "all serene" and in "capital health."

The chief members of the mess, apart from Taylor, were
Greathed, Chesney, and Maunsell. Wilberforce Greathed,
witty, dashing, and quick-tempered, had been appointed con-
sulting engineer to the Government at the time of the outbreak, and so became known as "the insulting engineer."

Apart from his hot-headed urging on of the General to assault, one of his best-known exploits to date had been a dash from Agra to Meerut which he had made at the beginning of the month—the last Englishman to penetrate that route for four months—carrying dispatches to Brigadier Wilson. On arrival, he found that Wilson had already left for Delhi, and so he followed alone and overnight, across the robber infested country to Alipore, where he caught up with the column.

Lieutenant George Chesney, the Brigade Major, was a scholarly young man with considerable organizing ability, whose skill with his pen as well as his tact endeared him to Wilson. This was fortunate, because, towards the end of the siege, relations between Wilson and the Chief Engineer became so strained that all Chesney's capabilities were called into play.

The daily—or rather nightly—routine of the Engineer Officer was described by Captain Julius George Medley, who joined the Corps early in August from the Frontier.

The Duty Officer's day started at five in the afternoon, when he went to the picket at the Subzi Mundi *serai* and relieved the Duty Officer there. Then he went with the Directing Engineer to the "Sammy House" to see what work must be done during the night. At dusk the working party would arrive under a junior officer, for all their work had to be done in the dark; the collecting of brushwood for the making of fascines, tracing out new breastworks, digging them, and so on. They worked by night for concealment, and because the nights were cooler.

Overnight a new breastwork might be nearly completed, and then the Duty Officer would have the further responsibility of looking over a battery which needed some repair-work to its defences. Medley, on his first night's duty, described how he had to visit a newly finished mortar battery, which was firing every quarter of an hour throughout the night.

"The unfortunate officer and two men were alone awake from necessity, and the rest were comfortably snoring on the ground, perfectly undisturbed by the noise of the mortars," he reported with some surprise. "Every fifteen minutes the officer gave the command, 'Light portfires.' At this, the men awoke, discharged the shell, proceeded to unload again, and then lay down and went off to sleep, their turn being over till it came round again."

The other most senior of the Engineer officers was Lieutenant Frederick Maunsell, who had served before with Alex Taylor. He had had a narrow escape at Meerut, where he was Adjutant of Sappers.

Some of these officers, although still subalterns, had seen as much as a dozen years' service, for promotion was not quick. About a month later, Lieutenant Edward Thackeray, twenty years old, and the youngest and most junior member of the Corps, wrote to his brother that because of the number of deaths he had had "about ten steps in the Corps since being out here." He was a cousin of W. M. Thackeray, the novelist.

Many of the officers who lived in that mess throughout that strange summer rose to General's rank. They included Taylor, Maunsell, and Chesney (who also received knighthoods), and young Greathed and Captain Medley. Others, however, like Baird Smith, who appeared marked for equally successful careers, died prematurely from the results of wounds and exposure during the siege. Thackeray became a Colonel and lived to be the last Engineer survivor of the siege. He died in 1927 at the age of ninety.

With an English genius for rising to awkward occasions, and a philosophy which could turn almost anything into a joke, the Engineers became "a very jolly party," with their own name for everything and everybody. Thackeray, for example, with his exacting standards still set by civilized life at Addiscombe, was known as "My Lord" (or occasionally as "Tall Boot," from his second name, Talbot). He rather fan-

cied himself as a dandy, and was prone to criticism of those
who were careless of their dress.

He had quickly settled on a suitable uniform for himself,
which had done him good service at the Battle of Hindun—
white clothes and a pith helmet, which gave him protection
from the sun, whereas the Riflemen in their small cloth caps
suffered badly. In his love of clothes, Thackeray was in sharp
contrast to an eccentric young Scot, Charles Thomason, the
son of a former Governor of the North-West Provinces.

Thomason had such odd ideas on dress that he became
known as "Robinson Crusoe." His earlier service was spent
in a very solitary station, where he had fallen back on clothes
designed and put together by his servants. Besides evolving
a style of his own, he believed that the heat of the sun was
best combated by the colour green, and he therefore arranged
that his clothes should be patched with great pieces of bright
green cloth which the sun soon bleached to a sickly yellow.

"My Lord" Thackeray thought very poorly of this, and
disgustedly proposed a subscription for his benefit. However,
it was not long before he too was reduced to wearing more
or less a collection of rags, and, like everyone else in camp,
was bidding smartly for the possessions of officers killed in
battle or by disease.

Among Thomason's accomplishments was a specialist's
knowledge of bagpipe music—the mess could provide plenty
of amateur musicians and had a quartet of its own—and he
had carefully gathered together a manuscript collection. This
and an heirloom, the "Grant Pipes," had been destroyed in
the May outbreak. Thomason was undeterred. He spent years
painstakingly repairing his loss, until, several decades later,
he was able to publish a large collection of bagpipe music
which he had rescued from oblivion.

Another young Lieutenant, James Tennant, was accomplished in both mathematics and astronomy and was already
a distinguished member of the Indian Survey. But his fre-

quent criticisms in the Corps earned him the name of "Objector-General." Later, he also became a General.

The nucleus of the Engineer Brigade at Delhi consisted of
500 Roorkee Sappers who had been part of a draft ordered
to Meerut in May. There some took fright and fled to Delhi
to join the mutineers. Maunsell's presence of mind saved the
remainder, for he suspected that the insubordination had been
due merely to panic, and brought the 500 down to Delhi
with the Force, even going so far as to send two volunteers
into the city to try to persuade any of their Sapper comrades
to return under the promise of a pardon. No one took advantage of this offer. These men were the only sepoy corps
allowed to keep their arms. Nevertheless, they were fully
aware of the veiled mistrust from not only the Europeans,
but also from Gurkhas and Guides as well, and the mutineers,
with their old comrades, would jeer at them from the safety
of the city walls. They were the only trained Sappers available, and under their officers they supervised all the engineering work, a service which was greatly valued.

Eventually death and disease reduced this corps to barely
100 men, but by then others had arrived—800 Muzbi Sikhs,
sent by Lawrence, and 600 Pioneers from Roorkee, brought
by Henry Brownlow, who was made Director of the Engineer
Park.

For the heavy, unskilled work of digging trenches and felling trees, about 1,000 local road coolies had been rounded up.

In more normal conditions of war, this Engineer force
would have consisted of a specially trained brigade of officers
and men, the former skilled in training as well as leading;
the latter blacksmiths, carpenters and the like. All would be
experienced in building and maintaining batteries, in con-
structing breastworks and trenches, and in making such Engineers' devices as powder-bags, sandbags, fascines, and gabions and fuses.

Instead, nearly all these men had to be trained, few of them
could be trusted with arms, and their equipment had to be

provided locally. On the site allotted to the Corps for its operations—its "Park"—they carried out daily drills. Magazines of different kinds were built, experimental batteries set up, and the pack-animals—of which there were thousands, elephants, camels, bullocks and mules—loaded and unloaded, and loaded again with supplies and materials for the batteries.

From the Ridge, the British could see new hosts of enemy marching over the bridge-of-boats, often to the familiar strains of "Cheer boys, cheer" and other English marching songs, and with their colours proudly displayed, so that they had a most peculiar feeling in realizing that these scarlet-coated figures in the familiar British uniforms were, in fact, their enemies.

By 3 July four more Artillery guns had arrived, two British and two native, more European foot Artillery, half of the Queen's 61st Regiment under Colonel Jones, heralded by its band and all dressed in khaki (such a good idea for camouflage, everyone thought), and a wing of the 8th Foot or King's Regiment under Colonel Edward Greathed. Both of these infantry regiments came direct from the Punjab and so the three Greathed brothers were together in the camp.

Finally, Major John Coke's Rifles marched in with some other cavalry, Sikhs and Sapper units, so that nearly 6,000 men with guns, mules, camels, elephants, and bullocks were assembled altogether outside Delhi. The time was surely due for a fresh attempt at assault.

This was kept a secret in the camp generally, but the British civilian leaders in the Punjab were anticipating it, for the news they received from the north was serious.

"Mutiny in every station," reported Herbert Edwardes, "and disorganization in every district."

Edwardes, in his letters to Sir John Lawrence, who had still been toying with the idea of abandoning Peshawar in order to strengthen the hold on a more limited region, announced his conviction that Reed would successfully storm the city now that those last reinforcements had reached him, but that if this was not so "another thousand will not turn the scale, while their removal will endanger the Punjab."

"Don't get engulfed in Delhi," he added to Lawrence as a final warning.

Now that Barnard had so many reinforcements, he could think of no reason to postpone an attack any further, and called a conference to discuss the matter. Reed might still be in titular command of the Delhi Force, but no one took much notice of him, for he was still confined to his bed and had nothing to add to any plan that might be prepared.

Plans similar to those of the abandoned attempt of 13 June were at last agreed on; the various regiments (unknown to themselves) were allotted their positions and duties, and the Engineers, since the enthusiastic Wilberforce Greathed still had the General's ear, were in the thick of the plot.

Baird Smith had a very swift insight into the state of indecision that prevailed at the camp. A messenger rode out to meet him as he arrived, and explained that the British Force was going to assault and his presence would be urgently needed. He hurried on his tired column and arrived in camp at three o'clock in the morning of 3 July—the exact hour when the intended assault was to take place. But all was quiet. The General's resolution had failed him at the last moment. There was no assault.

Two things contributed to change the General's mind. Some irregular cavalry were found to be treacherous, and were trying to undermine Coke's men; and the Bareilly force were now in the city, 3,000 strong, with six guns they had seized from a British battery, plus ammunition and treasure. The General felt that the odds were too great, and so called off the operation.

And then the rains began. They had long been expected, and now they finally arrived the immediate results were that the camp was transformed into a pool and began to smell even more offensively, so that regimental quartermasters had to pay rather more attention to the drainage problem. Not surprisingly, more cholera also came with the rains.

The first fall lasted for some hours, pouring down on everything like hail, flooding out the camp, exposing the shallow graves and drumming on the tightened canvas tents.

The air was heavy and oppressive, though much cooler, and the blessed relief of sleeping out of doors was now no more. By next day, however, save in the hollow where the staff officers had their tents, the water had drained away. For the first two days of the rains the enemy remained inside the city. About this time the Engineers cut the canal that served the city, and some thought that this had "thrown them into confusion," although, in fact, the tanks and wells already in Delhi were sufficient for their needs.

But the mutineers had enough worries, without any the Delhi Force attentions could give them. With their numbers, their arms, and their defensive position, they had every reason to succeed in their revolt; all they lacked were leadership and discipline.

The poor old King had neither the physical strength nor the personality to control the vast forces in his city. His sons, dissolute and self-seeking, idled about, made fine speeches, intrigued, drank and slept the time away, but did nothing to help him rule his people. Swarms of fresh mutineers, who arrived almost daily, terrorized the streets, looted the shops and brought trade to a standstill.

Bahadur Shah, well-meaning and devout, attempted often enough to assert his dignity at the councils. He tried to pacify the angry shopkeepers, he withered the sepoys with blasts of sarcasm, he prayed ceremonially in the mosque, and he insisted that more of his forces should camp outside, to the south and south-west of the walls, where the so-called besieging force could not reach them.

His officers complained that camping out was "inconvenient" in the rainy season, so on sufferance he allowed them

to come in "until it had passed." They swarmed through the
Delhi, Lahore, and Turcoman Gates, and occupied the Civil
Courts and the Mohammedan College. Those who could not
squeeze in there forcibly billeted themselves in houses.

Money rapidly became short, for all this time nothing was
being produced, no new goods were being made and sold,
and the thousands in Delhi were just squandering the treasure which fresh mutineers brought with them. Time after
time, the King warned the commander of his troops that his
treasury was empty. On the fateful 23 June on which so much
was felt to depend, sweetmeats were issued as an encouragement to the rebels to fight harder, and an ancient gun dating
from the time of the great Shah Jehan was mounted.

"When ready," wrote one who was present, "a he-goat
was tied to the mouth, and twenty-five *seers* of sweetmeats
placed inside and a necklace hung round the muzzle. Several
Brahmins and astronomers were summoned and directed to
consult their almanacs as to whether the mutineers would be
victorious. The astronomers replied that great disturbances
would last for a year. Several thousands would die, but the
shadow of peace and security would spread over the land.
Beyond this, the astronomers would say nothing."

At the Durbar, which was held nearly every day, fists were
shaken, threats uttered, and angry accusations levelled at
the most unlikely people. Some Sirdars, for instance, complained that Kuli Khan, the best gunner in the Fort, had
fired so carelessly that he had badly wounded three sepoys
and killed three camp-followers as the troops were returning
to the city.

Kuli Khan had been at that post since the beginning of the
siege, and soon after the English arrived he put to excellent
use the training he had received in their Artillery, keeping
up a running fire for so long that his praises rang round the
city, and the King himself had ordered the preparation of
enough gunpowder to keep the hero supplied. But hardly a
fortnight later he was the centre of a threatening mob, who

seized him and dragged him under arrest to the King, where he was charged with being in collusion with the English!

And day after day the exasperated but powerless King told his subjects that "they were destroying the kingdom that had lasted for 500 years." He would remark ironically on their curious failure to dislodge the English, and forbade them to make off with all the brushwood on the river-bank, with which they made cooking fires.

In the high winds the bridge-of-boats over the Jumna sank, and the mutineers from Bareilly, arriving on the other side, were held up there while a large party of sappers, miners, and coolies went out to repair the bridge. The King examined the troops through his telescope and remarked peevishly upon the number of elephants and cavalry they had brought. Meanwhile, the English bombardment was un-usually heavy; Kuli Khan's battery came under heavy fire and was partly dismounted. But although he did not know it yet, the King had some good news that day. The Bareilly contingent was commanded by a man who was to be worth more to him than any one else in Delhi. His name was Mohammed Bakht Khan.

Within the British camp the Duty Officers were beginning to complain at their task of visiting the picket posts in the rain, which meant a round trudge of six miles, taking them three hours every night.

Many of the troops hardly ever managed to undress com-pletely, but snatched what sleep they could, merely taking off their sword-belts and loosening their uniforms.

The mess dinner at night was an important part of the officers' social life. They would eagerly discuss the day's events, and those who had not actually taken part in them had probably observed them from the Flagstaff Tower. The Artillery mess was perhaps the best stocked, (with alcohol as well as food), but others, like Anson's Lancers and the

60th Rifles, were short of food and drink, and so had to keep up their standard in other ways.

The Rifles, for example, maintained a strict standard of etiquette. No one could appear in their mess in the evening without his green jacket. Nor might any officer smoke until the cloth was removed—even though there was scarcely any beer or wine to drink, and with shells bursting all round, so that any moment could bring the sounding of the bugles and a turn-out of all hands.

Their doctor, Innes, a neat, spruce little man, managed in some miraculous way always to look as if he had "just jumped out of a bandbox," whereas Young thought that the Staff, better fed and wined, were very slovenly, in "all kinds of disguises and strange coats, and such a thing as uniform, except the helmet and sword, is not to be seen amongst us."

In the mess each evening, by the light of candles and hurricane *buttis,* the strategy of the siege came in for some fierce criticism. Hodson was still unconvinced that passive resistance was the right policy. "The mismanagement of matters is perfectly sickening," he would say. "Nothing the rebels can do will equal the evils arising from incapacity and indecision."

He was thankful that Neville Chamberlain had arrived, who "ought to be worth a thousand to us," for "with our present chiefs I see no chance of taking Delhi."

Hodson had a personal reason for condemning inefficiency. During the march down, he had been at great pains to secure for the British the bridge at Bhagput, about twenty-five miles up the river. To hold this crossing, a British officer, Captain McAndrew, was left in charge of a large party of the Rajah of Jheend's men, horse, foot, and guns. But McAndrew heard rumours that a party of mutineers were moving that way, and abandoned his position without even waiting to see whether they actually arrived. As a result, a very small party of mutineers seized the bridge and burned the boats, which McAndrew, in his hurry, had left behind him. This was a serious matter, for it meant the breaking of communications with Meerut, and on 28 June General Barnard told him to try and salvage these boats.

"I can trust your judgment quite as much as your energy," he said drily, and so Hodson set off.

In the cooler, wet weather the journey was tolerable, "though not exactly what one could wish," and he found the charred remains of three boats, which he swore could easily have been saved if McAndrew had had the sense to draw them up on the other side of the river.

With another officer, he worked like a navvy on them for the best part of two days, and spent a night on the river-bank. They had nothing to shelter them from the streaming rain and high wind, and by some extraordinary lack of fore-sight had scarcely anything to eat—only a couple of *chapatties* each, a small tin of soup, and a little tea. When he returned to report that the boats were serviceable again, he heard that he had missed a fierce attack. Some of the camp elephants had been seized by the enemy when they withdrew, presumably with the connivance of the *mahouts*. It was a costly day's victory, and June had been a costly month. The 1st Battalion 60th Royal Rifles had in that month lost three officers and forty men, with twelve officers and 108 men wounded, and two men dead from disease; and other bat-talions had equally heavy casualties.

But now that so many reinforcements had reached them, most people there were convinced that "another week" would see them inside the city, and the Mutiny at an end.

Just before the end of June, when young Fred Roberts arrived, officers were so short that although Roberts was only twenty-four, General Barnard wanted him to be his Deputy Assistant Adjutant-General, but Roberts asked to be attached to the Cavalry Brigade, since it was "his own line." He was a modest, likeable young man.

The very next day he was under fire for the first time, and more than a little distressed to learn that two officers of the

4th Sikhs were wounded, apparently as the result of treachery among their own men. One died of his wounds, and the other was shot through the ankle at an angle that made it "scarcely possible for the bullet . . . to have come from the front."

This was not the only example of such injuries, and, as a result, all the regiment's Poorbeahs (who came from Oudh) were disarmed and turned out of the camp. They straggled over the rough ground to the city and joined the rebels.

On the day of Roberts's arrival, General Barnard wrote to John Lawrence defining his difficulties once again. When he first reached Delhi, he said, he had "fondly imagined" that he could bring his heavy guns (such as he had) to fire on the walls and so silence the Moree and Kashmir Bastions at once, opening the way in for his troops.

But since the enemy outnumbered his force so strongly, and as his own guns could not even reach the walls, it was impossible to silence the enemy's deadly artillery unless he could build batteries closer in to them—and he had no sandbags, tools, or equipment.

"You may ask why we engage in these constant combats," he wrote, forestalling the question. "The reason simply is that when attacked we must defend ourselves, and that to secure our camp, our hospitals, our stores, etc., every living being has to be employed. The whole thing is too gigantic for the force brought against it. . . ."

The mutineers were now at least 40,000 strong, with nearly double this number of desperate and warlike Mohammedans and other civilians, all under arms and willing to join in any fight. Their ammunition seemed inexhaustible, despite a rumour that they were short of percussion caps and could make no more.

Mohammed Bakht Khan, the King's new Commander, a stout, shrewd man, had been a subahdar in a British battery of field artillery. When he arrived in Delhi, he had been appalled at the state of discipline which existed. He asked the

King for orders for his troops, but all the old man could say was to appeal to him not to plunder the city.

"It is no use my giving orders," the King complained bitterly. "They are never obeyed, and I have no one to enforce them. But my decree is that the English should be caused not to exist."

Bakht Khan looked at him, sizing up his man. Then, on the impulse, he offered himself as Commander-in-Chief. The King seized his hand in gratitude. Bakht Khan could not believe his good fortune. He wondered whether this was all an elaborate joke, and pointed out that he was a descendant of the same family as the King of Delhi. The old man nodded.

"A greater man than the General does not exist," he agreed willingly.

"And," continued Bakht Khan pointedly, "I will be entitled to the honour of Bahadur when I have driven the English out of Delhi and Meerut."

Bakht Khan had brought with him 400,000 rupees worth of treasure, and so he was in a powerful bargaining position, for the treasuries in Delhi had long ago been looted.

An Indian who was in Delhi at the time said afterwards that "the sepoys . . . put the money in their own pockets; they did not give a farthing out of this to the King, so the sepoys of four or five regiments possessed thousands of rupees each, and under the weight of silver they could hardly walk, consequently they were obliged to change their silver for gold . . . (in which they were cheated by the *mahajuns*).

"The poor regiments are very jealous of those who are rich, as the rich sepoys don't wish to go to fight or to the field of battle. . . . They are very often insulted by their poor companions. . . ."

Bakht Khan demanded proper quarters for his men, and explained to the King that if he did not have full obedience from everyone under his command, princes included, he would cut off their noses and their ears.

"You have full authority. Do whatever seems good to you,"

replied the King resignedly, and presented him with a shield and sword and the title of General.

Bakht, for his part, agreed to promote the young Prince Mirza Mogul to the sinecure of Adjutant-General, and then started to inject some discipline into the mutineers.

He warned the *kotwal,* the chief police officer, that if any more plundering occurred he would be held responsible and hanged. A proclamation was made by beat of drum ordering all shopkeepers to keep arms; no person could leave his home unarmed. Those who had no weapons could apply for them free from Headquarters. Any soldier caught looting would at once lose an arm, and all civilians had to surrender any ammunition they might have.

Such stern measures were needed, for discipline was nearly dead. The princes had been made officers, but they did not understand the low-class dialect of their men and so had to give orders through interpreters. Then they were much distressed at having to go out of doors in the heat of the sun, and they started visibly when the cannons were fired. This did not pass unnoticed, and soon the sepoys were jeering at them openly. The sepoys were little better themselves, though. "When they wish to leave the field of battle they tie a piece of rag on their leg and pretend to have been wounded, and come into the city lame and groaning," a civilian noted sourly.

The streets of Delhi were unswept. Garbage and ordure piled up, and the smells and flies were almost as bad as in the British camp. The British troops organized games of cricket and even pony races to keep their minds off the siege, and the mutineers copied these attempts at escapism. They ran their cavalry horses thin in races through the streets, until their beasts' shoes split on the bad roads, and passers-by cried out in alarm at the danger of a dozen horses racing along the crowded thoroughfares.

Others went out on looting expeditions. They would arm themselves with a loaf of bread and a bottle of rum, and then pick a large house and knock on the door. When the householder appeared, they would rush at him, shouting, "Where is the Englishman you've been keeping in your house?"

When he protested his innocence, they would look at him knowingly and produce the bread and rum.

"Then how is it that we found *this* here?" they would ask and at once arrest the poor man. In most cases of this kind he bribed them to set him free. If he did not bribe them, then they looted his house anyway, and then arrested him.

With Bakht Khan's arrival and his sense of leadership, these outrages ceased temporarily, and the mutineers recovered some of their initiative. On 3 July they sallied out, several thousand strong, to prove their mettle.

Hodson saw them on their way out in the evening some five miles to the right of the camp, but although he reported their position at seven o'clock, it was not until three next morning that a force was sent out against them.

This attacking force consisted largely of newly arrived troops, who were all anxious to prove their quality and have a taste of action. After an artillery duel, the enemy fled, so that the only excitement they had was some of the artillery shot striking "unpleasantly close." In the burning heat of morning, the infantry lay down in the shade of the trees on the canal bank to enjoy their tiffin, which was brought out to them from camp by servants still in their long white mess uniforms, all balancing trays on their heads as they trotted barefoot to the battlefront.

Charles Griffiths of the newly arrived 61st was enjoying a bottle of ale with a friend—"the sweetest draught I think I have ever tasted"—as they idly watched a troop of elephants which had been sent out to carry the wounded and the sick, for many men had been struck with apoplexy in the heat.

Suddenly, "without warning," as Griffiths said with annoyance, a volley of shots whistled out from the jungle to one side, and struck several of the men lying on the ground. The others leapt up and rushed towards the jungle. Then the elephants, trumpeting with panic, trunks raised high above their heads, stampeded down the canal bank, struggled over the water and disappeared into the trees. They did not stop until they had reached the safety of their own quarters back in camp.

The infantry, advancing under very heavy fire, came at last to an open space where they could see the mutineers. After heavy musketry fire on both sides with many losses, the British fell back, still firing, and drew up on the other bank of the canal on either side of the bridge. Griffiths crept with his men along under the bank, and was loudly cheered by the others, who did not dare show their heads above the Ridge, for behind it the rebels were shouting taunts as they poured down a hail of bullets on them. Things looked as though they might go hardly should the vast numbers of enemy succeed in getting over to the left, when suddenly they heard the welcome sound of galloping horses and the crunch of wheels. Major Tombs and six Horse Artillery guns thundered along the road, passing the infantry with a cheer, galloped over the bridge, and, unlimbering with practised speed, opened fire.

With them came the cavalry, who had been called out yet again, but they had little to do, since the enemy fled rapidly and with little loss under the artillery fire. By this time everyone had been out for at least eight hours, and some of them, particularly the infantry, for seventeen, mostly in the blazing sun. Many died from sunstroke.

Their faces turned quite black in a few minutes, a sight which shocked their comrades, who helped load them on the backs of a fresh troop of elephants and then, scarcely able to crawl, they made their painful way back to camp.

Hodson was still not satisfied that the column had done "half as well as we ought." Brigadier Wilson was just as disappointed.

"We have been making another mess of it today," he wrote to his wife. "Using up four corps where two would have

done, and losing the chance to follow up the insurgents' retreat and make something decisive of it. Our position is now
worse than ever, and we have really no good head to extri-
cate us."

Those who had taken no part in the action were more exultant. "Cowardly loons," wrote Daly, still laid up from his
wound and disgusted with the mutineers. "Little honour they
do us in fighting. They *never stand....*"

There was plenty of material gain as the result of the fight.
They had seized all the plunder the enemy had taken in their
raid on Alipore, and which they abandoned in their hurry to
be off. They had thrown away even their belts and shoes, and
Colonel Young was amused to see that the irregular cavalry
were riding back with their horses piled up with captured
tents and saddles.

Roberts, who had accompanied the cavalry as staff officer,
was pleased to find, tied to a tree, a "nice-looking, white,
country-bred pony," and having liberated this beast, to use
the jargon of a later war, he was annoyed when he found
that it belonged to an officer—Younghusband—who claimed
it smartly.

At this time the enemy batteries, manned by highly trained
artillery-men, were the mutineers' most effective weapon, and
the deadly Moree Bastion fired almost continuously at the
right flank of the Ridge, and with terrible effect. A few days
earlier, the British had shelled the Moree for an afternoon,
and silenced two of the guns and brought down in ruins part
of the wall and parapet.

But by next morning the breach was repaired with sandbags, fresh guns had been brought forward, and the bastion
continued its deadly fire as before. Huge cannon, 32- and 24-
pounders, that the troops nicknamed "Whistling Dick" and
"Tambourine Sal," fired tirelessly from the walls.

The Europeans, on the other hand, only had two guns of
heavy calibre—24-pounders—and these had been seized from
the enemy, but were useless, as there was no ammunition to

fit them. Battery commanders thus offered a half-rupee reward to camp followers for the recovery of each cannon-ball
that fell in the camp, so that they could fire them back at the
mutineers. Such was the desire to earn these rewards that the
khitmutgars vied with one another to seize the precious metal.

Griffiths saw a party of them one day on their way up the
hill from camp, bearing the meals for the pickets on their
heads, when two round-shot from the enemy batteries struck
the top of the Ridge and began to roll down.

In a moment, the cooks had set down their burdens on the
ground, and were racing towards the balls as if on the football field. The first two each seized a cannon-ball, but forgot
they would be nearly red-hot, and they dropped them on the
spot, yelling and rubbing their hands. Then followed an ani-
mated conference, and finally, when the shot had cooled sufficiently, the first two men placed them on their heads, and
the others accompanied them eagerly to the commissariat
quarters to make sure that they had a share in the reward.
Lunch was a little late that day.

Even when there were no sorties, death was never very far
away. There were executions for treachery almost daily, as it
had long been known that spies were at work for the enemy
in camp, as well as for the British in Delhi, and, generally,
the former came off worst. In addition, there was a good deal
of attempted sedition, and the penalty for this was hanging.
Trust was not mutual, and Brigadier Wilson summed up the
prevailing attitude in camp when he wrote to his wife: "I
believe our Sikhs and Gurkhas to be as true as steel, but not
another native soldier is to be trusted."

Meanwhile, Colonel Baird Smith had not wasted a moment of his time.

"The Empire will be all the stronger after this storm," he
wrote to a friend not long after the outbreak, "and I have
never had a moment's fear for it. It is not five or six thousand mutineer mercenaries, or ten times the number, that
will change the destiny of England. . . . There is that vitality

in the English people that will bound stronger against mis-
fortunes and build up the damaged fabric anew. . . ."

Unfortunately, he had a delicate constitution and did not
take kindly to camp life. A wound he received about five
weeks later, a trifling affair which should soon have healed,
proved unexpectedly obstinate, and was aggravated by the
camp complaints he contracted: dysentery, camp scurvy, and
trench mouth. Nevertheless, he was of such a buoyant dis-
position that he was able to combat all his ailments for as
long as his services were required. Within two days of his
arrival, he made his report to General Barnard.

> The defences of the city against a regular and formal at-
> tack with adequate means in men and material . . . were
> extremely feeble [he wrote]; . . . Against an irregular attack
> with ordinary means they were formidable; and finally, as
> against a *coup de main* by a feeble force unprovided with
> siege artillery or engineers' stores—then only strong political
> reasons could justify the General in commanding such an
> assault . . .

These last conditions, unfortunately, were those which prevailed. A garrison of not less than 40,000 trained men and
irregulars were scarcely threatened by a tiny force of so-called
besiegers amounting now to about 6,000, and the natural
enemy reaction must be to attempt to drive the British from
their position and so to cut their communications with the
Punjab.

Had they used judgment and boldness in attacking the
weakest spots of the besiegers' position—the right flank and
the rear—and had they followed up their advantages instead
of melting away at setbacks, they could possibly have driven
the British out altogether. They did manage to attack convoys and harass the rear, and so the besiegers had to be prepared to be besieged as well.

The average daily loss to the British side was between
thirty and forty, and on a bad day might be well over 100.
Baird Smith pointed out that this rate of using up men in

the "ordinary process of the siege" showed, by "a simple cal-culation," how short a time it could go on. Either the siege must be shortened or greater care must be taken of the lives of the troops.

To shorten the siege meant, of course, investing it regu-larly or making an "assault *de vive force.*" Baird Smith pro-duced an official return of the entire supplies in the Artillery Park on 4 July, and these amounted to less than 800 round-shot for the heavy guns, and rather more than 5,500 shells of different kinds, and they would have to keep on using enemy cannon-balls to fire back at them. There was, indeed, barely enough powder for one day's active firing of the siege guns, and they had only 13,000 rounds of musket ammunition.

The Engineer Park was in similarly poor case. Even if siege batteries could be built—and there was not enough equip-ment available—they would still have scarcely any revetting material to maintain them.

For an assault, the same desperate circumstances made the situation risky indeed. Nevertheless, Baird Smith considered that the situation *did* justify an assault, and in a consultation with the General which lasted for three hours on 4 July he told Barnard so, without reservation and with full recogni-tion of his own responsibilities in the matter.

The General listened gravely to all he had to say, but his eye was dim and his reactions slow and heavy. As the discus-sion progressed, however, he became more cheerful and told Baird Smith that he would give the matter "further consid-eration," and they would discuss it again.

Barely an hour later, however, Barnard was struck down with cholera, and when Baird Smith returned to Headquar-ters for his second interview the old man was seriously ill and could see no one. By afternoon he was dead.

General Barnard's tragedy was that the occasion demanded men of outstanding military powers with decision, foresight, and active youth. Such qualities as he had—personal bravery and devotion to duty—were not enough. He was always seeing personally to small details, but though such actions were welcomed by the men, they were not essential to victory. The campaign was beyond him, mentally and physically. He had served in the Crimea, but, as Hervey Greathed wrote tactfully, "a Crimean education is not the best for this service."

Wilson shook his head at the "fearful indecision and want of firmness" which "made him unfit for his position."

However, old General Reed was still alive; although as Wilson said, "more fit for an invalid couch. . . . It is a sad state of things in such a crisis not to have someone capable of leading and directing us properly. . . ."

The day after the General's funeral, his effects—with those of the late General Anson—were put up for auction, as was customary. The 9th Lancers mess actually paid £400 for all General Anson's wine and beer, and bacon—a luxury—sold at four rupees a pound, and candles at three.

The command of the camp now devolved nominally on the even more elderly General Reed. Things might have gone ill had not Brigadier Chamberlain, as temporary Adjutant-General, been really in control. Reed, too infirm to act himself, delegated full authority to Chamberlain to issue orders without further reference to the General, except to tell him what he was doing.

Colonel Baird Smith—to whom Barnard had sent a message on his deathbed that if his professional reputation required any defence he was relying on him "as having received his last explanation, to guard him from misrepresentation"—now obtained General Reed's consent to destroy all the canal bridges to the rear, except one, and to blow up the Poolchudder aqueduct, which carried the canal water into the city and which could also serve as a road to carry the enemy into the camp's rear. Hodson accompanied the column to explode the Bussaye bridge—(a "beautiful" piece of work, said Baird Smith approvingly afterwards; a "perfect" demolition). Hodson, though, was disgusted to think that they had had eleven hours in the saddle, and in the baking sun, for the trifling result of an exploded bridge. Not a soul was to be seen except the local villagers, who came out with protestations of loyalty and bowls of cold milk. The latter were the more appreciated.

The Artillery shared Hodson's grouse at such an expenditure of energy of such a large body to so little effect; they had not had so much as a shot at the enemy for several days.

Hodson was in a grousing mood. He was beginning to doubt Chamberlain, regarding him excellent as an active leader of irregulars, but poor as a man of business; and indeed Chamberlain hated office work and so was out of place as Adjutant-General.

"Prompt decision in council is what we want," said Hodson. "There is no lack of vigorous action. There are plenty to obey, but we want someone to *command*." It was a terrible state of affairs, he thought. "Enough to fret one to death—no head, no brains, no decision."

He was rushed off his feet—or off his saddle—all day, for one of his officers was down with fever, a serious loss to what was beginning to be called "Hodson's Horse"; and he had hardly anything left to wear, because, like everyone else, he was contributing towards the clothing of refugees, who still straggled into the camp.

The sun had burnt his skin to the colour of a pickled walnut, and his hours in the saddle stripped all the skin off his hands, so that he could scarcely hold his sword.

But in the quiet days in camp, life seemed less earnest, and even tranquil.

"It is a pretty sight," wrote Daly, "to see the soldiers of the various corps in front of their tents amusing themselves, chatting in groups, jumping, and throwing round-shot, as though nothing serious was going on, nor has it ever occurred to them that there was anything doubtful in the conflict."

Once the King of Delhi sent out secretly to the camp to sound them out on terms for surrender, making sure that on his side the terms would include his personal safety and even the continuation of his pension from the Company, a request which was greeted by jeers in camp.

Now that the General was dead, new messing arrangements had to be made for the Staff, for Barnard had been entertaining a number of officers at his own table, for which he received no allowance. Various members of the Staff had battened eagerly on his generosity, naturally preferring to spend his money rather than their own.

There followed a brief lull, broken just after breakfast on 9 July, when heavy artillery fire began to rumble through a drizzle of rain away to the right of the camp down in the Grand Trunk Road.

A sowar from the 9th galloped up to the picket of two Horse Artillery guns and found two lieutenants, Stillman, commanding the duty post of Carabineer cavalry, and James Hills, who was Tombs's subaltern of the Horse Artillery, at breakfast. Their men were dismounted and huddled together in the rain. The sowar told them breathlessly that enemy cavalry were in sight, and did not add that his own picket had made not the slightest attempt to stop them further along the road. Even as he spoke nearly 100 horsemen dashed up while the two officers were still ordering their men to re-mount, and getting the guns limbered up for action. Stillman ran to the Mound to see what he could see from there, and Hills was horrified to find that his young Carabineers, all untrained soldiers and not even very good horsemen, at once fled in disorder, shouting: "The enemy are upon us!"

He yelled to them to come back; but no one returned. Within seconds, he was alone. He spurred his horse at the leaders hoping that, while he delayed them a little, the guns could get into action.

The first man he cut down, the second he hit, and then he was unhorsed himself. He groped desperately for a hand-hold, but his terrified horse was slippery with rain. His sword was gone and he would certainly have been cut to pieces at once but for his heavy cloak, which he had put on against

the rain and which muffled the blows, although ripped to
tatters by a dozen swords.

Then the enemy left him to chase the fleeing Carabineers,
and Hills freed himself from his horse and seized his fallen
sword, just in time to defend himself against three other cavalrymen, two of them still on horseback, who surrounded
him. He beat them back with a rapid alternation of weapons—now a thrust from his sword, then, when this was flicked
out of his hand, he fired his pistol and finally threw it at one
of them.

The man dug at him with his lance, and Hills seized the
weapon just behind the blade, and pulled his opponent off
his horse. Then a third man, towering above him, wounded
him in the head. Half-blinded with blood, down in the mud
on his hands and knees, and gasping for breath, Hills was on
the point of being run through when Tombs, who had heard
the shouting and commotion, came running from the camp,
his revolver in his hand.

He was thirty yards away when he saw Hills writhing and
slithering in the mud, surrounded by horsemen. He raised
his revolver, held his breath, took aim, and fired.

The mutineer rolled over, dead.

One of the other horsemen struck a wild blow with his
sword as Tombs raced up, but the turban Tombs wore wound
round his head saved his skull, and his life. The horseman
galloped after the main party and left the two officers alone
in the driving rain.

Meanwhile the rebels had penetrated the camp and were
making for a troop of native horse artillery, their progress
quite unhampered in the general confusion. As they rode,
they shouted to the men to join them and to harness the
horses to bring away the guns.

So totally unexpected was the situation that the British
Troop Sergeant-Major, thinking the intruders were some of
the camp's own irregulars, actually started to obey before he
realized that they were mutineers. His men stayed loyal. They

shouted to Major Olpherts's European troop to fire through
their ranks.

"Never mind us! Don't spare them! *Fire away!*"

One officer, Captain Fagan, who had been writing in his
tent, rushed out with no better weapon in his hand than a
pen, gathered his men together, seized a sword and carbine
from someone, and pursued the sowars. It was a breathless
and bloody little encounter with a great deal of noise and
shouting, in which the enemy cavalry hacked at some of the
Artillery and Carabineers (who were still in their shirt-
sleeves), then made away with several artillery horses which
they untethered, and cut down some harmless camp-grass-
cutters and women who were in their way.

Corpses were lying about in the rain, some even entangled
with the tent ropes, and men of the 75th, who had come up
in the general alarm, were firing away near the cemetery wall
at the trees in which some mutineers were hiding, with as
much glee as if they were potting at game. One European
drummer chased an Indian who jumped into the canal and,
in vain, tried to escape by bobbing up and down in the yellow water, but was at last shot down. Tombs and Hills found
one of Hills's opponents actually walking off with Hills's pistol, which he had found in the mud.

The duel then started all over again, the two officers in
turn fencing with the sowar until at last Tombs ran him
through with his sword. One man had got away with a
charger all ready for mounting, and another with a doctor's
horse, while Hope Grant, who had joined in the general
mêlée, forced two sowars to abandon the stolen horses they
were trying to swim across the canal. By the end, about thirty
mutineers were shot down, while the remainder retreated
over the canal bridge.

The invaders had been some of the 8th Irregulars from
Bareilly, whose uniforms so resembled that of the loyal 9th
that they had been mistaken for them.

Indeed, while they fled back to the city, Brigadier Cham-

berlain wanted to open Scott's 9-pounders at them, but he
was persuaded by others that the men they saw "must indeed
be their own 9th." Hodson and Brigadier Grant, who were
stalking the enemy separately, were also deceived. They saw
cavalry moving slowly along and Hodson followed them, convinced they were from the besieging force. Only when they
neared the cross-roads branching off towards the city did they
break into a gallop and disappear down the turning. The dis-
comfited pursuers came in for some jokes that night at mess.

What with the constant rain, the steamy heat, the general
feeling of futility and the vast discomfort, anything that pro-
duced a laugh or even a smile in camp was an episode to be
cherished and remembered. The dampness was such that a
pair of boots polished one evening would be green with mil-
dew by the next day. Everyone and everything was clammy
and wretched; and in the occasional bursts of sunshine, the
ground and the tents steamed and stank. The area was a lake
of foul mud in which the troops slipped and slithered, for no
one had thought to lay duck-boards or stepping-stones. In any
case, no such stones could be found. Any stones had long ago
been trodden into the slime.

In addition to these basic discomforts, cholera was on the
increase, and the ruined houses and streaming tents that
served as Army hospitals were full of vomiting, gasping
patients who lay awaiting death in an atmosphere of misery
and putrefaction.

Sometimes it rained for twenty-four hours or longer, and
the normal miseries of camp life were further aggravated.
The Rev. Rotton often felt that he could hardly have kept
going at all had he not succeeded in buying at one of the
sales of dead officers' effects a buggy in which he drove round
the camp every day. He was a fairly young man, and in good
health—as far as anyone was at the time—but even so he
found that the task of visiting no less than fourteen hospitals
each day was almost more than he could manage. All this
time he had no other Protestant chaplain to help him, nor

did one arrive until the middle of August; but he magnani-
mously admitted the help of the Catholic priest, Father Bertrand, as being "without risk of offence to any, except the
most bigoted." Father Bertrand did not spare himself for a
moment; he lived like a hermit and worked like a cart-horse,
and the good Protestant chaplain could not withhold from
him his whole-hearted praise.

On these rainy days the Chaplain left off his clerical robes,
and put on instead jackboots and breeches and "a dusty-
coloured *choga*." He was slightly ashamed of the fact that, to
save shaving, he had allowed himself to grow a voluminous
and coal-black beard and moustache.

The hospital building of the 8th and 61st infantry regiments was on the extreme left flank of the camp, and nearly
all the patients were suffering from cholera, without a hope
of recovery. No women nurses graced the scene, despite Miss
Nightingale's repeated offers to Lady Canning to bring out a
party to India. The stench of death and illness hung over the
place, and the constant retching and moaning of patients was
almost the only sound, for most of the men were too ill to
walk.

In the hospitals, the greedy flies were more numerous than
outside. They crawled all over faces and heads, through collar-
openings, and even, the Chaplain found, down his throat
when he was reading the Bible or praying with a dying man.
His Bible was indelibly stained with fly-marks, and he could
never afterwards look at it without being forcibly reminded
of the hours he had spent in these terrible surroundings.

Soon, the number of dying was so great that he could only
hope to carry on his duties by kneeling on a chair in the
centre of the building to make a general supplication on behalf of all the patients together; after this he would deliver a
sermon from the same position.

All this while, the rain went on falling.

"Rain, rain, nothing but rain," wrote the despairing Anson

to his wife. "Sometimes soft, sometimes hard, making everything, particularly books, horribly damp, and every person dull and miserable."

He wrote this letter at six o'clock one morning, having woken to the periodic misery of Duty Officer's ride round the pickets. Like many others, he had set out expecting a short campaign and so had hardly any kit. Had he expected the extraordinary fate of being stuck already five weeks outside Delhi, he would have brought some warm clothing, but as he had none he compromised by doing physical jerks whenever there was an inch to move in the tent, and when his partner was out of the way.

Hodson and Colonel Young both thought it would be "an excellent idea" if the ladies safely in the hills were to make flannel shirts for the soldiers—who because of their unsuitable uniforms were always either too hot or too cold. So many stores had fallen into enemy hands or were out of reach in the rear that no supplies were available.

But, despite the flooding, Hodson, vigorous and active now that he had got over his bronchial attack, could declare that "everything is wet and wretched but ourselves," and join in the laugh against himself at being "the victim of such a sell," in being taken in by the irregulars. All agreed that a "crack" with Hodson was as good as a glass of champagne. The greater the odds, the higher rose the spirits of this tall old-young man with his thinning yellow hair, unusually pale complexion, and heavy, drooping moustache.

On the day when it was learned with alarm that the Delhi force was cut off from Calcutta, so that no reinforcements could possibly get through from the north, Hodson gave a whoop of joy.

"Hurrah! Hurrah!" he cried in genuine enthusiasm. "Snug as a bug in a rug. No more orders from Headquarters—we can do what we like!"

His hard eyes would bore into a situation and he never hesitated to communicate his thoughts to the authorities and to his friends. It was even a little grim comfort to him, when the scandal of the irregulars occurred, that he had "repeatedly warned" everyone of the danger of letting Hindustani troops remain under arms.

With 500 reinforcements at the end of the month came an addition to his officers: young Hugh Gough, the friend of Commissioner Greathed (and late of the 3rd Native Cavalry) who had been in Meerut on the Sunday the Mutiny began. Greathed introduced the two men.

"I found him sitting, booted and spurred, talking to a native who was one of his spies from Delhi," Gough recalled later. "He looked up with a quick, sharp glance, which seemed to go through me—as he told me afterwards he 'liked my looks'—and then said, 'You are just the man I want, Gough. Are you fit for a ride?' "

The young subaltern was practically dropping on his feet after his journey down from Meerut, but he was keen, and he had his career before him.

"Yes, sir!" he replied promptly.

"Well," said Hodson, "come along with me. I'm going out for a reconnaissance."

He allowed Gough enough time to have a quick breakfast and then they set out with a troop of Hodson's Horse for a sixty-mile ride round the camp.

"I was struck with Hodson's marvellous knowledge of the language, and the quick way he seemed to extract all the information he wanted, and his great powers of endurance," Gough said afterwards.

Another new arrival was Edward Vibart, formerly of the 54th Native Infantry, who had endured such adventures in his escape from Delhi in May. He found that the Flagstaff was the most popular picket; it was safe, and out of reach of the flies that hung in swarms and clouds above the stinking and festering corpses of animals which lay all round. No working parties were detailed to dispose of these foul, bloated hulks of camels, bullocks, elephants, and mules.

On the day of his arrival, Vibart saw "a little afternoon's outing," which was Hodson's usual afternoon exercise. He was studying the layout of ground in the region of Ludlow Castle, which was held by an enemy picket, and this entailed crawling along *nullahs* on his own, every minute in danger of being picked off by the enemy. The enemy soldiers craned their necks to see him, sometimes under cover and sometimes in the open, peering at him through a telescope and anxiously debating whether they could shoot him down. They in turn were the subject of a similar debate up at the Mosque, which was really too far out of range to do much damage. So both sides held their fire—and wrote reports about what they had seen through their telescopes.

It is difficult nowadays to realize just how isolated each British station was in India at that time. The electric telegraph was still regarded as little more than an ingenious toy; and since India only possessed 273 miles of railway line, the quickest means of communication was by horse and rider. But horses could go lame and riders could be robbed; thus news from home or from other formations was delayed by a thousand accidents.

The mail-carts, or *dak*-carts, had two wheels, and were drawn by two horses that kept up a steady jog-trot. The routes they took were divided into stages—as for the stage-coaches in England—but because of the heat and the rough surface of the roads these stages were only about six miles apart. Since the only serious alternative to the mail-cart was a palanquin-*gharry,* a heavy carriage with an average speed of three miles an hour, most officers arrived for duty outside Delhi on the springless but speedier mail-carts. Mail, especially official mail and messages, was treated with a surprising contempt.

Hervey Greathed, the senior civil servant in camp, had a tent next-door to the Post Office tent. His pillow was stuffed with letters that no one had bothered to deliver—"futile Agra correspondence," as he described it.

The Post Office clerks were, in Young's opinion, "a drunken set," and those who had friends among them always knew when a *dak*-cart was leaving or arriving. These favoured people would go down to the postal tent and rummage undisturbed among the mails for all the camp in the hope of finding a letter for themselves. Many of the *peons* or postmen had no idea where even the General's tent was, and since they could not read and many did not dare ask the sahibs for directions, they took the easiest way out and threw the letters into shell-holes to get rid of them. This casual arrangement for the distribution of official letters, orders, and reports led to many delays.

Some dispatches travelled less openly, but were still liable to delay or loss. Messengers rolled up the thin papers into tiny cylinders and hid them in their hair, in turbans, or in boots; even in a hollow tooth. Others chose more personal places of concealment, so that these messages were subjected to the same assaults of nature—covered with mud, soaked and stained with sweat—as their bearers.

Messages were often written in French to confuse the enemy if they were captured. If in English, the writers would use Greek characters, which led to some curious phonetic spellings of Hindu names.

India is roughly 1,900 miles from east to west and the same distance north to south—containing a total area of 1,500,000 square miles—and against these vast distances such primitive methods of communication meant that important dispatches which were topical when written were of only historical value by the time they were delivered.

Thus on 4 July Lord Canning, the Governor-General in Calcutta, could sit down in good faith and write to Queen Victoria a report on the situation that was out of date before he began it, for it was based on details from Delhi that had been posted in mid-June.

Lord Canning [he wrote] presents his humble duty to Your Majesty, and although unable to give to Your Majesty

the complete details of the capture of Delhi, and of the defeat of the rebels in that city, as he has long desired to do,
he can at least announce to Your Majesty that the city is in
the possession of the British troops, under Major-General
Sir Henry Barnard; and that nothing remains in the hands
of the insurgents except the Palace or Fort, in which they
have all taken refuge. This was the state of things on the
13th or 14th of June, the latest day of which any certain accounts have been received from Delhi; but nothing was
likely to interfere with the completion of the capture within
48 hours. . . .

This event has been long and anxiously awaited, and the
time which has elapsed has cost England and India very
dear. Many precious lives have been lost, and much heart-
rending suffering has been endured, for which there can be
no compensation. The reputation of England's power, too,
has had a rude shake; and nothing but a long-continued
manifestation of her might before the eyes of the whole
Indian Empire, evinced by the presence of such an English
force as shall make the thought of opposition hopeless, will
re-establish confidence in her strength.

Lord Canning much fears that there are parts of India
where, until this is done, a complete return to peace and
order will not be effected. Wherever the little band of English soldiers—little when compared with the stretch of country over which they have to operate—which Lord Canning
has at his disposal has shewn itself, the effect has been in-
stantaneous.

Except at Delhi, there has scarcely been an attempt at
resistance to a European soldier, and the march of the smallest detachments has preserved order right and left of the
roads . . .

After a short lull outside Delhi a new attack began on
Hindu Rao's, and the General, up for the day with his staff
and other officers not on duty, sat in the sunshine on the
grass by the Mound and listened to the crackle of musketry
while the slow, heavy shells whistled harmlessly above them.
Up to the middle of the afternoon casualties had been very

few, but then it was decided to send out a column of 800 men against them. They moved off with a noticeable reluctance, for, as Fred Roberts said afterwards with unusual naïvety, "men do not like advancing from cover when they are being pitched into by a heavy fire from some unseen enemy hidden behind trees and rocks."

Suddenly, and quite unexpectedly, the mutineers began to retreat—and at once the whole British force were after them with such speed that within minutes they were actually within sight of the city walls. The enemy's heavy guns and howitzers had a range of at least 1,000 yards and the sepoys withdrew until they were almost beneath the ramparts, which were lined with mutineers excitedly firing cannons and muskets and pouring down a fearful shower of grape and shot on their pursuers at virtually point-blank range. Men fell like leaves, for the enthusiasm of the pursuit had led them into a trap, and the column they had chased became a disorderly crowd, with horsemen stumbling over infantry, and infantry falling over themselves in their zeal to reach the safety of the gates. There was nothing left for the British but to retire as well.

The sight of the hated *sahibs* withdrawing in haste gave courage to the mutineers, who increased their fire. Brigadier Chamberlain, who commanded the column, was wounded in the left shoulder, and began to lose blood at such a rate that he became dizzy and decided to delegate his command and make for camp at once. Before he collapsed, however, he insisted that two guns should be put in place to guard the retreat, and he sent off Roberts with one of the General's A.D.C.s to carry out this order.

Roberts turned to steady the nervous, rearing horses in the shafts of one of the gun carriages, and at that precise moment felt such a violent thud on the back that he was almost sick and nearly fell off his own horse. For a moment he hardly realized that this must be a wound. Giddily, he dismounted, and one of the Fusilier officers sent two men to his aid. The ball had struck his leather pistol-cap pouch, which had slipped round to the back, and this saved him. With great relief, he climbed on his horse again and set off after the guns.

A good deal of criticism followed this escapade, in which twenty died and 200 were wounded. But the rebel casualties were put at nearly 1,000, and for hours next day they carted away the bodies that lay outside the walls in heaps.

Fred Roberts's wound gave him an insight into the conditions of the wounded and the hospitals, which by now were becoming so overcrowded that there were not enough *doolies* to go round, and many desperately wounded men were forced to lie on straw on the ground in the pitiful shelter of tents.

Scarcely one of the dozens of amputations performed without anaesthetics survived the ordeal. Gangrene was very common, and also hospital fever, which might almost have been called "gaol fever," for sick and well alike laboured under the horrors of the worst season of the year in torrential rain, muggy heat and the everlasting and revolting flies. Roberts would lie on his back watching the canvas roof of his tent, which was always black with settled flies.

> At the first ray of light or the smallest shake of the ropes [he wrote in *Forty-one Years in India*] they were all astir, and for the rest of the day there was no peace; it was even difficult to eat without swallowing one or more of the loathsome insects. I had to brush them away with one hand while I put food into my mouth with the other, and more than once I had to rush from the table, a fly having eluded all my efforts to prevent his going down my throat. . . .

No sooner was a dish of food uncovered than it was almost invisible under them. Even a cup of tea would quickly become a solid mass of drowning black specks. The men on picket duty used to amuse themselves when things were quiet by tracing patterns of sugary water on sheets of paper, then shaking gunpowder over them and, as soon as the flies had settled into a black mass, they would light the powder trail. Others would trap them in cups of water.

Those of the sick and wounded who were thought unlikely to be fit for duty for some time, and who were thus sent back in convoy to Amballa or Meerut, found the hospitals there already swarming with the overflow from Delhi. Such a convoy was sent out on the evening of the 17th, when things were quiet again; and on this journey the unfortunate General Reed was a passenger.

No one could honestly feel sorry to see him go. The wonder was that he should have been appointed to such an arduous duty in the first place—but it was in keeping with the administration of the Company's Army.

Chamberlain, because of his wound, was not able to succeed Reed. Brigadier Archdale Wilson of the Artillery Brigade was the only other possible choice. This meant passing over the heads of two other more senior Colonels—Congreve, the Acting Adjutant-General of the Queen's troops, a fussy individual, very fond of his own comforts, who became easily excited if his opinions were not immediately accepted; and Longfield, of the Queen's 8th Foot. Neither of them wanted the job, but nevertheless felt pangs of jealousy when it fell to Wilson. Congreve took the opportunity of leaving the camp for Simla, and Longfield took over from Wilson as his Brigadier.

Archdale Wilson was then within a few days of his fifty-fourth birthday, and considerably younger than any of his three ill-fated predecessors. Although never a great leader, a fact that had been amply proved at Meerut, he was certainly the best of the remaining officers available for the command. "Just a stout, gallant Englishman," Daly called him, and added: "I should not expect anything very distinguished from him, but always firmness and gallantry. He is decidedly the best we have."

Colonel Baird Smith was also pleased with the choice.

"Another change," he wrote to his wife. "The kaleidoscope

scarcely gives more or more varied, only they are generally more beautiful. . . . It is one comfort that we have at last a man. Be he good, bad, or indifferent, he will be a real and not a sham commander. It has been such miserable work since I joined from the want of a head for whom one could feel the faintest sense of respect. . . ."

The new General approached his formidable task with modesty but Christian resolution.

"This is a fearful responsibility that has been thrown on my shoulders," he wrote to his wife, "and knowing as I do my own weakness and incapacity, I feel as if I should faint under the burden, but the Lord God in whom I put my trust will surely give me strength and support."

On the day after Wilson was promoted, Baird Smith, as Chief Engineer, went to ask his views on an early assault. Wilson was not keen; he felt that this would be "too desperate a measure." The prospect was thus indefinitely postponed again until they should have more reinforcements.

Wilson felt that if he had even "another 2,000 men" he would be prepared for a regular battery attack.

"I am ready for this," Baird Smith assured him, "whenever you are."

A few days after their meeting, Baird Smith received 300 more Punjab Sappers and 600 unarmed Pioneers, all volunteers from the workmen on the Ganges Canal at Roorkee. These untrained coolies proved excellent workmen under fire and, despite their tremendous casualties, they performed a most valuable service to the Engineers and to the camp.

Baird Smith used them for clearing away trees, walls, and buildings which provided thick cover for enemy patrols quite near Hindu Rao's picket. By the end of July nearly all these hiding-places were cleared, and a breastwork completed which ran from the picket uphill to the Ridge by Hindu Rao's, so that the men could cross safely under some kind of cover.

This was the first attempt to consider the safety of the force

as men. All these weeks they had been beating back the mutineers in something approaching disorganization and without
the slightest practical regard for their own security. Even the
batteries were not adequately protected. Baird Smith was determined to change this state of affairs, which had arisen
through the ineptitude of Major Laughton, the first Chief
Engineer.

All through that summer the Engineer Brigade rarely re-
laxed. They were always repairing batteries or making traverses; building up magazines, digging ditches, trying to locate
enemy miners, and, in any free time, training the newly arrived Pioneers.

"Jumps" were made on the road to prevent further cavalry
charges on the camp and the small temple, the "Sammy
House," which stood in the way of the advanced picket, was
blown up—an explosion that caused great alarm in the city.

General Wilson was also a Pioneer. For the first time he
introduced some method into the daily duties of the men. A
properly organized rota of picket duties was drawn up, which
allowed a certain number of troops to be sure of a night's
rest when they were not on duty. The General also ordered
that in future attacks there must be no more foolhardy rushing after the enemy, which had brought such disastrous con-
sequences.

During the first weeks of the siege the idea of being in
action had been so strange that men would sit on the parapets and watch for the flash from the enemy's guns. Then
they would shout, "Down!" and down everyone would duck
while the shells trundled harmlessly above their heads. Wilson's orders stopped this foolishness.

General Wilson had inherited from old General Hewitt of
Meerut a love of smart turn-out, and he deplored the fact
that uniforms were sloppy and that many troops went about
in their shirt-sleeves.

"*Some* kind of uniform," he insisted, must be worn. More
patrols under an officer or an N.C.O. were to go round, and

officers on the outlying pickets must send in written reports
every day to the Field Officer. Every picket was to have a
bugler to sound the alarm in case of a night attack, and if this
should happen, the posts were to be defended "to the last
extremity," while supporting troops, who must go to bed
already accoutred, were to move out to their assistance. Those
troops not on picket duty were to move always to the same
positions—which were laid down—when they were ordered
out. None of these obvious arrangements had been made
before; the men were grateful that they were being made
now.

As soon as Fred Roberts was convalescent, he was given
some duties to perform. One of these involved the disposal of
the hundreds of corpses of camels and bullocks that littered
the camp. Gangs of coolies carried these loathsome hulks of
rottenness out of the camp to be buried or burned, but far
too many were left as prey to the jackals that prowled around
through the night, and to strange birds of prey of species
which before this had not been seen within hundreds of miles
of Delhi.

The other notable invalid, Brigadier Chamberlain, was
slower in his recovery, for his wound was more serious. When
he first arrived up at the camp and coolies were helping him
out of his litter, the sudden rush of blood as he tried to stand
up made him stagger and he fell on his wounded arm. This
caused him so much pain that even the surgeon who was
waiting to operate could hardly help crying out in sympathy.
It was an agonizing operation, for several fragments of the
shattered bone had to be removed.

The Brigadier made a restless patient, and passed two or
three days half stupefied with morphia. Then he lay on his
back for several weeks, and the rubbing of the rope mattress
of his bed gave him carbuncles. The camp outside Delhi was
not a very comfortable place for convalescents.

By this time misgivings were beginning to be felt about

Sir Hugh Wheeler's force, which was supposed to be coming to the assistance of the besiegers of Delhi.

The most disquieting reports were coming through from Cawnpore, and although at first everybody tried to discredit them, and kept such news from their wives in the hills, at last they could no longer be denied.

Wheeler, seventy years old and hard-pressed for three weeks by the mutineers, with his force weakened by sickness and death, had made the fatal error of putting faith in promises by the supposedly Anglophile Nana Sahib that he would grant safe conduct for his troops if he surrendered.

He did surrender, and his men were slaughtered as they stepped into the boats to be taken downstream. The fate of the women was still more horrible. The mutineers herded them into a small house, and kept them there for two or three weeks. When the Nana learned of Havelock's approach, he had them killed and their bodies flung like stones into a well.

Young Edward Vibart, whose father, a Major, was there with the rest of his family, was shocked and horrified to realize that they had been killed, for scarcely a survivor remained from that large force.

Everyone was so numbed at the news, that, with the reticence of their generation, they could hardly bring themselves to pass on the details to their wives and families.

The Delhi Force, which already regarded itself as the avenging instrument of God, was now filled with even greater hatred of their enemies. As a result, their rage was directed against everyone in Delhi, and not merely the mutinous sepoys.

Lieutenant Charles Griffiths, who had been in Ferozepore with the British 61st Regiment of Foot when a small revolt was crushed on 13 May, now recalled how, a month afterwards, twelve Mohammedans and high-caste Hindus had been punished for their part in it by being blown from the mouths of guns. Many who heard his account of this in the camp were for carrying out a similar vengeance on the mutineers in Delhi.

This punishment was the established way of dealing with mutiny and rebellion under the old Mogul Emperors, and was equally dreaded by Hindus and Moslems because, in both their creeds, it destroyed the soul as well as the body.

The Hindus believed that unless their corpses were burned to ashes or consigned to the sacred waters of the Ganges, they would not dwell among their gods; the Moslems held that the Koran taught that all true believers must be buried unmutilated. Only those who had lost arms or legs fighting the infidel would be exempted from this condition.

. . . The order was given for the guns to be loaded [recalled Griffiths], and quick as thought the European artillery-men placed a quarter charge of powder in each piece. The guns were 9-pounders, the muzzles standing about three feet from the ground.

. . . The twelve stood two deep, six in front and six in the rear, calm and undismayed, without uttering a word.

. . . Arrived at the guns, the culprits were handed over to the artillery-men, who, ready prepared with strong ropes in their hands, seized their victims. Each of these, standing erect, was bound to a cannon and tightly secured with the small of the back covering the muzzle. And then all at once the silence which reigned around was broken by the oaths and yells of those about to die.

. . . They were still yelling and raining abuse, some even looking over their shoulders and watching without emotion the portfires about to be applied to the touch-holes, when the word "Fire!" sounded from the officer in command, and part of the tragedy was at an end.

A thick cloud of smoke issued from the muzzles of the cannons, through which were distinctly seen by several of us the black heads of the victims, thrown many feet into the air.

While this tragic drama was enacting, the two sepoys to be hanged were turned off the platform.

The artillery-men again loaded the guns, the six remaining prisoners, cursing like their comrades, were bound to them, another discharge, and then an execution the like of which I hope never to see again was completed.

All this time a sickening, offensive smell pervaded the air, a stench which only those who have been present at scenes such as these can realize—the pungent odor of burnt human flesh.

The artillery-men had neglected putting up back boards to their guns, so that, horrible to relate, at each discharge the recoil threw back pieces of burning flesh, bespattering the men and covering them with blood and calcined remains.

. . . The drama came to an end about six o'clock [a.m.] and as usual, even after a funeral or a military execution, the band struck up an air, and we marched back to barracks, hoping * soon to drive from our minds the recollection of the awful scenes we had witnessed. . . .

Happily the camp soon had a new subject for conversation. A prisoner was taken: a woman, wrinkled, unattractive, and wearing a sowar's green uniform with a green turban, with a musket in her hand. She led a cavalry charge against the 75th Foot—"Fighting against us like a fiend," said Hodson with relish. He had known about her existence for some time. She contemptuously referred to the mutineers' cavalry as "women."

This woman was said to have killed two of the Delhi force and the troops said she was worse than five sepoys in the field, but because of her sex she was brought back to the camp while interested officers and men stood around and discussed her prowess.

Keith Young wrote, a little disappointed, to his wife that "as she is old and ugly, not much romance attaches to her." She was derisively called the "Maid of Delhi" or "Pandy

* That hope was not realized. This account is taken from Griffiths's book, *A Narrative of the Siege of Delhi,* published by John Murray in 1910, fifty-three years later.

Queen," and she looked like an active little man or a female impersonator. At Hodson's earnest request, however, the General determined that her continued presence among the "superstitious Moslems" would be represented as miraculous, almost like a Joan of Arc, and he ordered her to be caught and brought back.

Colonel Greathed thought that, despite the uniform, she was no more than "a dispirited old woman." Anyway, the courageous old soul was sent up with an escort to Amballa, and the siege saw her no more.

There was so little to talk about in camp that this incident provided fuel for conversation for days. It took everyone's mind off the smells and squalor of their position—and the fact that beyond waiting for reinforcements no real plan of campaign existed.

The Chaplain found that, like so many others, he was borne down by the evil miasmas of camp, and he just could not face the prospect of visiting his hospitals after such prolonged overwork and such continued anxiety over his family away in Meerut. He gave himself the luxury of a day's holiday, and viewed events through borrowed binoculars from the Flagstaff Tower.

Captain Anson and Hope Grant, both men of extreme piety, had asked him to hold a mid-week service in Anson's tent—an unusually large one—so that officers could hold prayers at eight o'clock, a time which would allow the Brigadier to visit his pickets comfortably first. Anson was impressed by the Chaplain's good memory, which allowed him to preach extempore from the Bible; Colonel Young occasionally yawned in the Sunday services and thought that Rotton's sermons were far too long and dull. Rotton, for his part, wished that the officers would contribute something towards the success of these prayer meetings instead of sitting silently and leaving all the initiative to him.

In short, the waiting game was telling on the tempers of everyone, and only self-discipline kept people from falling out with their friends over trifles. Many had come out in boils, scabs and rashes on their faces and hands, and still the rain poured down, so that everyone was soaked, in tents or out, and boots and belts and other leather equipment were covered with a green mould that sprouted afresh every night.

The foul smell from the dead in their shallow ground and the cesspool soured the damp breezes which blew in the evenings.

Men and officers lay on *charpoys,* on doors scrounged from ruined houses, sometimes on just a blanket in the mud, and tried to will themselves to sleep in the foetid atmosphere.

Despite these foul conditions, many believed that the darkest days were past. On their arrival at Delhi, for instance, all Indians thought that the British Raj was doomed and at an end, and nothing was brought in for sale in camp.

"Sheep, poor and thin," one soldier noted in his diary then, "could only be had at the commissariat and at 5 rupees each! Grain 10 *seers* the rupee! Fowls unknown. Now sheep are as common as were jackals at Sekrora; grain is 45 to 50 *seers;* poultry of all kinds abundant; boots, shoes, even macassar oil!"

In the evenings there was often quite a turn-out in the main street in camp; several buggies and a *palki gharry* were proudly displayed by their owners when off duty. One buggy was sold at an auction, but, Daly wrote, "a pot of jam nearly fetched as much."

Jam was indeed a great delicacy, and Colonel Young was fortunate, for his wife busied herself in making apricot preserves which she sent down to him in the mail-cart, as he liked jam with his breakfast. For the rest, the danger, the discomforts, and the lack of leadership had been with them for so long that they accepted this unwelcome trinity as being an inescapable part of their lives. They had nothing else to do but soldier on.

"What they want just now," wrote Anson, to his wife, thinking of the incidence of sunstroke among his men, "are padded curtains to their cap covers. Their heads, owing to the small size and shape of the forage caps they wear, are very inadequately protected from the burning sun."

But what the Army wanted and what they got were, as always, two quite different things.

CHAPTER V

Still Waiting

THE EFFECTIVE FORCE, then, both European and Indian, officers and men, amounted to 4,023 Infantry, 1,293 Cavalry, and 1,602 Artillery and Engineers—a total of only 6,918. The sick and wounded, on top of this, amounted to 1,116—more than one-seventh of the total fighting strength.

Baird Smith was impatient at the continued hold-up in reinforcements, especially of the siege-train and ammunition. Like many others, he did not understand that there was very little more to send. He complained that "at present we get everything in driblets, which seem to do little more than supply our daily waste."

He was losing promising young Engineer officers in battle or from disease at a tremendous rate.

Their entry into Delhi was now only a question of time—so far as he was concerned, the shortest time possible. Yet the wrongness of the situation could not be denied, when "one has the feeling that the whole do only tends to repair a gigantic blunder of our own growing for years and years, and of which we have been disgracefully ignorant until its effects burst on us as they have done. . . .

"The errors must be corrected, but you can't sponge out history, and this business will stand for ever against us, as an outstanding instance of a ruling Government and Community having been taken utterly by surprise."

Heartening reports had been received, however, that the
mutineers were equally discouraged. Once or twice the city
was so quiet that it was rumoured that they might all have
gone away "in despair."

This was, in fact, far from being the case, although General
Bakht Khan had thoughtfully taken the precaution of ordering 500 ladders to be made, so that, should the English capture the city, the sepoys could escape over the walls and be
away across the desert.

The redoubtable gunner Kuli Khan was still in form, and
the King had sent him a *tawiz,* or charm, to put round his
arm, and so make him invincible.

One of the deserters from the British camp warned the
King in his durbar that if he used, say, 30,000 of his men to
attack the troops now in the British camp, they "ought to
defeat them"; but that if the attack was delayed, then reinforcements would arrive from England, and they would probably be defeated. The King was too distracted by other problems to pay much attention to this good advice. Even the gift
of an elephant, which had been captured from the British,
could not cheer him up. He had indeed much on his mind—
not least the fact that someone had been caught digging a
mine under one of his Palace walls. Although the man was
promptly blown from a gun, the King was alarmed that any
one of his subjects should have been so disloyal. He withdrew
into the cocoon of royalty, and tried to concentrate his
thoughts on other things.

To sepoys who arrived from distant stations he said bluntly
that he had no money to pay them. To those who asked for
muskets, he explained he had no arms. The Princes were dis-
credited—although one pointed out bitterly that nearly two
and a half hundredweights of oil were being smuggled into
the British camp every night for cooking and to light lamps.

The houses of more and more rich people were being broken into and plundered on the pretext that the owners were
harbouring Europeans. Moslems and Hindus were indulging

in the luxury of religious riots, and casualties became so serious that the King issued a specific order that no Moslem should kill a cow during the festival of Id or help anyone else to do so on pain of being blown from a gun. His Chamberlain said that he would have to consult the *moulvies* on this matter—a reply that so enraged the old King that he returned to his private room in a fury and refused to see anyone.

Then someone spread the rumour that the British were abandoning their camp, and at once about 3,000 horsemen and 1,000 fanatics on foot, armed with clubs, swords, spears, and guns, rushed out to share the loot. They were astonished to be met with rifle fire and at once fled back to the city even more discontented than before.

The officers were complaining that they had received no pay; but the King had no money to pay anyone. The Jhansi troops and others had seized large sums when they mutinied, and would not pay them into the treasury, which was empty.

Even the General had his complaints. He told the King in durbar that he had been accused of being in collusion with the English and of "slinking home and leaving his men to fight without orders."

From the look he gave the three Princes and the words which he whispered in the King's ear, it was fairly clear whom he suspected of making these accusations. The Princes retaliated by charging him with bad manners in "violating the customs of good society" by whispering. The matter finally ended with much apologizing and insincere flattery on all sides.

Bakht Khan held a review to enliven his troops' flagging spirits, and asked all faint hearts to fall out and go home. None accepted this offer, but all pledged themselves to fight to the end. This pleased the King, who turned out and inspected 2,800 pounds of sweetmeats which had been made for the delectation of the soldiers.

But the review and the gifts and the flattery and superstition were all remote from any real action. It was part of a dying world of make-believe that carried no meaning, and had no answer to the problems of survival and victory. Bakht Khan tried to stop the continual plunder and looting in the city by announcing that no guilty man would take part in "the coming victory." No one seemed to care. Like the British troops on the Ridge outside, they suspected that no plan for victory yet existed. They were quite right. The Munshi Jeewan Lal's last entry in his diary for July read almost like a commentary on the whole affair: "A *moulvie* said to the King today that, if he would permit him to recite a verse of the Koran over the entrails of a goat, then the guns of the English would become useless."

On a lower level, the sepoys tried to keep up their own morale by inventing stories of British cruelty: how they had sent back some captured camp followers after cutting off their noses and ears; how they thought of putting to death all their own Hindustani soldiers; how their chiefs in Calcutta and London were dying of disease, and two of their Cs.-in-C. had already committed suicide. The King listened patiently to these chronicles; to mend the situation was now beyond him.

"Whatever happens," he said wearily, "happens by the will of God."

Archdale Wilson thus wrote reassuringly to Sir John Lawrence: "I shall hold my position to the last, for it is of the utmost consequence that the enemy should be confined within Delhi to prevent their ravaging the country about. To effect this object it is absolutely necessary that I should be strongly reinforced as quickly as possible." Soon afterwards, Lawrence sent him down 4,000 reliable reinforcements ("not a Poorbeah amongst them"). More than a quarter were Europeans, and Lawrence was nearly draining the Punjab of British troops to build up the Delhi Force. He knew that once Delhi was captured then the Mutiny elsewhere would collapse, for Delhi was a natural rallying point and the heart and core of the struggle.

For some time the British had vaguely supposed that a large-scale attack would mark the great festival of the Bukra Id, when the King of Delhi used to go out with a large Mohammedan escort to sacrifice a camel or goat at a *serai* beyond Subzi Mundi in honour of Ishmael, the Mohammedan equivalent of Isaac, and his sacrifice by Abraham.

Thus it came as no surprise when lookouts reported on 31 July that they had seen a large enemy force marching through the rain as if making for the rear of the British position. This force might have passed unseen in the dark, but some delay in starting led to their discovery by daylight.

The enemy were bound for the site of the Bussaye bridge, destroyed two or three weeks back by the Engineers, and they carried timbers to rebuild it, so as to cross over to attack the rear of camp, under cover of a feint attack to be made on the front in the usual way.

Although the rain and the liquid mud clearly hampered the enemy's movements, General Wilson felt obliged to follow them up with a movable column. By some mistake, instead of issuing the order verbally, as should have been done, someone sounded the "Assembly" on a bugle, so that the whole camp turned out too soon for a false alarm. The mutineers had just finished their bridge, and had sent the cavalry across, when a storm burst overhead, and in the sudden flooding of the stream, the whole structure was swept away, cutting off the cavalry from the rest of the force which were about to follow. The broken timbers roared down on the foaming river past the camp, where with some relief British troops saw them float by harmlessly. The column of mutineers had no choice but to march back to the city, wet and wretched.

Almost with exasperation, Commissioner Greathed wrote of the mutineers: "Their characteristic is to do the wrong

thing at the wrong time." This characteristic was not confined to them.

Greathed was the senior civilian in the camp. Others included the urbane Sir Theophilus Metcalfe, who had been
appointed his assistant, and Henry Marten, Baird Smith's
assistant. There were also collectors and other members of
the Civil Service—in Anson's words, "treasureless and powerless." Save when these civilians were aroused early by the
noise of guns, and were inconvenienced by shot which fell
too close to their tents, they passed a very easy time during
this strange siege.

Hervey Greathed, outlining his activities to his wife, wrote:
"I get up between five and six, go out for a ride, or walk, or
lounge over to Edward's [Colonel Greathed] or Tombs's tent,
or to the knot of gossips who sit daily before Colonel Thompson's tent in the street.

"We breakfast at half-past eight, and when that is over I
have writing to employ me until three, when there comes a
difficult bit of time to get over till five or six, when the turn
for riding or strolling comes back and then mess, and so to
bed." He added that "on fighting days, the course is a little
altered."

But if Greathed and some of the Staff had difficulty in
filling in their time, others found every moment of their day
taken up. The Chief Engineer described his day's work thus:

I get up about four, and immediately set off to go round the
batteries and defences to see if I can do anything for their
security. I have generally a lot of demands from the artillery
officers and others, and when I return arrangements are
made for satisfying these.

I get home about eight and work till breakfast time, about
nine or nine-thirty. I breakfast on some fish, of which we
have a daily supply, tea, and toast, and then back to my
writing-table again. The daily reports of the Field Engineers are then gone over, abstracted for the General's information and sent off; all routine business is disposed of,

and then I take up the matters connected with our future progress in our work, all of which I am getting into form for future use. These occupy me until the afternoon, when, unless people call, I go out again round the works, and get back in time to dress for dinner.

I go to bed almost immediately after dinner, and so the day ends. It does not look tempting, does it? However, it has not been of my seeking, and so I take it quietly.

The Engineers had divided the camp into two parts, right and left, with a directing engineer in charge of each. Working parties coming on duty at dusk knocked off at dawn, when there would be danger of discovery, and at one o'clock, tiffin-time, the order-books came round with the next twenty-four hour's allocations of work. They made breastworks, laid batteries, cleared cover, strengthened posts, and cut up acres of brushwood for gabions and fascines.

Jules Medley, one of the numerous junior Engineer officers in the camp who was to become a General in later years, arrived on 7 August. He had been serving on the Frontier since the start of the Mutiny, and it had taken him two months to reach Delhi. His first task was the least enviable—at Azadpore picket, a cavalry post close to the one remaining canal bridge which had been kept intact for foraging purposes. This was kept ready mined, with an Engineer officer on duty in case of emergency; because of the post's distance from camp it took a spell of forty-eight hours' duty and the officer had to accompany the patrol on its round over the flooded country, reporting on the canal's depth. This duty involved a ride of twelve miles through slush and water, often many feet deep, and a return to a tent where clouds of flies all day and persistent mosquitoes at night virtually prevented sleep.

After the failure of the attack of the Bukra Id, the enemy began to lose heart and confidence in their ultimate success. What was more, John Nicholson, the great "Nikkul Seyn,"

was known to be expected to aid the British. Sir John Lawrence was alarmed at the rate of loss of senior officers, and
the danger of allowing the stalemate before Delhi to continue any longer. So Nicholson, the tall, bearded one, who
was regarded as a god on the Frontier—a rôle which his
Puritan heart detested—Nicholson was leading a special
"movable column" to Delhi. Once they arrived the assault
would not be long delayed, for Nicholson was a man of immediate and tremendous action.

On his way to Delhi, for instance, he reached Amritsar to
be told that mutineers from Sealkote had already left for the
same city. He believed that they might pick up more recruits
on the way at Goordaspore, and so resolved to race them to
the town, which was forty miles away. The mutineers already had two days' start on him, at the hottest time of year.
Nicholson did not argue these difficulties; they argued themselves. He impounded every gig and cart, horse and pony
he could find to carry his troops. Men who had never ridden
a horse in their lives were faced with snorting chargers or
tough ponies. Officers clambered up two by two to ride on the
backs of the camels. Light carts designed for two passengers
carried four or more; and even so hundreds marched.

They started at dusk and by dawn were twenty-six miles
nearer. Nicholson halted the long, strange convoy, not to
rest, but to cut down the branches of trees to make awnings
to cover the men who rode in carts or on gun carriages from
the pitiless heat.

"We look like the road to Epsom on Derby Day!" said
someone amid laughter. Then they set off again to march as
Europeans had rarely marched before, through the terrible
heat of the Indian summer. As the sun moved up the sky,
soldiers, their red jackets soaked through with sweat, fell in
the dust delirious with sunstroke, and were left where they
fell. Some went mad, others dropped dead with strokes. The
rest marched on.

At noon the bedraggled column reached a small clump of

trees, where some of the officers begged that they could halt. "No," said Nicholson. "We must press on." But unexpectedly he relented and he agreed to allow a brief halt.

As they slept, one officer suddenly started up, crying out, "Where's the General?"

Others staggered up, sensing danger, but Nicholson was where they had left him, astride his horse, bolt upright in the burnished glare of the sun, waiting with unconcealed impatience for them to have their sleep and then be away. The sight had its effect. Within minutes everyone was up and marching.

Despite these efforts, the mutineers had reached Goordaspore before them, and were trying to cross the Ravi River, nine miles away, by a local ferry. Nicholson pursued them to the river banks and, leading his men like a subaltern, attacked them. Not one mutineer escaped. The revolt at Sealkote was over.

Now, as if the news that Nicholson was on his way to Delhi was not enough to depress the mutineers, they were further downcast by the tales of those who had escaped Havelock's vengeance at Cawnpore, and stories of terrible fighters who had come from Ceylon (the Highland regiments), who wore petticoats like women and fought like tigers. Compared with these fighters, they said, "the Gurkhas are mere mice."

It was also expected that Sir Patrick Grant, previously commanding in Madras, the new C.-in-C. appointed temporarily until Sir Colin Campbell arrived from England to take over, would soon be taking the field in person, and would be arriving almost before Nicholson, with plentiful reinforcements at last. But fast on the heels of this encouraging news came a dispatch from Agra confirming the Cawnpore massacre and describing the death of Sir Henry Lawrence at the Siege of Lucknow, an almost irreparable loss to India. Hodson was greeted by the news on returning worn out after a day in the saddle.

"To the country," he wrote in his diary, "his death would be worse than the loss of a province. . . ."

As usual, then, the expected reinforcements could not now be sent to Delhi, for although Lucknow was expected to be relieved in a few days, neither Grant nor Havelock could come to their aid.

Many of the mutineers in the city were equally sick of the stalemate and the Begum and the Princes had already started secret negotiations for the best terms they could get. They got nothing. By now the only condition the Force on the Ridge would accept was total surrender.

The rainy season progressed, and slowly the temperature fell and health in camp improved slightly. The *daks* were held up, but, as a consolation, no cholera cases were reported for several days. When there was a slight lull in the rains, it was regarded as a chance to celebrate with sports in the Rifle lines—cricket, quoits, and an impromptu pony race. These were such a success that little else was spoken of for days. As a talking point, indeed, this gymkhana rivalled a shell which had fallen within the lines and burst near the Artillery mess tent—a calamity for the mess, which prided itself on its *cordon bleu* cook, its habitual six-course dinners, its mutton and pastry, its famous beer—and a cause for sly smiles and grins on the part of the private soldiers who had no share in these delights.

During a lull, the Engineers, particularly Wilberforce Greathed, decided to put into practice an idea they had considered for some time—blowing up the bridge of boats the mutineers had built across the river. This might have been listed among the sports items, for it misfired and caused a great deal of excitement to those who watched from the Flagstaff Tower.

Two rafts were sent down from a point a mile upstream with barrels of gunpowder lashed on them. A slow-match was lit to fire the powder by the time the rafts reached the bridge.

It was an ingenious idea, but not ingenious enough. No one had taken the currents into consideration, and the strong swollen tide turned one raft against a sandbank, where it stayed until it blew up. The other was spotted by the mutineers from the bank. A couple of men on *mussacks*—inflated sheepskins—paddled out and towed it ashore and dismantled it. The disgusted Engineers made one more attempt with a huge raft which was to act "by pressure and obstructing the waterway," but the same thing happened. Those who saw the third failure remarked wisely that if only they had sent them down after dark they might at least have frightened the enemy.

Hodson was as busy as ever, riding on special expeditions of reconnaissance. He was very pleased with the exploits of his little force, and Commissioner George Barnes had written him a most complimentary letter about it. He believed that, at last, past blots on his career were wiped out, and his future was assured.

Regular officers like Brigadier Hope Grant, whose Army experience had been the strict routine of the Lancers, could never bring himself to believe that such a "rabble" as Hodson's Horse could ever make good soldiers, and took a long time to accept the value of irregulars.

Nicholson was expected to arrive not a moment too soon, for the toll on officers and men had been so heavy that the force had dwindled amazingly through disease, deaths after hospital treatment, and outright killing by the mutineers. General Wilson was ill from a severe attack of dysentery, and even when he recovered his old vigour was lacking. His nervousness and over-anxiety about trifles were noted with concern by Baird Smith and others, who, if they felt they could not rely on the judgment of their commanding officer, found their own problems much aggravated.

"Would we could have had Sir Henry Lawrence as our leader," wrote Hodson only the day before he heard of that commander's death. "We should have been in Delhi weeks ago."

Men like Barnard and Wilson were "brave as lions, but they have not big hearts or heads enough for circumstances of serious *responsibility*. This word is the bugbear which hampers all our proceedings."

On the morning of 7 August there was a clear sign that things were going to move at last: Nicholson came in on the mailcart a week ahead of his troops to consult with the General before returning to bring in the column.

On the afternoon of his arrival he was galloping round the posts and batteries to see for himself the layout of the positions. Despite his simple uniform, which gave no clue to his rank, everyone recognized his tall, spare commanding figure with its unmistakable black beard, and the inscrutable eyes full of cold power. On the Frontier his appearance enhanced his reputation among the hill-men, who reckoned a leader without a beard as only half a man. Nicholson was all man.

Despite his size and physique, he suffered from poorish health, and this shortened his temper. He would work from ten to eleven hours every day, and had a sharp way of dealing with regulations or people he did not like.

Once, riding through a village in Peshawar, he passed a mosque and saw that the *mullah,* instead of salaaming him, was staring at him in a way he took to be contemptuous. That night Nicholson sent his orderly to bring the *mullah* to him, and when the holy man arrived Nicholson set to with a razor and lather brush and shaved his beard off there and then.

Another time he was standing with a few friends at the gate of his garden in Bunnoo when a man with a sword in his hand approached him and asked which of the group was Nikkul Seyn. Something in his face made Nicholson seize a musket from a sentry and ram it into the man's chest.

"If you don't drop your sword, I'll shoot you dead," he said by way of reply. The man rushed at him. Nicholson kept his word. The bullet killed his attacker instantly, and went through a copy of the Koran which was turned down at a page that promised Paradise to those who fell trying to slay unbelievers.

Nicholson's official report of his action to the Chief Commissioner was as blunt as the man. "Sir," he wrote, "I have the honour to inform you that I have just shot a man who came to kill me. Your obedient servant, John Nicholson."

Nicholson had many friends and well-wishers in camp, including Captain Alex Taylor of the Engineers and Fred Roberts, but he also had to combat a fair amount of envy among the older officers, over whose heads he had been promoted and who resented him not only because he was young, but because he was a Company's man.

But as his admirer, Henry Daly, wrote: "Put all the Queen's colonels together who are in the camp—Greathed inclusive—and you could not extract a *man* who would be willing even to incur the responsibility of commanding this force. All here rejoiced at Nicholson's arrival, and not one would have attempted to urge a word which would throw the command on himself."

Nicholson was an officer of the East India Company, and was held by officers holding the Queen's Commission to be their junior, and something of an upstart. The British were not only at war with the mutineers, but, in a subtle, well-behaved way, with themselves.

The Queen's officers took most offence at their supercession by so young and junior a commander, as being "unauthorized by the terms of the Queen's warrant." To get round this difficulty, therefore, it was arranged that on his arrival the Queen's 52nd Foot, which was serving in his movable column, should be transferred out of his command to another brigade, so that Dennis and Campbell, the two Queen's commissioned full Colonels of that regiment, should not feel the humiliation of continuing to serve under so junior a Brigadier. By this means Nicholson would from now on have a brigade none of whose officers was senior to him. In these efforts to save face, a good deal of material discomfort had to be undergone, while a general post took place in the arrangements of the camp. The 9th Lancers had to move their lines to make way for the 1st Fusiliers, who were to be transferred to Nicholson when he finally came in, but when the tents were struck to move them elsewhere, it was found that the canvas had perished and was so rotten that many could not be pitched again.

The mess tent came entirely apart at the seams, and let the rain through in streams. The officers had often to eat their meals sheltering under the table.

John Nicholson was lit by the burning fire of zeal that seems to kindle only in Presbyterian souls. He was taciturn and inhibited, even in dealings with his own brother Charles —a Lieutenant in rank, but a company commander of the 2nd Punjabs. They could never talk freely, despite their deep feeling for one another.

John Nicholson brought an awed and uncomfortable silence to the mess on the first evening he attended. The laughter and the exchange of the latest camp anecdotes died under his cold gaze. Yet all who had served under him respected him; the fact of his arrival put fresh vigour into the jaded camp. He was a living symbol of victory, and in that wet and feverish August outside Delhi such a symbol was precious indeed.

Nicholson, having satisfied himself about the situation, then rode off to rejoin his troops back at Kurnaul, and to bring them in within another week. This reinforcement almost doubled the effective force, and even General Wilson had to admit that at last the capture of the city—excepting only for the absence of the siege train—was within the bounds of possibility.

On the following Sunday, 9 August, the Chaplain was obliged to hold Communion in the midst of thunderous interruption from all sides, since the previous week—the occa-

sion of the Bukra Id—he had deferred it. Colonel Young, together with many others, observed the sacrament, but even
the not very deductive mind of the Judge Advocate-General
had slight misgivings on their fitness to receive it. ("The roar
of cannon which was continually going on during service, and
the aspirations of all of us that each discharge from our guns
would send some of the wretched mutineers to perdition
seemed hardly in unison with the peaceful and sacred duties
in which we were engaged.")

About this time, the first letters and newspapers from home
with news of the Mutiny began to arrive, and the officers were
appalled to learn in what light they were being represented.
Because of the delay in the mails to England, the true state
of affairs was even now not known, and it was galling to men
in camp to find that instead of Parliament, as they fondly
imagined, discussing this greatest of threats to their Empire
since the American Rebellion, they were gravely talking of
"cotton and courts of justice." Lord Ellenborough (except
that he made the foolish mistake of supposing that they should
be able to cut off the enemy's water supply, quite ignoring
that the rebels had full command of the river) was allowed
to be "sensible"; Vernon Smith, President of the Board of
Trade, who had foolishly supposed that they could surround
Delhi and starve the mutineers into submission, and was bitterly condemning them for not having done so, was solemnly
booed in the Headquarters mess, when Sir Theo Metcalfe
read out the speeches.

"We have some six hundred European Lancers and Dragoons," wrote Young indignantly to a friend at home, "and
the same number of reliable Native Cavalry—a pretty force
with which to surround a place like Delhi, a city seven miles
round."

Such furious letters took at least a month to arrive, but they
might as well disabuse the glib critics who were so gratui-
tously running the campaign from London, Westminster, and
Whitehall—"arrogant civilians," wrote Young, "or purse-

proud mercantile men, all totally ignorant of everything connected with the Army, and more particularly of the causes of
the outbreak who, without a show of reason, attribute the
Mutiny to the misbehaviour and inattention to their duty of
regimental officers."

Young felt that the Mutiny was the fault of the Government, if anyone, and the home authorities who supported
the Government. "Of course, there *are* individual instances
of misconduct, but the way in which the European officers
generally have behaved throughout the late mutinies ought
to secure them from such attacks. . . . These fault-finding
gentlemen would do much better to confine their reviews . . .
to the acts of the members of the Civil Service during the
present trying time. With a few rare but bright exceptions
. . . they have shown off most lamentably, and I begin to
think Lord Ellenborough was right when he talked of its
being the 'correct thing to abolish the Civil Service and fill
up all civil appointments from the Army.' "

What hurt the men on the Ridge most of all—and what has
hurt the English in India ever since—was the ignorance of
the critics about that far country. They had no conception
of the small numbers available to cover thousands of square
miles, of the difficulties in communication, and most of all,
the convoluted Oriental mentality that could exasperate a
European so quickly and so often.

About this time the mutineers discovered a store of rockets
in the city, and these added to the explosives which they
dropped on the camp.

The besiegers were distressed to find that their own rockets were inferior and less effective—although, by an irony,
both sides had drawn them from the same arsenal, although
at different times. The enemy were still vastly superior in
artillery. Even the heavy guns, such as the 24-pounders, could
be replaced in a twinkling of an eye if they were damaged.

In the camp, though, the British could boast only one or

two captured earlier in the siege which were now so worn with work that they were of little use.

Baird Smith, however, was very pleased with his protective work round the batteries, and had ridden round continually these last few days to see for himself how they were standing up to the shells. On one of these trips an excited Irish rifleman rode up to him in a great state for his safety. "Och, sir, and take care of yerself. Don't be going on there," he advised his Colonel.

"Why?" asked Baird Smith.

"Why, a big shell has just busted."

"But," said the Engineer, "if it *has* burst, it isn't dangerous any longer!"

From holding a position of their own which appeared to be impregnable, the mutineers now found that they were also facing an impregnable siege camp. Here indeed was a unique situation that promised indefinite stalemate.

On 12 August, however, the General decided to take the first big offensive action against the enemy since 7 June at Budli-ka-Serai.

At three o'clock in the morning the column began to assemble under Brigadier Showers: about 1,200 men, including Horse Artillery, the Bengal Fusiliers, Gurkhas and Coke's Rifles, with guns and protecting cavalry. Baird Smith came out to see them set off, and was struck by the scene.

"It was a beautifully moonlit and starlit night," he said later, "perfectly still and quiet, except for the hum of a crowd, that rose and fell on the fresh breeze." Soon after four, the column moved quietly off through the gardens in the direction of Ludlow Castle, where the enemy battery was established.

The matter had been kept secret from all except a very few, and the intention was to surprise the enemy completely to try to capture some of their guns. Henry Daly, one of those in the know, was waiting anxiously in the camp, along with the unwilling non-combatants who, as the bugles announced

"Reveille," were also roused by a heavy burst of musketry, and thought for a moment that the Metcalfe pickets were under enemy fire again. But that first volley was quick and sharp; it showed that the column had achieved its purpose in getting close up to Ludlow Castle walls unseen by the enemy.

They crept right up to the walls and found the enemy sound asleep. In the murderously short engagement that followed, the mutineers had not a chance of success. One sentry alone had seen the advancing column and, challenging them, was shot down at once as the musketry opened up. The mutineers—chiefly soldiers of the 74th, one of the old Delhi regiments—did succeed in firing off two of the guns, but one of their artillerymen was bayoneted in the very act of putting the portfire to the breach. It was a brilliant little engagement, and not least because for once the besiegers were taking the initiative. Within two or three hours of leaving camp the column was on its way back.

The engagement had cost more than 120 killed and wounded, but then there were the guns, three light pieces and one 24-pounder howitzer.

Hodson thought the return to the camp worth seeing—and everyone who could was seeing it—with "a soldier with musket and bayonet fixed riding each horse, and brave young Lieutenant A. G. Owen of the 1st Fusiliers (who was wounded) astride one gun, and dozens clinging to and pushing it, or rather them, along with might and main, and cheering like mad things.

"I was in the thick of it by accident, for I was looking on as well as I could through the gloom, when Coke asked me to find Brigadier Showers and say he was wounded, and that the guns were taken. I found Showers himself wounded, and then had to find a field officer to take command, after which I assisted generally in drawing off the men—the withdrawal or retirement being the most difficult matter always, and requiring as much steadiness as an attack."

The men of the 1st Fusiliers rode the leading horses and

dragged in the first guns, stopping from time to time to cheer the Brigadier who had led them so well.

The mutineers retaliated by sending over large rockets and by making night attacks. Then they placed some heavy guns over the river and shelled the picket round Metcalfe's house so effectively that the camp of the 1st Punjab Infantry, which was on the near side of the camp and within their range, had to be moved. But nothing could damp the spirits of the camp now. Once more they were counting the days until they could be inside the city.

Even the weather seemed cheerful. It had not rained for more than a week, so there were pony races in the lines, and games of cricket and quoits. The band of the 8th Regiment gave a recital in the Headquarters camp, and the main street of the camp was crowded with gentry displaying their fashions, which were legion, since no two of the Staff or the Artillery dressed alike.

Even a shop had been established—"Peake and Allen's"— two merchants who had arrived in the sopping rain just before the fight of the Bukra Id when artillery and musketry were deafening the camp with their roars. They surmounted their initial dismay, and, despite high prices, became a highly popular establishment. Allen was a notable dandy and held to be "the best-dressed man in camp."

But no music, no distraction, could take away the smells that hung over the camp. Anson, cursed with abnormally sensitive nostrils, was continually offended by the terrible stench of death and putrefaction. At one picket in the rear of the camp, he was so overcome by the foetid air that while the other officers were dining with relish off their roast goose, rice pudding, and stewed guavas, liberally washed down by beer and wine, he could scarcely eat his own meal for nausea at the scores of rotting animal carcasses not half a mile away.

A friend obligingly sent him down a bottle of eau-de-Cologne to ease his sufferings, but he was relieved when news of a promotion heralded a reshuffling in his regiment, so that he was likely to become second-in-command and so could avoid the stinking picket duties in future. The only cure for the smells was distance.

Hervey Greathed had plenty of leisure time to ride about, but he, too, could not venture far beyond the confines of the camp because of the filthy smell from the fly-infested camels' bodies lying thick on the ground.

After nearly two months, it had not occurred to anyone that of all urgent jobs the burial of dead animals ought to have a priority. One or two officers on pickets passed their time, when not catching snakes or stalking muskrats, in blowing up the flies with gunpowder.

Many people were ill with dysentery—including the General, who was able to eat nothing save arrowroot. His command was increasingly a burden to him, and during the past few days signs had appeared of differences between him and his tireless Chief Engineer. These were to reach alarming proportions before many more days had passed.

It had all begun on 1 August, when Wilson was still not quite recovered from his earlier fever and dysentery, and only a day or two after Baird Smith had pronounced himself, though cautiously, "in no mood for complaint" about his commander. The General, still convalescing, had a long talk with him and was alarmed by the vigour of his proposals for disposing of the enemy force. The strain of waiting for weeks in blinding, baking sunshine, and then torrential downpours, of being exiled and in fear of death in this strange wild country half a world away from home, was telling on the senior officers far more than they realized. They were out of their depths professionally and psychologically, and they had no one to turn to but each other.

Wilson's great fear since Bukra Id was that the mutineers should again get to the rear and cut them off. Every movement during the next few days which looked as if this might be their intention set him off worrying and begging Baird Smith for his reassurance. This was given freely and several

times a day. "If they can move," he would say, "so can we."
Their first argument was over the responsibility for some road
work. General Wilson afterwards explained to Baird Smith,
"how he was worried to death by many contretemps, and
would be very grieved indeed if he hurt his feelings." Baird
Smith begged him to forget his impatience, and insisted that
he had only wanted to establish the justice of the affair. But
both remembered the angry words, and might have returned
to the subject but for one of far greater importance—the arrival of Nicholson's force, 2,000 strong. They also brought a
large convoy with five heavy guns, plus ammunition and powder, and several *lakhs* of treasure.

The band of the 8th played, the camp turned out to see
them march in, and remarked on their smartness; in the evening the parade in the main street was colourful indeed. The
newcomers in their British scarlet jackets gave a fillip to the
fashion of dyeing summer whites a variegated khaki hitherto
unknown except north of the Indus.

Because of the unreliability of native dyes, even men in
the same companies found that their uniforms varied between puce, slate-colour, drab, grey, and true khaki. Almost
the only ones to keep their original colours were the shabby
but proud Coke's Punjabis and the Sirmoor Gurkhas, who
remained faithful to their tattered and dilapidated green.

The Staff, and the Engineers particularly, swaggered about
in all imaginable varieties of dress.

Boots of all kinds were in use. Young noted officers wearing "top-boots, jack-boots, antigropelos [a pretentious syn-
thetic-Greek name for waterproof leggings], with trousers and
breeches of every description, coats of every variety and colour and cut, and head-dresses including the turban, the helmet, the *solah-topee,* the wide-awake, and half a dozen others."

Young Sir Edward Campbell of the Rifles, who fancied
himself as a dandy, was especially noticeable in a costume of
flannel, no two pieces of which were the same colour. Nor
did he make the slightest protest one day when a Sikh, with

cool familiarity, curiously fingered the various pouches he wore, White Knight fashion, to carry numerous different necessities. A Gunner standing nearby remarked to him with flowery politeness: "We are obliged to bow to circumstances now, sir. *Any other time I would have knocked that fellow's bloody head off!*"

If uniforms were anything but uniform, so were the faces to be seen crowding the camp from now on; pale Europeans, darker Gurkhas, Pathans, Moslems, bearded Sikhs, and men from the coasts; for every white man in camp there were twenty coloured ones, and all of them eager to assault the city.

Besides the untiring and unfailing *khitmutgars,* or table-servants, possibly the most loyal were the *bhisties,* the humble servants who everlastingly carried water up to the batteries and pickets for men as everlastingly parched with thirst. Several were killed or wounded, and it was generally agreed that if any decoration were to be awarded, one should go to the *bhisties.* They staggered along, carrying water in the skins of beasts, sewn up cunningly, holding the throat with one hand to control the flow into a cup. These skins were still slightly porous, and glistened with the water they contained, and so kept it cool.

More and more mutineers, plus armed civilians, were making off from Delhi; others stayed, but sent off their wives and children, fearing that the city was doomed. From their camp they could see the bridge black with their carts and carriages, and there was some belated argument as to whether this vexing means of communication should be destroyed.

The Princes were sending letters to Hervey Greathed "declaring they have been all along fondly attached to us, and that they only want to know what they can do for us. They must find out for themselves," Greathed added sardonically, "for I shall not answer and tell them."

The mutineers made no more sorties, but continued with

the rockets and 24-pounders. The shells and rockets had the range of the river bank, but could reach little farther. Not much damage was done, but two British 9-pounders tried to destroy the house in which the rocket battery was placed, and wasted forty rounds or more to no purpose.

Sickness was a little less. Convalescents were brought out in their beds in the evenings to enjoy the cooler air. Chamberlain did not like to do this, though, lest it should be thought that he was seeking to make an exhibition of himself, and so he forfeited the chance of making his recovery easier. Officers made a point of visiting their men in hospital whenever possible, and the General visited whatever hospitals he could, but he was distressed to find that "the poor sick and wounded had nothing to while away the long dreary hours," so exerted himself to find light reading for them. His own wife and many other officers' wives were still busy collecting and sending down flannel waistcoats and other comforts, but the appearance of pocket handkerchieves provided the General with some innocent amusement, as "the men won't know what to do with them."

The General was by no means well himself, so fagged with unaccustomed work and anxiety that he was suffering from cramps and could not sleep. He and most other officers in camp were satisfied that the long delay in attacking the city was "for the good of the cause." No one "who understood the situation could wish to advance against the enemy at this moment," he thought, and since the siege train had not been ordered until the project for "assault by *vive force*" had finally been abandoned, and as 1,000 ammunition carts took a long time to collect at Amballa and longer to bring down to Delhi, there was no delay which did not seem excusable.

The siege train had reached Loodianah, but, like everything else, it was held up, and was not now expected until the end of August, or even the beginning of September.

"I believe at home some credit will be given to the handful of English in the North-West having held at bay the whole

native army," Greathed told his wife. "Lord Canning has
made use of impatient expressions about the delay, which he
will regret." But the Governor-General found it a sore point
that Delhi was proving so difficult to take, "for by it will be
measured the extent of the mistake of leaving Delhi and its
magazine in the hands of native troops when a spirit of mutiny was known to be abroad."

People in Calcutta were too ready to talk of the weakness
of the walls of Delhi. But they forgot its additional protecting glacis, ditch, enfilading bastions, arsenal, and huge artillery mounted a dozen and more on each bastion. Their own
infantry force, now 5,000 strong, faced an enemy, admittedly
reduced since so many armed civilians had gone, of about
30,000 trained men under arms.

"In European warfare, the siege of a fortified town, with
such a garrison, would not be undertaken with less than
60,000 men," wrote the Commissioner, "if the truth were
known the world would wonder."

The arrival of *chicks,* or hanging screens, had given Anson's tent a blessed relief from flies (though they made the
tent stiflingly hot), but on picket it was still as bad or worse.
Despite the stench and filth, everyone made themselves as
comfortable as they could.

There were compensations, even for the smells, and Anson
and another officer had what he called "an exquisite little
dinner" with Hope Grant. "Grouse soup from P.A. and Co.
[Peake and Allen's], to remind Hope of the grouse shooting
season at home, and a green young goose, with some very
good, fresh-looking peas from a Parsee merchant just come
here, hash and fricassee, and a nice pudding. We drank a
bottle of beer each, and enjoyed our dinner very much."

For the officers, life bordered on luxury. For the men, conditions were much less satisfactory, but still their spirit stayed
cheerful. They were less demanding and less critical. They
had endured worse conditions before, and expected to do so
again. Anyway, their duties kept them occupied; there was

little time to feel depressed. The cavalry was chiefly in demand for bringing in convoys of ammunition—250 carts at a time—which they met at Alipore. The road was in a fearful state with the bloated, crawling corpses of camels or bullocks every 200 yards or so. Camels were dying off in droves. They seemed unable to survive in the already putrescent atmosphere, and their bodies were dragged off, where possible, by elephants.

"We stopped about two hours by the roadside to let the convoy pass us and have a good start, and Evans took the opportunity to go to sleep in a puddle," Anson wrote in a letter.

"He is the strongest man I know. Yesterday he was for two hours up to his breast in water under a burning sun surrounded by alligators, which he was attempting to catch by their noses." Anson, who had a streaming cold himself, added with some astonishment: "He has only got a slight cold today."

Some wit started a pleasant rumour in camp to the effect that a mob had pulled down the Leadenhall Street office of the Company and hanged the East India Directors from lampposts.

"I do not suppose it will quite come to that," said Greathed drily, "but I think the days of the India House are numbered."

When not discussing this probable result of the Mutiny or inventing new names for Hodson's Horse—"The Allo bokharas" and "Ring-tailed Roarers" were among the latest—the great piece of gossip in camp concerned the arrival of Mrs. Leeson.

One morning a bullock cart drove out from the city carrying a Pathan with an *ayah* sitting beside him. Some little distance from the Subzi Mundi pickets they stopped and continued on foot as far as the sentries, where the young *ayah* fell on her knees, raised her hands in an attitude of prayer, and thanked God aloud, in English, that she was now safe at last.

The astonished soldiers led her to their officer, who found that she was a Christian, the daughter of a man named Collins and an Indian woman. She had been married to a Company's officer's son, a Government clerk in the Engineering Department named Leeson. The husband had been murdered during the outbreak of 11 May, and with her two small children she had been lying in bed that morning when a sepoy burst in, fully armed. Seeing the little boy and girl—who were only four and three years old—he first seized the boy by the hair, cut his throat and gashed him about, and then set upon the girl Mrs. Leeson clutched in her arms and slit her throat likewise. With a final shot at the young mother, he rushed out, leaving her with one child dead and one dying.

Fortunately for the nearly demented mother, a friendly family of a neighbouring Afghan came in and rescued her.

Although the girl died, Mrs. Leeson was taken in and nursed back to health, and kept closely hidden away from danger.

There she had remained for more than three months, learning that many of her relations in the city had been murdered, but hearing rumours of other half-castes and Europeans who were also in hiding. From time to time, however, these unfortunates were discovered and put to death at once, and her Pathan protector determined to take the risk of flight to the camp. They reached the picket in safety, and Mrs. Leeson was taken up to the camp in a *doolie*.

Although her arrival astonished most of the camp, it was no surprise to Hodson (who was away at the time), since about ten days earlier he had managed to get in touch with her through one of his spies. He had even sent her money and one or two comforts to ensure that, if she could not be rescued, at least she could continue in safety until the city fell.

The exhausted young woman was put under the care of Mrs. Tytler, who, with her French nurse, had successfully resisted all attempts to get her to leave the camp.

By a fortunate chance, about a fortnight before, a Commissariat officer in Simla had, as a kindly gesture, sent down on behalf of the well-meaning busybodies in the hills an enormous parcel of women's clothes of all descriptions, which caused great embarrassment in the camp. However, as they were much the worse for their journey in the rains, they were washed and hung out to dry in the Headquarters camp, where their presence caused some ribald comment. On Mrs. Leeson's arrival, these clothes came into their own, and she was able to exchange the Indian woman's garments that she had been obliged to wear for so many weeks for clothes which, since they had been collected for charitable purposes, were hardly smart, but at least were serviceable and of European style. She remained with Mrs. Tytler, an object of much compassion and curiosity to all, until the General, who distrusted her story, had her sent off to Amballa out of harm's way.

Food and necessaries in camp were plentiful now that Peake and Allen's had established themselves with brandy, beer, and soda-water. Two Parsee merchants, Jehangir and Kowasjee, had also opened a shop, and so Peake and Allen's had been obliged to lower their prices a little. Their stocks were brought up by bullock-cart and camel-wagon—testimony to the adventurous spirit of the traders. Soon a bazaar such as always sprang up round cantonments was functioning.

Spies brought in some of the new percussion caps which the mutineers were now obliged to manufacture for themselves in the city. They were found to be very well made, but they lacked detonating powder. The spies claimed that the mutineers had tried in vain to supply this by their own manufacture. But to balance this, an attempt at sabotage was revealed in camp. Some of the guns in the Hindu Rao's batteries were found to be carrying too far, and others falling short, and sometimes they flashed several times in succession before they discharged properly.

It looked as though some of the gun lascars had been spoiling the priming powder by mixing it with powdered glass and small stones. Natives were not supposed to be admitted to the magazines, but in future it was ensured that nothing would be left to their hands at all. In the end the sabotage was tracked down to *classies,* or tent-pitchers, and two of them were hanged at once.

General Wilson had never trusted any natives who handled the guns, although so far they had given no cause for suspicion. But the General never forgot that he was an Artillery officer. He could never pass artillery of any kind without looking over them carefully, putting his thumbs into the vents and trying with his own hands whether they were loaded or empty. Finally, he would give them an affectionate pat.

The Chaplain had at last been relieved by the arrival of a colleague, the Rev. F. W. Ellis. Greathed was amused to notice that "the presence of a clergyman at mess is working a reform, and Colonel—whenever he forgets himself and uses the word 'Damnable' corrects himself and says 'Devilish.' "

Then a young Guards officer, roving over the Subzi Mundi suburb with his irregulars, discovered in a house he entered a huge and beautifully bound book, large and imposing as a family Bible. But the noble-minded young man was horrified when he opened it and found pages filled with what he called "the most obscene pictures imaginable, beautifully, nay artistically, executed."

Confronted by his first sight of erotic Hindu art, this young man, who might have made away with it as a rich prize, resolutely tore the shocking book to pieces under the very eyes of his men who "fully understood the import of the devilish work."

So August grew older and the bands played in the evening, the siege train was awaited, and as day followed day the expected date of the assault was reluctantly put back and back. The prospect of victory was indefinitely remote; the way of life was accepted as being almost permanent.

A visitor arrived from Simla for a few days, "just for the

change," in the person of Lord Frederick Hay. He had a perfectly bald head, now unprotected, since he had had the misfortune to lose all his wigs in the recent upheavals; Fred Roberts thought him "the image of his mother, and equally mad."

There was more time to grouse about the mail, which came in by different routes, some of which took longer than others and lost a day, causing a great flutter among the wives back at Simla. Mrs. Young was very proud of the fact that she had written eighty-two letters to her husband since the Mutiny began.

The mail was delivered after dinner at the mess table. "All the Headquarters letters are brought together in a large bag, and the contents being emptied on the table, one or two of the party sort and throw them across to the different proprietors," Colonel Young noted with disapproval. "Poor Arthur Becher was much distressed last night at not getting his usual letter, and sent and had the whole Post Office ransacked for it, but without success."

The General received a brusque letter from Lord Canning in which he requested Wilson's reasons for his supposedly unnecessary delay and hesitation. Wilson drafted his reply, describing the true situation and its bristling difficulties, and urged the Governor to send either Havelock's or another force to Delhi as soon as humanly possible. Up to now he had considered the co-operation of Havelock's army as "the only chance of safety to the Empire," for with the force he now had, however fast he beat back the enemy attacks, they could always reoccupy their old positions and meet them again.

"As an Artillery officer," he wrote, "I have no hesitation in giving my opinion that the attack on Delhi garrisoned and armed as it is now, is as arduous an undertaking as was the attack on Bhurtpore in 1825–26, for which 25,000 troops and a hundred pieces of artillery were not considered too large a force. . . ."

Submitting this to Baird Smith for his comments and

emendations, he received in reply a memorandum favouring immediate action, since, whatever the perils of an assault, those of inaction at such a time were still greater. While there were any chances of success, he felt it was worth taking the risk. Baird Smith pointed out that Wilson's army and its officers possessed more skill, foresight, and organization than the enemy, and the only course was to make the breaches for assault as early as possible, before the enemy got wind of their intentions.

This was the last thing that the General wanted to hear. He had hoped for an argument that his policy of waiting was the best one. Instead, he received a suggestion to attack.

He was fast approaching a breakdown due to the anxiety of responsibility which he was not of the calibre to handle. This, in turn, reacted on his actual ability to deal with the situation. It was fortunate for the Delhi Force, and for the future of the British rule in India, that he had to support him—even to lead him—two men like Nicholson and Baird Smith, but unfortunate for his own reputation that they were both of so inflexible a mould that they made no allowances for any man whose resolution did not approach their own.

Baird Smith, indeed, was fast becoming openly impatient. "I am beginning to suspect that Wilson has a good deal of the ancient dame in him," he wrote to his wife. "He so prefers small designs and incomplete conceptions to doing anything thorough, that I fancy his mind is of limited range."

Wilson was slowly being forced to a desperate decision—to act without waiting for the now almost legendary supporting force. At last he forced himself to make a personal visit to Baird Smith, whose foot was painful and inflamed, so that he was unable to wear his long Army sock, and had to have cold-water compresses applied throughout the day, chafing at the limitations thus imposed on his active mind and body.

Just as the Engineer was finishing a quiet dinner in his tent, the General walked in, to find him "with no stocking on one foot and no shoe on the other," but perfectly composed at the unexpected honour, despite his unorthodox appearance. He had, in fact, been up until one that morning poring over the draft letter to Lord Canning and his own latest memorandum to the General.

Wilson had evolved a little speech with which to open the batting—that he considered as "most able" his Engineer's exposition of the condition of the force, and wished to thank him for it, and meant to send it to the Governor-General just as it was, but wanted to consult him over a few additions, and so on.

These rehearsed preliminaries disposed of, Baird Smith for the first time put to the General his own project for the attack upon the city, which differed from all the earlier abortive plans, not only in its fuller organization, but even in the direction it was to take.

They sat together for a good hour, while Baird Smith unfolded his design and thrashed out the only difficulty which he regarded as serious—that, in carrying it out, as they would have to do, in the early days of September, recognized as the worst and most unhealthy part of the rainy season at Delhi, the soldiers might be struck down by the sun, and the plan fail for that reason.

At dawn on 25 August the chance for action came. Brigadier Nicholson left the camp once again in pouring rain, which began as soon as they set off, with a movable column of 1,600 infantry and 450 cavalry, plus sixteen Horse Artillery guns. Their orders were to overtake the mutineers and bring them to an action. Nicholson would have liked Hodson, just back from his own expedition to Rohtuck and down with dysentery, to go with him, but, despite their pleas, Dr. Mactier was adamant. He pointed out how bad the weather was, roared with laughter, and said that Hodson's job was to nurse himself and not seek more trouble.

The force had a fearful and killing march after the rebels, who were making for the nearest bridge over the canal, at Nujufghur, sixteen miles away. To follow them, Nicholson, with Sir Theo Metcalfe acting as guide, had to lead his men across country that had all become a treacherous bog, in torrents of rain that made every step that they took worse than the last. Before they had gone nine miles they had waded through two swamps at least waist-high through the water, with their ammunition pouches on their heads. Metcalfe, who rode ahead to spy out the way, nearly fell into the hands of some enemy sowars, but got away safely.

They could not follow the road because it had become impassable for artillery; but Tombs, recovered from his illness, was not one to give way before obstacles, and rode round his men encouraging them on as they heaved at the guns which had stuck fast in water and mud up to the axles. At one point the water was over the foundering horses' backs.

When they had struggled as far as Nangloe, nine miles from camp, Nicholson received word through his scouts of the enemy's position twelve miles ahead, and despite the experiences so far, which warned him what to expect as they pushed on, he ordered the advance to continue.

By four that afternoon, fatigued and blown, they were a short distance from Nujufghur, and found that the enemy, 6,000 strong, had drawn up in a position a mile and three quarters long, between the canal bridge and the village, with a strongly fortified *serai* with entrenchments, parapets, and embrasures to the left of their column. Four guns held this, and nine more were between it and the bridge. The village behind the position was also strongly held, and also the *nullah* or drainage canal and its bridge on the other side, their right, swollen to a great height by the recent rains.

It was late for a battle when Nicholson brought his force round by a side road to a point where the wide and swollen *nullah* separated him from the enemy lines. He took them over by a ford, but even here the water was breast-high, and as they pressed forward with difficulty and delay they came under the inevitable fire from the *serai*. There was time only for a hasty reconnaissance and Nicholson swiftly decided to make an attack on the *serai* first, as the strongest point, and then, changing front, to sweep his force down the enemy lines towards the canal again and seize the bridge.

The infantry advanced to within about 300 yards of the enemy *serai*, and then deployed and halted, while Nicholson and his staff rode out to reconnoitre. Soon afterwards he was riding down the lines, addressing the men, who heard him with a cheer. "Hold your fire to within 20 or 30 yards, then fire and charge, and the *serai* is yours," he said, shouting to make himself heard above the streaming rain.

He ordered everyone below the low ridge on which their flanking guns were posted to lie down, but remained on horseback in their centre to see what would happen next.

The artillery opened up with their comforting thunder. A horse battery galloped forward and unlimbered at close range, treating the face of the embattled *serai* to a few minutes' shower of round-shot. Under cover of this, he ordered the infantry to stand and advance.

Soaked, wretched, ill, and filthy, they fixed bayonets and then, in an unbroken line stretching for more than 100 yards, with Nicholson at their head, they advanced with sloped arms over the slush and marshy ground, ignoring in an astonishing way the enemy fire which poured down upon them. A little over 30 yards from the enclosure, Nicholson's hoarse command was taken up by the regimental officers, and the whole force rushed forward with a volley and a shout.

"In less time than it takes to relate," wrote Edward Vibart, who was with them, "we had scaled the walls, carried the *serai*, and captured all the guns by which it was defended."

The fortification was carried at the bayonet point, some of the mutineers still loading and firing with cool deliberation until the infantry were actually upon them. Vibart had a narrow escape when a bullet struck his sword blade only a few inches from the hilt, nearly knocking it out of his hand, and was greeted by a fervent shout from the ranks behind him: "Thank you, sir! That saved *me!*"

The mutineers saw that their strongest point had fallen and fled in confusion, leaving behind them thirteen guns and all their ammunition, treasure, tents and baggage. Tombs and his men shot them down in dozens and, supported by the Lancers and the other cavalry, followed them up until it was dark.

Since the baggage was far behind and had not been accelerated by hearing the sound of battle, the troops were without any food or covering, and settled down to bivouac for the night on the sodden ground, the kind of gratuitous physical endurance test which happened so frequently in this campaign.

It was "supremely uncomfortable," admitted Charles Griffiths, who was there with his regiment, the 61st. Hungry, wet through, lying on the ground, they slept only fitfully. Lieutenant Gabbett, a cheerful young man who had been quite a friend of his, died soon after of internal haemorrhage; and another Lieutenant Elkington, also of the 61st, died of a wound received that day. He was eighteen and had been in the Army for only a few months. He had a presentiment of his death in this engagement, behaving all that day with unusual quietness and reserve. When his friends went through his things afterwards, they found his most valuable possessions neatly bundled up with directions for their disposal.

Next morning the weary troops—too weary for Nicholson to attempt to order them to follow up their victory still further—set off back for camp again, and elephants were sent out to bring in their wounded.

The baggage and camp followers came in first, with quantities of plunder. One man rode on a pony with a live peacock under his arm, and there was a good deal of money and cooking pots and *lotahs* (drinking vessels).

It was a rather costly victory in comparison with recent experience—twenty-five killed and seventy wounded, and twenty horses lost. But, of course, again there were the guns, possession of which in the eyes of the camp made every victory worth while; and the enemy were thought to have lost at least five hundred.

They were all cheered vociferously as they re-entered

camp, limping, sodden, and exhausted, at sunset on 26 August, played in by two regimental bands and greeted by soldiers lining the road and waving their hats.

The General was delighted. He had been very uneasy at the enforced absence of his strongest supports. He issued an official order which read: "To Brigadier-General Nicholson's judgment, energy and determination I mainly attribute the glorious results of the Nujufghur expedition, and next to the steadiness and gallantry in action and the cheerfulness under great privation and fatigue exhibited by the officers and men placed under his command."

John Lawrence, up in the Punjab, was equally delighted. "I wish I had the power of knighting you on the spot," he wrote to Nicholson.

This was their first decisive victory in the open since Budli-ka-Serai, and the expectation was that as things had now begun, so they would go on.

In the city, too, everyone felt the same. The King no longer pretended that reinforcements of fresh mutineers would be anything but unwelcome. When he had heard that the Gwalior troops were ready to march on Delhi, he replied that as the treasury was empty there was no point in their coming. Learning from Nussereebad that 6,000 more rebels were there and about to start for Delhi, he peevishly sent them word that since the 60,000 in Delhi could not drive off the English, then what could 6,000 do?

When Bakht Khan complained that the soldiers were becoming too undisciplined to obey his orders, the King replied wearily: "Then tell them to leave the city." He told a deputation of officers that he foresaw that "the English will ultimately recapture the city and will kill me." These officers, impressed by his gravity, swore that they would be victorious; but oaths were becoming meaningless in these days. No one seemed to care any more. The initiative had been lost, and no one knew how to regain it. The King had to go into the Red Fort himself and order its artillery to fire.

Denunciations and treachery were the order of the day.

The powder magazine blew up and several hundred people with it; Hassan Ahsanullah, one of his Court, suspected of being in league with the English over the disaster, came running to the Palace, a troop of soldiers at his heels, and calling out to the King to protect him.

The King had the palace gates closed and hid him in an underground washing-room, but Ahsanullah's house was plundered before Mirza Mogul, at the King's orders, could arrive there and salvage a few belongings with the help of some cavalry.

Angry soldiers then surrounded the Palace, demanding Ahsanullah "for justice," while the King pretended as long as he could that he knew nothing of his whereabouts, but at last had to surrender him to the inflamed troops while insisting that his life was spared. The wretched Ahsanullah was imprisoned and had plenty of time to meditate on the dangers of spying for the *Feringhees* while the King anxiously negotiated for his life, under hourly threat of the plunder of his own Palace.

The Begum Zeenat Mahal, trying to keep a foot in both camps, diplomatically sent the King a message that the soldiers were (falsely, of course) accusing her, too, of complicity with the English. Ahsanullah's house and property were burned, and everyone with any property or possessions closed their shutters and sat quaking with fright inside their houses. Then feelings simmered down when a council of officers agreed that Ahsanullah was absolved from the charge of conniving at the explosion.

But although this crisis was weathered, and Ahsanullah was escorted honourably to his ruined home by the Princes, matters generally did not improve. Nobody was trusted, and the latest suggestion was that anybody who had been a servant to the English was probably in their pay for information and should therefore be confined.

Despairing of ever receiving any pay, many sepoys had already deserted the city, speeded on their way by a sigh of relief from the unlucky King. The Princes requisitioned money from the bankers under the pretence that it was for paying the troops, but General Bakht Khan complained to the King that "not one pice" had been handed over. The King angrily ordered that it was to be given up "at once," and that in future any such impressed money was "to be paid to the General in the presence of the citizens."

The leader of the mutineers from Neemuch, one Ghost Mohammed, was a rival of Bakht Khan, and lost no chance to try to discredit the longer-established commander, not excluding an attempt to condemn him for being in league with the English. By now it was surprising that everybody was not in league with them: there was no money, no opium, no leadership, no security and no hope.

At last the King learned that Ghost Mohammed and his Neemuch troops, having refused to join Bakht Khan at the latter's invitation to attack the English with the Bareilly Brigade, had suffered their ignominious defeat at Nujufghur. After a hurriedly summoned council, he sent out a force under Mirza Mogul to attack the supposedly deserted camp, but Mirza Mogul discovered the unfortunate mistake and returned precipitately with his troops. Altogether the city was in great anxiety and distress after this day's news. Even Bakht Khan was accused by the King on his return, for in his absence the Neemuch force had got in first with the story that the Bareilly troops had quarrelled with them and left them in the lurch! Bakht Khan complained in writing to the King of the bad advice he was receiving from everyone else, and the distracted monarch assured him that he was "perfectly satisfied" with him as commander.

After this the Princes began fresh, secret, and independent negotiations with Greathed and Hodson. The latter sat and listened to strings of promises and fair words, but made no promises in return. As he told his wife, "If I get into the Palace, the house of Timur will not be worth five minutes' purchase."

Hodson had other things to occupy him as August drew to its hot and cloudy close—daily averaging 90° in the shade. He had just received the two new troops to join his cavalry, and already had horses to mount them, so his new corps was progressing from its infancy.

"Such an experiment as raising a regiment actually in camp on active (and very active) service, was never tried before."

All this time, the camp was rather in the situation of someone who knows there is a serious and important job to be done, who has an idea how it is to be done, and yet lacks the will-power to act on his belief.

The situation in the north-west was dangerously fluid; a decisive blow must be struck as soon as possible if the whole Punjab were not to rise.

The siege train was close, though inevitably it would be yet another two or three days later than expected; and still the sun shone on the tents now dotted about on many different levels, and in the evenings bands played, and sports were arranged for those corps not decimated by disease—for by 31 August the total number in hospital in camp had risen to 2,368.

And until "Tattoo" was sounded officers and men would walk up and down the main street to the canal bridge and back, neatly dressed as far as their motley uniforms would allow, or ride or occasionally drive in buggies, laughing, talking, and gossiping together about the day's events and the latest "shave" in camp.

But behind all their gaiety there was the knowledge that "something" was impending, and since it was generally thought that Baird Smith was the man most likely to know what, people would look at him very meaningly and say: "Well! What are we going to do next?"

The Chief Engineer would look at them with his square, expressionless countenance and innocently ask: "Well, what?"

CHAPTER VI

The Last Days

THERE WERE two possible ways to capture Delhi: by surprise and assault, blowing in the gates and then scaling the walls on ladders; or by "regular approaches," a traditional bombardment which would make a breach through which troops could swarm into the city in far greater numbers than by scaling ladders alone.

This second way seemed the best, but to blow a hole big enough meant having guns close to the walls. This, in turn, called for extensive and secret surveying of the ground, most of which was in enemy hands, a task of great delicacy which fell largely to the exuberant Irishman, Captain Alex Taylor.

Nothing depressed him for long—not even the irony that the walls round Delhi had been strengthened by the great engineer Robert Napier, with whom he had worked for years making the Grand Trunk Road, which ran from Peshawar to the outskirts of Lahore, 256 miles away.

When Taylor had first been posted to the Punjab years before, there was not a single worthwhile road in all the province; nor even a map.

"When I was told that I had to make a road to Wuzeerabad or Jhelum," he admitted later, "the first question that occurred to me was: Where are they, and how can I find them?"

249

He *had* found them, and then he set about raising a labour force of locals. He surveyed the road, levelled it, was his own draftsman, clerk, and accountant. Today, the road that Taylor made is still his best memorial.

The final assault could be made only from the north and north-west, which were the only parts of the walls that faced the Ridge even indirectly.

But if positions for batteries could once be established, then the bombardment would take an entirely different direction from that hitherto contemplated, and this was the plan upon which Baird Smith had been working, from Taylor's reports and suggestions.

These new positions depended not only on the nature of the walls which the guns would have to command, but also on the nature of the ground on which they would be built, and on the routes by which they could be reached in safety.

Robert Napier, fifty years before, had reconstructed the seven miles of walls round Delhi to withstand just such a siege as was now to be brought against them. The size of the city and its natural position gave it immunity from all save the most concentrated attacks, for the front on which the force would be able to operate was less than a mile long, and consisted of a curtain wall tapering from 13 feet thick at the base to 8 feet thick at the top, with no ramparts in the proper sense, but a parapet 16 feet above the berm or projecting ledge which surrounded the walls. This berm varied from 15 to 25 feet in width, and rose to a height of 8 feet above the ditch, which was between 20 and 30 feet wide and 20 deep.

The counterscarp up which Salkeld, Vibart and the others had so painfully scrambled in May, with the enemy's bullets singing past their ears, was worn by water and weather, and not difficult to descend. Beyond the crest of this the glacis sloped gently down to the rough ground outside the walls.

The parapet of the walls was only a thin masonry 3 feet thick and 8 feet high, with musketry loopholes, and it gave little protection against artillery. The bastions were not particularly large on this front either, but they mounted from nine to twelve guns each. Beyond, overlooking the river, the massive old Pathan fort of Selimgurh mounted a dozen guns which could rake the banks as far as Metcalfe's park.

The glacis, also part of Napier's fortifications, was designed to shield the masonry walls, so that a shot which cleared it must be aimed too high to make an effective breach—which obviously would have to be low if an entrance was to be made. If, however, the artillery aimed at an angle, and fired at the flank of a bastion, the shots would strike lower and so more effectively. Taylor had calculated that the best position for a breaching battery, therefore, was somewhere on a line continued out from a bastion's flank, near enough to demolish the walls, and able to cover that portion of the curtain adjoining the bastion where it could strike low. This sounds fairly obvious now, when set down in a few words; but it took weeks of dangerous patrols, by day and night, before this conclusion could be reached.

For the purposes of the survey it was, of course, impossible to occupy the ground with troops. For one thing, there were no troops to spare for anything except action and picket duties, and for another the success of the scheme depended upon secrecy. Baird Smith's plan, which he laid before the General when the latter had surprised him, shoeless, in his tent, was simple: the breaching batteries were to concentrate, not on the right or north-western portion of the north face, which was where all the fighting had taken place and where the enemy would naturally expect them to attack, but on the left, where the river would give a certain protection and where there were open spaces which would allow for freer movement. A larger and more powerful battery towards the right would silence the Moree, and as a means of entry for guns and supplies, the Kashmir Gate would be blown up when the assaulting columns were about to make their entry.

The essential factor was time. Since there were not enough men for a full-scale attack with trenches, every inch of ground had to be known in detail, none of which was shown on the existing plans of Delhi and its environs. There was nothing left but for Taylor to examine it himself and make his own maps.

The enemy held Ludlow Castle, though not with any great regularity, and Taylor noticed that sometimes it was deserted for a short time after one picket left and before their relief arrived—a slack arrangement by which he profited one day when he slipped out from Metcalfe House, armed only with a pistol, and with a small party of Guides as escort.

He reached the Kudsia Bagh, and left his men with strict orders not to fire—a very necessary caution with men as excitable as the Guides—and then, climbing the wall of the garden nearest the city, he found himself gazing almost into the face of the sentry on the city walls. The man seemed so near that he could hardly believe he had not been heard. Taylor lay clutching the top of the wall for a good hour, examining the derelict Custom House, which was immediately before him. He knew that the roof of that building, having been burnt on 11 May or after, had fallen in, but the brick walls were standing. Here was a ready-made site for screening one of his breaching batteries.

He also discovered that neither the Custom House nor the Kudsia Bagh was occupied by the enemy, even spasmodically, for there were no signs of occupation or of disturbance in the thick vegetation. In fact, in this area of dense lime and orange groves, only Ludlow Castle was occupied.

Taylor repeated his reconnaissance expeditions whenever possible, often accompanied by Charlie Thomason of the "Robinson Crusoe" clothes. Once or twice the enemy surprised them, and they had to retreat smartly. Another time, as they set off with their prismatic compasses, and some chainmen and an escort of Coke's Punjabis, they found that the boundary wall of the Kudsia Bagh suddenly bristled with muskets, and a volley exploded above their heads. Two hundred turbans ducked down as the mutineers reloaded.

Taylor said with elaborate nonchalance, as he saw their escort vanish towards the camp: "Here's a go! What's to be done?"

"Well," said Thomason reasonably, "we can't take Delhi by ourselves."

"But don't let's *run*," rejoined his Captain in the Anglo-Saxon tradition. So they walked back as calmly as honour demanded until they reached a deep *nullah,* and then, said Charlie Thomason afterwards, "once out of sight we put down our heads and legged it as fast as we could along the stream-bed."

Sometimes Taylor went on his own, making the excuse that, since it was a risky business, he ought not to endanger other valuable lives. He was an athlete, too, a fact of which he was grateful one day when, entering the turret of Ludlow Castle, which was empty at the time, he was nearly surprised by the arrival of the new enemy picket. He escaped only by sprinting downstairs six at a time and then shinning up the compound wall behind, as the sepoys raced round the wall of the house and fired on his hastily retreating back.

"It was a shave," he admitted afterwards. "It was a shave."

Thomason also ran into danger on these expeditions. Once his Gurkah escort vanished while he was taking some figures on the Kashmir Gate road, and to his horror he tracked them down gleefully catching peacocks in the jungly surroundings, careless of the dangers all around them.

Another time, he was making a detailed theodolite survey from the Observatory, which was on the base line. He had a very bad head for heights, and was still weak from a bad attack of sunstroke and dysentery, from which he had suffered, off and on, all through the Mutiny. Rather than back out of the job, however, he forced himself up the narrow, steep outside stairway of the 60-foot shaft, leaving below him (for there was only room for one on the top), James Tennant, the "Objector-General," who was particularly strong on mathematics.

Following Thomason went his Sapper orderly, Gurmukh Singh, a splendid, tigerish-looking Sikh with bristling beard and whiskers. He carried the theodolite.

The Observatory was very exposed; enemy snipers could get within 50 or 60 yards of its batteries and as the Engineer and the Sikh, with their theodolite, were silhouetted on the skyline, half the guns on the ramparts opened up against them. To add to Thomason's dizziness there was no parapet on the tower, and to shout his readings down to Tennant below he had to crane his reeling head out over what seemed to him a yawning gulf into which he might topple at any moment.

This and the precision of his work sufficed to keep him oblivious to other dangers, and just as he had made his last reading he was quite astonished to find himself seized unceremoniously by the leg and flung like a log into the little circular trench which had been cut in the platform as a concession to security. Bruised and startled, Thomason found Gurmukh Singh standing over him and shouting indignantly, *"Sunta nahin? Main bola:* 'Down!' " ("Didn't you hear? I shouted: 'Down!' ") And where his head had been an instant before was the mark of a round shot.

Eventually a six-gun battery was made on a little plateau 300 yards out in front of the House and 900 yards from the Moree Bastion, which it was to command. Since the site was so near the enemy position, the working parties engaged there came under heavy grape fire, but as the mutineers did not know exactly where the work was going on under cover of darkness, it proceeded with little interference.

At the end of August, as the work continued, Commissioner and Colonel Greathed went up to Hindu Rao's to view it from above and, being friends of Reid, who commanded the battery, they were allowed on the roof, where Reid had made a watch-tower with sand-bags, from which either he or a Gurkha was always on the lookout. He and his men had been in every fight at Delhi and half his Gurkhas had been killed or wounded, yet he so far had not been touched.

After each new engagement Reid's friends used to look at him incredulously and say: "What! Are you *still* not wounded?" In the top storey of the battered house he had his Gurkhas' hospital, since they refused even to contemplate being moved back to camp when wounded. In this fearful spot, the vortex of nearly every attack, where the windows had been protected by traverses to let the wounded have any chance of surviving at all, they lay throughout the firing and counted the hours until they could be on duty again.

Down below, on the walls, the enemy guns started up against the battery. The Engineer officer on duty there, Lieutenant Edmund Warrand, had just been relieved, and before he left the site he took the sergeant to look through the embrasure from which they had been clearing faggots of brushwood, to make sure that it opened directly on the right spot. As they leaned together in the opening, a shell burst through between them and carried off an arm from each man.

An officer of the 1st Bengal Fusiliers who had looked in on the battery helped Warrand out, dazed and streaming with blood, but as they were making their painful way to camp, the Fusiliers' regimental call to arms sounded. The officer was Adjutant of his regiment, and so had to abandon Warrand and fall in with his men.

A few days later he enquired at the hospital whether Warrand had been brought in, but the place was so full that he was asked to look around for himself among officers who had lost an arm—for he did not know Warrand's name. Only after he had found him and they had talked together for a few minutes and he was turning to leave did they exchange names.

"Whom have I to thank?" asked Warrand. The other man gave him his name.

"Why, not *Kendal* Coghill?"

"Why, yes. But what is *your* name? Not *Edmund* War-rand?"

They had not met since their schooldays; Coghill had been Warrand's fag at Cheltenham.

The first parallel which Major Reid had pointed out to his friends from Hindu Rao's was a long, dry *nullah* which ran in exactly the right direction for the Engineer's purposes.

It stretched from the Pagoda picket, behind the point where the first siege battery was proposed, between the future sites of the other three, into the Jumna in the middle of the Kudsia Bagh. This deep, narrow slit in the ground was a providential geographical feature, for not only would artificial trenching here have been costly in time and materials, but it would almost certainly have warned the enemy what was afoot.

Alex Taylor arranged for a large, two-winged battery about 300 yards before Hindu Rao's, where there was a small plateau sufficiently far to the right of the position to deceive the rebels. Its right wing could play on the Moree Bastion, and the left wing on the Kashmir Gate. Other supporting batteries would be made near Ludlow Castle and the Kudsia Bagh, and in the Custom House compound.

Now that the time for action was at hand, General Wilson was quite taken aback by the proposals and pleaded for time to adjust himself to them.

"He shows amazing ignorance of the first and simplest principles of fortifications," Baird Smith grumbled. "We differ, and I sometimes lose my patience with him, but we are very good friends, and I usually bring him round to my way of thinking in the long run. . . . If the General potters, my alternative is to put on record that he pottered clean against my will, and Government must judge between us. . . ."

By the early days of September, Wilson was showing serious signs of beginning to crack under the strain. "My work is almost more than I can carry through. I get so exhausted and my head so confused that I at times almost despair. . . ." Furthermore, he could not sleep and his nervousness brought on increasingly severe cramps.

Any suggestion became to him a further anxiety; the slightest check assumed terrifying proportions; he could scarcely even avail himself of the comfort of explaining his worries by letter to his beloved wife, since he had reached the point where his worries were too great to be spoken of. He was not only at war with the mutineers; he was at war with himself.

To the more evenly balanced Baird Smith, however, physical handicaps should be faced and conquered. His zeal for work prevented his ankle from healing as it should, and his constitution was so weakened that he also fell a victim to camp scurvy and trench mouth. Pained by a blackened, suppurating ankle, suffering acutely from dysentery, and confined first to his tent and then to his bed, neither his clear insight nor his iron resolution failed him for an instant. But to help him to keep the pain down, he admitted that he "consumed as much opium with as little effect as would have done credit to my father-in-law." His father-in-law was Thomas de Quincey.

At first, Baird Smith always persuaded Wilson to come round to his point of view.

Baird Smith regarded his wavering resolution as one of his "idiosyncrasies," and pointed out that "to be successful in such a work as ours we must be coherent, and stick to our plans like *wax*."

But as the days went by this became more than the General could do. Like wax, his resolution was melting.

The siege train was at last within a few days' march of the camp, and since the assault on Delhi was presumed to coincide with its arrival. Prize Agents were appointed to superintend the collection of loot expected to be found in the conquered city. Three officers were chosen to represent the interests of field officers, secondly, more junior officers holding the Queen's commission, and, last of all, officers of the East India Company. No one was very enthusiastic about taking on the job. No one even knew whether anything of value would be left in the city, or whether any prize money would be allowed to the Army. But at least everyone held that these appointments were a most encouraging sign; now surely the assault could not be long delayed.

But then there was yet further delay; the siege train commander had sent some of his elephants to help men of the Rifles over the Jumna in the low-lying marshland. An outrider came in to explain they would be a few more days on the way.

Sickness increased again, chiefly fever cases. When the rains fell, few or no fresh cases of cholera would be reported, but in the hot, heavy days the numbers rose alarmingly. Even Peshawar, Sir John Lawrence assured the General, reported that they were in no better case. They had barely 1,000 men fit for duty.

The stench of the camp on the Ridge still hung thick and foul on the air, and one night it was so appalling that Captain Anson could not sleep at all, but lay tossing about and wishing resentfully that he had not what he called "such superb olfactory nerves."

A couple of days later something was done about the smells at last, when a senior officer, Colonel Custance, finding himself driven nearly wild with nausea and disgust, explored the fringes of the camp. He found sixty-five enormous animal carcasses heaped together in a mountain of putrefaction, and once he had detailed a working party to remove them the atmosphere in the hot and foetid camp improved.

The escort for the long-awaited siege train fell to the cavalry and a horse battery under the command of a Captain George Bourchier, an old friend of Anson. The road out of camp was bordered with corpses of men and animals for seven miles. No one had removed them; none was buried. The stench of decay was appalling, and the sights of vultures at

work on the bloated corpses turned the stomach of the har-
diest man. The escort took six hours to reach the outpost,
where they bedded down as well as they could on the hard
and muddy road, and waited for the siege train to arrive.

Soon the long line of guns and howitzers and heavily laden
mortar-carts, pulled by ponderous elephants, came in sight
on the grey morning horizon; and then a convoy of ox-carts,
loaded with ammunition, stretched away into the distance
for more than six miles. Escorting troops of the Beloochi Battalion rode on the guns or sat in the carts; others marched on
either side. It was a cheering sight to the watchers who went
out to welcome them in, for the new armaments included six
24-pounder guns, eighteen 18-pounders, four 8-inch howitzers
and four 10-inch mortars, thirty-two in all, with about 400
rounds of ammunition per gun.

After camping at the outpost all day, the train and their
new escorts set off again for camp at the snail's pace of the
elephants; it was a wearying journey. Anson's Lancers in
the rearguard were continually catching up with the tail of the
line of carts and having to halt and move on, and halt and
move on again. Despite the slowness of their advance, they
arrived at the camp before dawn and many were already up
to watch them stream in, each gun drawn by its two elephants, who pulled their burden along like some little toy.

The Beloochi troops were admired for their unusual green
uniforms, which had broad red stripes across the chest.

Colonel Greathed had 250 men from his regiment, but was
disturbed to find that they were in a poor state of discipline,
for they had been very short of officers. They were also "a
bad class of low Irish," who had made the most of their
licence—very different from his "well-behaved set." However,
it was a task for the disciplinarian Colonel to undertake and
he accepted it.

A few more reinforcements were expected within the next
day or two, and then the Delhi Force would have received
every man that John Lawrence could spare—almost more

than he could spare. But there was no reason to wait now that the armaments had arrived. The layout of the batteries could begin at once, subject to the General's agreement.

Nicholson had seen with some annoyance how General Wilson was vacillating and postponing decisions; as a man of action, Nicholson had no time for hesitation of any kind. One morning, before a meeting of all the field officers, he was sitting in his tent with one of his few intimates, young Fred Roberts. Suddenly Nicholson turned to him.

"Delhi must be taken," he said urgently. "It is absolutely essential that this should be done at once, and if Wilson hesitates longer, I intend to propose at today's meeting that he should be superseded."

Roberts was astonished at this proposal. He observed cautiously that, since Brigadier Chamberlain was still unfit for duty, then if Wilson *were* to be so unceremoniously set aside, the next senior officer to take his place would be Nicholson. The young Brigadier smiled.

"I have not overlooked that fact," he admitted in his ponderous way. "I shall make it perfectly clear that, under the circumstances, I could not possibly accept the command myself, and I shall propose that it be given to Campbell of the 52nd."

He added that he personally would serve under Campbell, so that no one could say he was advancing his own interests.

They walked down to the Headquarters camp together, and Roberts waited with the greatest impatience until Nicholson had seen the General, wondering what the outcome would be. But when Nicholson emerged from the General's tent after the council, he was able to tell the anxious young man that the General had agreed to immediate preparations for the assault. Roberts walked back feeling profound relief, yet certain in his heart that, had the General refused to assault, Nicholson would have been perfectly right, in the circumstances, to declare against him.

That same evening Alex Taylor wrote home that "all is

arranged, and win or lose, a few more days will see the assault on Delhi ... The General has at last agreed and named the day." Nicholson was to command at the assault itself, and had approved the plan in detail, but since he held no official position other than commander of the Movable Column, he had been excluded from the private Headquarters council, and so knew nothing of the plan of assault until 4 September, when Baird Smith, and not the General, had shown it to him!

John Lawrence was hopeful of success, now that delay was to end. He had boundless faith in Nicholson, but sent him this advice: "Don't assault until you have given the mutineers all the powder and shot which the siege train can spare, and then go in, and may God be with you all!"

As excitement grew among the British, so the spirit of the mutineers began to fall. Spies told how they staged a great demonstration because they had not been paid for weeks.

Angry, shouting soldiers surrounded the palace, uttering such abuse and threats that the King had been obliged to come out and face them. A deputation of subahdars requested their pay, and the King replied with unpalatable logic that, as he had not invited them to come here, he did not expect any service from them, and, further, since he had no money, he could not pay them. After further arguments and threats, he made a vague offer of payment at some future date, but this was refused with jeers.

Another argument followed, and another offer. Suddenly enraged beyond endurance, the old King bent down, stepped back and picked up the embroidered carpet on which he had been standing. Then he flung it in the faces of the deputation.

At this, his faithful body-servants shed tears and prevailed upon the deputation to leave, which they did, grumbling among themselves. Part of the trouble was due to their resentment over the last fiasco on the battlefield. The guards due to go off duty refused to be relieved by the "fugitives," as they contemptuously called the Neemuch troops after their disgraceful flight at Nujufgurh. This led to two hours of the complicated argument and insult so dear to the Moslem heart. The insults led to blows, and the blows to bloodshed. Finally, to prevent a wholesale riot, the Bareilly troops somewhat complacently intervened and took over the guard themselves.

No troops were likely to come and reinforce the Delhi mutineers now; and some in camp thought that the great day of the assault would be an easy affair, with few enemies and those ready to run off at once.

It was rapidly approaching the fever season ("Delhi in September" was proverbial), and already nearly 50 per cent of the Europeans in camp were sick. The mood was for instant action. They must go in; and at once.

All the Artillery officers, horse, foot, and staff, who were still on their feet were told off to serve in the batteries, so short was the force of effective men. Every regiment which had come into camp had suffered an epidemic of fever and cholera; one of the latest was Captain Bourchier's troop, which went through a baptism of cholera from which very few recovered. Within a few days he had lost seven out of seventy-five men.

The numbers of sick in hospital throughout the camp had risen from 2,368 on the last day of August to 2,977 on 6 September. By then the last reinforcements which could be expected were arriving—200 more of the 60th Rifles from Meerut, and 100 gunners, all played in with the usual band accompaniment of "Cheer, boys, cheer!" and "Auld Lang Syne."

The reinforcements included men who had been invalided out, and who were now recovered and reporting back to be in at the last battle. That same evening Alfred Wilde's troop of Sikhs, the 4th Punjab Rifles, arrived straight from the Frontier, a rough-looking set of men of splendid physique; and the Dogras, a hill tribe, chiefly Rajputs. The Sikh riflemen entered camp with their long, swinging step, their short rifles at the trail, khaki turbans surmounting their fierce, bearded faces. They had come down direct by marches of twenty-five miles at night. A great roar of cheering greeted them; their white teeth grinned in appreciation of their welcome.

The Jheend Rajah had asked that he could bring in his men from their duties guarding the communication line to Kurnaul, so that they could be on active service at the assault. And finally, on 8 September everyone turned out to see the arrival of more than 2,000 troops from Kashmir. "Such a picturesque-looking lot," said Colonel Young, "dressed *so* gaily!"

They had brought their own artillery, four brass guns, "with lots of small guns on camels; cavalry, with bright brass mambrino-looking helmets (*à la* Don Quixote); and infantry, fine, strong, powerful-looking men, armed with long matchlocks fitted with flint locks."

Hervey Greathed, who was standing near General Wilson, expressed reservations: "A very fair lot," he said; "as good as any native state troops I have seen, and will probably do service after their own fashion—though not to be trusted in battle or in the open."

Despite these reinforcements, however, on 7 September, the total effective rank and file of all arms (including the gun lascars, drivers and recruits), amounted to only 8,748—of whom 2,977 were sick. Of the Europeans, only 580 artillery, 443 cavalry, and 2,294 infantry were available. So universal was the sickness that the 52nd, which had arrived with Nicholson only three weeks ago with 600 men, now had only 242 *not* in hospital.

This was the composition of the Delhi Force at the time of the last battle:

Cavalry

> H.M. 9th Lancers
> H.M. 6th Dragoon Guards (Carabineers) (and weak troops only)
> Guide Cavalry

Hodson's Horse
Detachments of 1st, 2nd and 5th Punjab Cavalry

Infantry
    H.M. 8th Foot ⎫
    H.M. 60th Rifles ⎬ part
    H.M. 52nd Foot
    H.M. 61st Foot
    H.M. 75th Foot
    1st and 2nd Bengal European Fusiliers
    Sirmoor and Kumaon Battalions of Gurkhas
    4th Sikh Infantry
    Guide Infantry
    1st, 2nd and 4th Punjab Infantry
    Beloochi Battalion (wing)
    Jheend and Kashmir contingents

Artillery (Horse)
    Tombs' troops (only 4 guns in camp), Turner's, Rem-
       mington's, Renny's and Money's (the latter now under
       Captain Blunt)

Artillery (light field batteries)
    Scott's, Bourchier's
    Siege guns, *c.* 40 heavy and howitzers; 10 heavy mortars;
       12 light; with companies of Foot Artillery attached.

Engineers
    120 regular Sappers
    Companies of Muzbi Sikhs, hastily raised and partly
       trained:
    Coolies

Now that the time of assault was at hand, action and energy took the place of apathetic lethargy which had gripped
the British for so long.

A Colonel Hogge, who had ridden in ahead of the siege

trains, was made responsible for the organization of the artillery park, and he had everyone there working day and night. They had much to do. The guns were overhauled and the gun carriages, hitherto harnessed to elephants, had to be adapted to being drawn down to the batteries by bullocks. (As Commissioner Greathed remarked drily: "Elephants cannot be trusted under fire—they have a great sense of self-preservation.")

One of the Engineer Officers, Henry Brownlow, had completely organized the Engineers' park, even down to getting all available labour pressed into making the necessary gabions or basket-like wicker defences which, filled with earth, would form the breastworks of the new batteries. He now had 10,000 of them ready, with 10,000 fascines or brushwood faggots, and 100,000 sandbags already filled, plus field magazines, bamboo scaling ladders, spare platforms, and all other equipment required for a regular siege.

Brownlow had also taught the Muzbi Sikhs how to build a battery and make a field magazine, which, when it came to the real thing, would be "under pressure and under fire."

His Pioneers, almost completely untrained, were taught how to dig trenches and throw up field works, and other teams of men practised the unloading of bullock-carts and pack-animals.

Brownlow had been ill for weeks, but even so everything was rehearsed as far as possible. For the vital ten days before the attack, he was at work almost incessantly, snatching food and sleep when he could—"living on bread, milk, eggs, tea, quinine and chlorodyne," as he put it—and taking off his clothes only to have a good scrub-down and change. He trotted about everywhere on his steady pony, his sole concession to the dysentery which tore at him being a cummerbund, with which he bound up his suffering stomach.

In addition to his work at the park, he was out visiting the new battery (Remmington's) with Taylor, and when Warrand was struck there he stayed overnight at the hospital—as many friends did with their wounded comrades—in case there should be anything he could do for him.

The camp breathed enthusiasm and activity. The gabions bristled like forests, the tools and ladders and platforms and frameworks and sandbags stretched for acres, almost as far as the eye could reach. There were even two new "infernal machines," which Wilberforce Greathed had never ceased to hope might be made use of after all. ("Baird Smith is not a man to forget the smallest trifle," noted his brother Hervey with approval when he was conducted round the area.) Every day's work had been chalked up on boards in elaborate detail, and the Engineers were confident of the success of their share of the work.

Baird Smith was convinced their operation would be successful. By day, the General irritated him with his indecision and his grumbling. At night, he hid the agony of his stomach with chalk and opium. The weather was stiflingly hot, the sickness in camp was serious, and "the General was a terrible bore."

The violent division between them had to be faced. General Wilson, still torn by that decision whether or not he ought to assault without reinforcements, had been warned by Lawrence in a letter dated 29 August that "there seem to be very strong reasons for assaulting as soon as practicable. Every day's delay is fraught with danger. Every day disaffection and mutiny spread. Every day adds to the danger of the Native Princes taking part against us. . . ."

But still he required reassurance; and he received it, not only from his Engineer, but from Nicholson, Chamberlain, Daly, Norman, and Alex Taylor, all of whom warned him repeatedly that if the chance were not seized at once, it might well be too late and the fight would end in being not for supremacy, but for the very existence of the British in the Punjab. Even the loyal Indians were beginning to hold back to see which way the cat would jump.

Several times the General thought that he was going mad.

In the ten days between the arrival of the siege train until the assault, he wrote Baird Smith no less than sixty letters.

My dear Smith [he began], we shall never get on in this manner; because I told you you were asking more than the means at my disposal would allow me to sanction. You say all your calculations are valueless, and even waste labor, and seem inclined to throw all the work as well as responsibility on me. I have already more than I can manage, and my head gets into such a state that I feel nearly mad sometimes. For God's sake, don't drive me quite so. . . .

They had been arguing about the building of the first siege battery, which the Engineers insisted they could build and arm in a single night; indeed, it was essential that they should if the secrecy was to be preserved and its effectiveness ensured.

The General was certain that it could not be done. The Engineers were just as sure that it could.

He is so peevish [wrote Baird Smith, exasperated], and positively so childish, that I have sometimes great difficulty in keeping my temper with him.

He combines a wondrous amount of ignorance and obstinacy, is so discouraging, has such a total want of *vim* and energy that he is literally the greatest obstacle extant in the vigorous capture of Delhi.

He is now in a towering rage with me, because I keep harping on the necessity of arming all the batteries in one night, which he says is impossible, utterly impossible. I say it isn't, and so we're at loggerheads just at present; but I conclude I will bring him right in time.

Their notes to each other were becoming increasingly strained in tone, and Baird Smith was devoting all his energies to converting Wilson to agree to his "impossibilities." At last, after another personal visit, the General exhaustedly gave in once more.

It is evident to me that the results of the proposed operations will be thrown on the hazard of a die [he wrote

wearily], but under the circumstances in which I am placed
I am willing to try this hazard, the more so as I cannot suggest any other plan to meet our difficulties. . . . The chances
of success under such a heavy fire as the working-parties
will be exposed to are anything but favourable. I yield, however, to the judgment of the Chief Engineer.

At this skilful passing of the responsibility, Baird Smith
felt bitter indeed. The story of the taking of Delhi would be
strange, he brooded. "But it will never be told, and all memory of the General's absolute obstructiveness will be buried
under the glare of success."

On Monday, 7 September, the General issued an official
statement—said to have been written by the Chief Engineer
—to the entire camp. It referred to the many hardships they
had so "cheerfully borne," and which he trusted would soon
be over and rewarded. He promised them "a cheerful endurance of still greater fatigue and exposure."

This was a call to the troops to assist in the building of the
batteries and trenches by giving cover to the Engineers, and
a warning that for the Artillery there was to be, for a time,
"even harder work than they yet have had." Nevertheless, at
the assault itself "the Major-General feels assured that British pluck and determination will carry everything before
them, and that the bloodthirsty and murderous mutineers
. . . will be driven headlong out of their stronghold, or be
exterminated; but to enable them to do this, he warns the
troops of the absolute necessity of their keeping together, and
not straggling from their columns." (A favourite insistence of
Wilson's.) "By this, can success only be assured."

All commanding officers were to impress strongly on their
men that no indiscriminate plunder would be allowed, since
the Prize Agents would collect all property for sale and fair
division. ("Any man found guilty of having concealed captured property will be made to restore it, and will forfeit all
claims to the general prize: he will also be likely to be made
over to the Provost-Marshal to be summarily dealt with.")

Next, the General reminded the troops of the many brutal murders the mutineers had committed all over the north-west, and ordered that no quarter would be given. On the other hand, no women or children were to be killed, both "for the sake of humanity, and the honour of the country you belong to." The General ended in the confident hope that "all will exhibit a healthy and hearty spirit of emulation and zeal from which he has no doubt that the happiest results will follow in the brilliant termination of all their labours."

The General's statement was much approved; Captain Anson took pains to copy it out in full for the benefit of his wife.

The project that Alex Taylor had first suggested to Baird Smith included the use of Ludlow Castle as a battery site, and before the building of the main battery farther to the right was begun, he recommended that for security's sake this should be occupied. On Taylor's information that it was carelessly guarded and that the picket holding it usually went off duty before the relief took over, Baird Smith assured the General that it could easily be occupied. But to the General this piece of uncorroborated evidence from a junior officer was enough to imperil at the outset the success of the whole plan.

Since nobody could confirm Taylor's evidence, Nicholson himself offered to go out by night with Taylor to provide the required proof; and so at midnight these two keen Scots-Ulstermen set out, nobody apparently feeling the least concern that two such key men as the Second-in-Command of the entire force and the chief executive of the Engineers should be skulking about unprotected in the dark within musket-shot of a supposedly enemy picket.

But Ludlow Castle was indeed unoccupied; Saturday night's expedition served its purpose. On the following night, the 6th, the building, its surrounding area and the Kudsia Bagh, were occupied by the Delhi Force. The task was carried out

by 700 men, including the ubiquitous 60th Rifles, under
Colonel Greathed's command.

Two or three days earlier, in visiting Commissioner Greathed's tent, General Wilson had found his brother Edward
sitting with him. Edward seized the opportunity to ask the
General that his regiment might "have a good place" in the
assault.

What, asked Wilson politely, was a good place? "The front
of the column," replied Edward Greathed—and immediately
claimed that position for the 8th as their right, for they were
the senior regiment in camp.

Wilson was very pleased by this eagerness, and so when
the Engineers asked him to appoint a General Field Officer
of the trenches in the siege operations he sent for Edward
Greathed—doubtless his other brother, Wilberforce, had made
a few hints in addition—and commissioned him with the task
of occupying the necessary ground. Greathed took his brother
Wilberforce as his Conducting Engineer; Sir Edward Campbell came in charge of the Rifles.

That same night, on hostile ground, the Engineers supervised the filling of 16,000 sandbags which were hidden close
to the spot where, two nights later, No. 1 Siege Battery was
to be built.

At sunset, Jules Medley joined Taylor at Hindu Rao's to
help him trace out the chief battery, No. 1, on the ground
they had already surveyed. It was to be in two parts; the right
half, 700 yards from the Moree Bastion, would take six guns,
and the left, 200 yards away and covering the Kashmir Bastion, four more, with a trench joining them which continued
as far as the "first parallel"—the deep *nullah*.

While they worked, camels laden with gabions and fascines,
the raw material of the batteries, waddled down, kneeled on
the ground and were unloaded. As the working parties of
sappers and infantry arrived with their pickaxes and shovels,
they were detailed off to their appropriate posts in dumb
show, for strict silence had to be observed. However, the

camels were not subject to such orders, and their normal groaning and roaring and grunting as the burdens were unloaded from their backs caused the whole party much alarm.

So far, the moon had not risen, and the work of felling trees, filling more sandbags and digging the trenches had to be done by starlight. There was no more soil on this rocky patch than there was anywhere else near the Ridge, and the shortage of time and men meant that they had to find some other method of building the battery instead of carting up loads of earth to the site.

They built the solid part of the battery 30 feet thick up to embrasure level, entirely of brushwood fascines; sandbags already filled and stored near by composed the merlons above, and their interior face, and the embrasures, were revetted as usual with gabions and fascines. The chief snag about this method was that the resulting structure was highly inflammable, as some gunners found out later on.

When the moon rose at ten o'clock it was on an industrious scene of dozens of camels arriving, depositing their strange burdens and returning for more, while hundreds of men, as busy as bees, raised up the battery, which had to be finished and ready to open fire in the morning. All this went ahead splendidly until suddenly, without warning, a brilliant flash burst from the Moree Bastion, followed by a loud report.

Presently a shower of grape came rattling down and ploughed up the ground where the men were working. Some of the Sappers and Pioneers fell, writhing in agony. A few minutes later another murderous shower burst overhead; more men fell wounded.

This was serious; if the enemy had the range so well, then the whole working party could be killed before morning.

Medley, whose job was building the three powder magazines for the guns—two for the right side and one for the left —conferred hastily with Taylor about whether they should stop work or carry on. They decided to work on, and luckily there were no more shots. The mutineers in the bastion had heard the noise of their work, but thought it was only working parties cutting brushwood, and so stopped after two rounds, completely unaware of the havoc they had caused.

It was a hot night, and sweat poured down faces and glistened on stripped bodies, but, fortified by constant drinks and by the excitement with which these active preparations filled every mind, no one had time to feel the heat or fatigue until it was all over.

Medley, returning after a trip to Hindu Rao's to drink some tea, found that the camel trains were finished with, and that strings of artillery carts laden with shot and shell were already lumbering down to the site, the bullocks urged on over the rough ground by the curses and oaths of their drivers. Then came the guns themselves, huge 24-pounders from the siege train, which took twenty bullocks each to drag them into position.

The sort of smothered row that ensued, beggars description, [he wrote afterwards]. At three o'clock the place presented a scene of awful confusion. Sappers, Pioneers, artillery-men, and infantry, all mixed up together with an inert mass of carts, guns and bullocks struggling together in a heap. . . . The confusion, however, was apparent, not real; everybody knew what his work was—and everybody did it. Men and officers worked like horses, and the chaotic mass of carts and animals cleared off to camp. The Artillery stowed their ammunition in the magazines, and as fast as our platforms were ready, the guns were dragged into their positions.

But however hard they worked, they could not achieve the impossible. By dawn the right-side battery, instead of bristling with six guns against the Moree, mounted only one, and for the other five not even the platforms were ready. But it was out of the question to keep the exhausted working-parties any longer; if the enemy realized what was going on, they could have mown down every man they saw struggling back to the Ridge in the open.

Thus the Sappers and Pioneers went back while there was still cover of darkness, and the front covering party was also withdrawn. Medley and two other Engineers stayed with the gunners to finish the platforms with a handful of workmen.

The moment daylight revealed to the gunners in the Moree what had been going on under their noses, a fearful broadside of shot and grape raked the defenceless battery time after time, and anyone showing his head outside its cover was felled in an instant. The single gun mounted could achieve little on its own, and at last in a fury of desperation Major Brin, who was commanding the Artillery party in the battery, rather than accede to the General's suggestion that they withdraw, personally dragged a howitzer, in the open, well to the rear, and fired it back over the parapet.

"We talk of Victoria Crosses," grumbled an officer, "Brin ought to be covered with them from head to foot!"

The night had also been a busy one in the Kudsia Bagh for Colonel Greathed. He was superintending the felling of the fine orange and lime groves which had to be sacrificed to make way for the batteries. The intention was to build inside the protection of the high garden wall, and when the time came, this could be knocked down and the guns would be ready for action.

Here, too, many a breath was held as the thudding of axes, as loud as the hooves of the galloping horses, echoed in the night air, and nobody was in the least surprised when in the middle of the night an alarm was raised that the enemy were upon them. It was a false alarm. Someone had shouted, "Look out!" to the men below him as he lopped off a heavy bough. So close were they to the city walls that when the moon rose the sweating troops could see mutineers actually peacefully asleep under the walls, quite unaware of the activity that was going on so close to them.

Hodson was certain that the actual assault would be child's play; the General was not so sure. He was less concerned about the assault itself than about the street-fighting which must follow inside, and the setback caused because the first battery was not ready to open was almost more than he could bear. Everyone else, though criticizing the Engineer's foolhardy insistence that they could perform impossibilities, was exuberant with joy that the first blow was being struck. The General could find nothing better to say than that all was "not as favourable as I could have wished," and he began to worry about the sunstroke which the men in the batteries must surely suffer.

He actually considered withdrawing the guns altogether until the next night, but Major Brin was adamant; despite his shortage of guns, the bombardment began.

At last the five remaining platforms were raised and their guns mounted; at last the whole side of the battery could fire against the Moree, and amid tremendous cheers from everyone watching on the Ridge that old enemy received a fierce reply to the three months of shot and shell which it had inflicted on the camp.

For the rest of the morning and afternoon, in the blistering heat and through a sandstorm, the battery pounded its objective ceaselessly, until it stood a heap of smoking ruins, and the guns had ceased to answer. Everyone grudgingly admitted admiration for the persistence and bravery of the mutineer gunners, who still kept a 9-pounder firing from the side, running it behind the ruins of the parapet to load and then bringing it up again to fire.

Fred Roberts had been writing to his mother on the eve of his new duty. He was looking forward to the opening of "the" battery—No. 2—which was to make the principal breach, and felt honoured to be allocated to it, for it was to be "manned by the 'pets,' i.e., staff officers"—who would have to stay at their posts until the assault, because the dangers of relieving them would be too great.

"I can scarcely realize that this is the last night I have to spend in my tent before these horrid walls," he wrote. "The next two or three in the Batteries, and then I hope many miles beyond, following up and punishing these fiends, wher- ever we may meet them."

That same evening work began on the second battery, in front of Ludlow Castle. This time the Engineers did not pre- tend that a single night would complete their work; but the General was infuriated to find that the proposed site at the Kudsia Bagh of No. 3, which should also have been started at the same time, proved on further examination by Medley to be screened from the city walls by a number of unex- pected obstacles, such as walls and rising ground, which had not appeared on the map, and which rendered it impossible as a position. Yet a further night's delay resulted while a new site was found.

"The fact is my Engineers, although very zealous, have little or no experience, and attempted to perform more in a cer- tain time than was possible with the means at their disposal," Wilson wrote bitterly to his wife. "There is also a sad want of arrangement amongst them. I told them all this before they commenced, but they would not believe me. . . ."

Wilberforce, Greathed, and Thackeray placed their No. 2 Battery 500 yards from the Kashmir Bastion, and in front of Ludlow Castle. Like No. 1, it was made in two parts, the right-hand for seven heavy howitzers and two 18-pounders; the left, about 200 yards off, for nine 24-pounders. These eighteen guns were intended to silence the bastion, to destroy its parapet on either side and so prevent the enemy gunners from taking cover there, and to open the main breach on the left of the bastion for the actual storming of the walls. The impossibility of the Engineers' original optimistic plan was clearly shown when the work on this battery had to continue for three nights, until 11 September.

The first battery was the key to the attack; all the remain- ing heavy batteries could be built under its protection; and on their speedy completion depended the success of the as- saulting columns. Engineers and Artillery were working with this aim in mind, and Brin's courage, coolness, and foresight

kept them at it, despite all obstacles. The 4th or mortar battery was traced out on the same night, 8 September, behind
the Kudsia Bagh, and beyond the first two. It was completed
and armed with ten heavy and twelve light 5½-inch mortars;
but they remained silent until the other batteries were ready,
since it was agreed that the working parties would carry on
better if not disturbed by the gunners. Impatiently everyone
was looking forward to the time—probably on the 11th—when
the thirty-five heavy guns and the twenty-two mortars would
all start firing—the most tremendous, concentrated barrage
the Army had ever planned against such a target. How long
could the great walls hold out against such an onslaught?

Commissioner Greathed, with other laymen and non-combatants, watched the firing in the evening as Brin's solitary
battery showered its shells on the Moree, each on target,
bursting with columns of dust and rubble inside the bastion.
The light guns and rockets of the mutineers were firing from
Kishengunge in reply. Greathed thought them "a very pretty
sight." In fact, all would have been most enjoyable if one
could only be sure that they were not doing any damage—
which unfortunately they were. He saw a rocket flying right
over into Metcalfe's grounds; another fell on the road only
300 yards from the Flagstaff, and several dropped in the
ravine below.

After dinner Greathed rode down to visit his brothers, accompanied by Captain Turnbull, the A.D.C., and an officer
of the 52nd. At Ludlow Castle they dismounted and walked
on through the gardens, which had been inaccessible to them
until only two days before. Soon they could hear the sound
of bills and axes crashing through the undergrowth and tree
trunks, and came upon the fatigue party at work on the mortar battery.

The Kudsia Bagh was pleasant and shady, the air cool with
the bitter-sweet scent of the ravished orange and lemon groves.
Greathed stood on the riverside terrace at the end of the
garden, breathing in the soft air of evening, while above his

head the shot whined and flew through the trees quite harmlessly, because high walls protected the enclosure from the city guns.

He had seen Wilberforce, but Edward was no longer there. It was clear that the operations were to take longer than at first planned, and he had been relieved and had gone back to camp to sleep. The Duty Officer, of course, had to be awake night and day.

Two Rifles officers were on duty, and sleeping soldiers lay about on all sides, taking what rest they could between their shifts. A working party went on filling sandbags for the next battery.

In the morning he was up again on top of the Mosque, gratified to see the parapet of the Moree so smashed and shattered that the guns had been drawn back and had to fire at random. Everyone was even more impressed by the bravery of the Indians.

"I never saw such plucky gunners in my life," said Major Reid, watching them from his post at Hindu Rao's. "Fight it out they will, and every gunner *will* be killed at his guns."

All through the day, a brisk enemy fire from the rifle-pits dug outside the walls harassed the men in the batteries, but still the work went on. There was no stopping it now.

All night again the digging and shovelling and the placing of sandbags and gabions went on with such success that the No. 2 Battery was also ready by daylight. Medley and Wilberforce Greathed directed the work incessantly, sustained in the heat of their exertions by pints of claret. The guns arrived and were hauled behind the battery until their platforms were ready; and then at last the embrasures were masked with stones and earth to keep up the appearance of innocence until the required moment when all the great guns could fire together.

Alex Taylor, who, since Baird Smith's disability, was looked upon as the real director of the active siege operations, had been looking for a site for the third battery. His Irish-Scots

dash and nerve got him safely through the enemy's hail of
fire to a small ruined outhouse of the old Custom House,
which was so well within enemy range—only 160 yards from
the Water Bastion—that the mutineers had never dreamed of
destroying it.

This was a superb site for a battery, perfect for range, provided it could be built under the hail of fire which any movement would at once provoke.

On the same night when Greathed, Medley, and Thackeray were toiling on No. 2 Battery, the uncomplaining, unarmed Pioneers who did so much of the hard work of the
siege started work there on No. 3. No one knew just where
their foes were and what treachery they were up to, for the
mutineers took care not to relax the pouring out of their
musketry and shells, and thirty-nine of the plodding working
party were either killed or wounded at the Custom House
that night. As they dropped, Medley noted that their companions "would stop a moment, weep a little over their fallen
friend, pop his body in a row with the rest, and then work
on as before." The survivors worked like machines, tirelessly,
silently, terribly.

In the morning, Wilson sent for Colonel Greathed and
asked him to take over down at the batteries again from that
night. He was given the command, alternating with Colonel
Burn, who had not long been in camp, and Major Brookes of
the 75th.

It was all very satisfactory. The enemy still thought that
the main attack was to come from the direction of No. 1 Battery. But Octavius Anson saw that the General was "not altogether pleased" at the way the Engineers had been "trusting
too much to dash and neglecting the rules of the art." He felt
there were too many young and inexperienced heads among
them in positions of responsibility too great for their limited
experience. General Wilson was fuming, in fact, because by
now he could scarcely allow any credit to them for the work
which had already been done. Very little, in his eyes, had

been achieved, and he was angry because Baird Smith had disregarded his advice to open fire. By now hardly a man could fall without General Wilson taking it as a major disaster; his failing sense of proportion had completely vanished, and even his most sycophantic subordinates were beginning to complain of his growing vacillation and irritability. The business of delay in opening the battery fire had forced from him a further barrage of memoranda to the now highly incensed Chief Engineer.

"I consider the two days' battering of No. 1 have been completely thrown away, and that a large number of artillerymen and a large quantity of ammunition have been needlessly expended," he wrote furiously.

Baird Smith scribbled testily in the margin: "Quite the reverse; the loss in the Key Battery was indeed serious, but trifling in comparison with that which must have resulted from General Wilson's plan, with the small help for working parties and manning batteries!"

Wilson wrote again that "great and useless delay" over the batteries was an unfair discouragement to the working parties, who were now expected to prolong what they had been led to believe would be a short if severe burst of exertion over at least four days and nights, and all "thanks to the Engineers' miscalculation and want of arrangement." He had wanted to have opened No. 2 Battery at once and so try to silence the Kashmir Bastion guns.

Wilson was by now in such a state of nervous frenzy that he finished by scribbling to his Engineer that "as I cannot coincide with you, it will be better that in future you make all your requisitions regarding the arming of the batteries direct to Major Gaitskill commanding the Artillery, and for working parties to the Assistant Adjutant-General of the Forces."

"How unjust!" wrote Baird Smith in his diary.

And so, on the eve of action, the open rift had come; the climax, towards which three months of waiting and preparation had at last led, would be fought with two of the three chief directors of the campaign not on speaking terms.

Baird Smith sat down to draft a long protest which he proposed to submit to the Governor-General; but then he thought better of it. Wilson's arguments and anxieties had kept him up to a late hour, and in the morning Smith wrote to his wife: "He is quite off his balance, and now he has cut me ... It is a great relief and I find myself somewhat in the position of commanding the army in a quiet way."

He believed that Wilson resented him being responsible for so much already. This was not wholly true. The General, over conscientiously, was trying to take upon his shoulders the anxieties of every officer and man in his army—and was paying the penalty for it. He received scant sympathy from Baird Smith. "All goes well," that Colonel wrote a day or two later, "except that I am satisfied Wilson has gone off his head. . . ."

By now it was thought that only one more night would complete the job, and that by next morning twenty-eight more heavy guns and twenty-two mortars would join in the roar of No. 1 Battery, whose salvos against the Moree and the Kashmir Bastion continued to draw the admiration of all who watched.

In the evening, those with nothing better to do found an aesthetic pleasure in seeing the shot flash over with a rattling noise; in the gathering darkness the flashes of the guns would light up the grey dark as they fired, and, seconds later, the deadly explosions of their shells flared in crimson petals.

The officers who gathered on the Mosque and the Flagstaff in the morning peered unsuccessfully through a thick haze which now obscured the view. All had spent the night asleep in their tents and agreed in abusing the Engineers (who had worked until dawn) for their foolhardy insistence that a single night would complete their task. It was a relief to have some whipping-boy, for as the assault, looming like a black cloud over the future, was perpetually postponed, their nerves became tighter and tighter.

In the afternoon the parapets of No. 1 Battery—which had been firing almost incessantly for more than two days—burst into flames.

"It must have been from great carelessness of the officer arming it," said the General bitterly. In fact, the fire was due to the method of construction, for building in such haste meant using a number of inflammable materials, like the brushwood fascines. Within seconds, the whole thing was blazing like a torch.

Panting *bhisties* struggled over the open plain with buckets and goat-skins of water, while bullets sang about their ears, but the small quantities they could bring up were useless, and the Gurkhas in the trenches had to jump up on the parapets and beat out the flames with sandbags. Two of them were struck by one shot at once, and their officer, a Lieutenant Lockhart, fell over the parapet with his jaw smashed by a bullet.

But the fire was not a disaster, for the battery's work was nearly done and the time was almost here for the others to take over.

That evening, Thackeray had to take out a working party of British infantry to finish No. 2 Battery, because the shortage of trained Sappers and Pioneers was so acute that none could be spared for the job. The British troops were quite unaccustomed to this manual work in the great humidity and began to collapse with exhaustion long before the task was done. Alex Taylor was called upon to provide substitutes, and he picked on some of the Kashmir contingent, 120 of whom, "armed to the teeth with matchlocks, swords, and shields," came marching down prepared for colourful action.

When they found that the task was only a matter of piling their arms and filling and heaving sandbags, they protested that this was not the kind of work they were prepared to do at all. Medley looked at them with exasperation and then set to work to provide an example of the dignity of labour. After a few minutes the native officers decided that what Engineer officers would do, they could do, too, and before long the whole party was working hard without more trouble.

At about four in the morning a rattling musketry fire burst about them from the ground in front, and, in a twinkling, the militant Kashmiris had flown to their arms and were replying with such a volley that the unfortunate Medley, caught between them and the enemy, expected every moment to be his last. Shouts and signals were useless in the deafening noise that was going on. The only way of stopping it was to push the warriors forcibly over the parapet one by one, bellowing at them that if they wanted a battle they could carry it on in the open.

At last the battery was completed and gunners filed in, ready to begin.

The embrasures were still masked by sandbags, and once the heavy howitzers had been dragged into place on their platforms Dogra volunteers were called forward to throw off the protecting sandbags and expose the guns for action. In the meantime, on his side, Thackeray had the nine 24-pounders all ready. The chief breaching battery now awaited the order to fire.

The mortar battery, with Major Tombs in command, had been allowed to start firing, and from the Kudsia Bagh, about 300 yards behind them, they were already banging away. The shells, marked on their flight by the lighted fuses, soared overhead and burst among the enemy between the Kashmir and Water Bastions with a thundering report that made the earth tremble. With this noise, plus the continuous firing of Brin's six guns from the No. 1 Battery portion which had not been burnt out, plus the enemy's replies with shot, shell, musketry, and rockets, Medley thought it was "as good as a fireworks exhibition at Vauxhall, with the additional charm of the risk of being killed and having nothing to pay for your fun."

The scene was indeed magnificent. The low ground between batteries and city was illuminated by continuous flashes
and brilliant orange bursts of flame, which lit up the thick
undergrowth of jungle and gardens. Each shell, as it burst
over the city, set a glow on the delicate spires and domes.
And always in the background was the heavy roll of mortars
and guns, the rattling of musketry, and the frightening hiss
of huge and dazzling rockets that soared above no-man's-land
like comets. At about one-thirty in the morning there came
a brief lull, and so Colonel Hope Grant, his aide, young
Anson,* and his nephew, Frank Grant, Adjutant to the
Lancers, set off to see what was happening nearer the enemy
positions. The moon was in its third quarter and the night
seemed deceptively quiet. Indeed, the only obvious signs of
war were an occasional musket shot from the ramparts or the
hoarse challenging whisper of a sentry. But this peaceful appearance from a distance was misguiding.

Near Ludlow Castle trees were split asunder by shells,
others had been lopped by the battery builders, and an overturned ammunition wagon was abandoned with its dead and
bloated bullocks still in the shafts.

Farther on were long strings of camels, grunting and groaning on their way to the batteries, laden with gunpowder barrels, and teams of bullocks—drawing the 24-pounders for the
No. 2 Battery. It seemed incredible that the mutineers could
have no inkling of these immense activities which were going
on within shouting distance from their walls, but they slept
on none the less.

The Custom House battery, No. 3, which Wilberforce
Greathed regarded as his special pet, was not expected to be
ready until that evening. But the word had gone around that
at last the real bombardment from No. 2's eighteen guns was
about to start, and so, at daybreak, crowds of non-combatants
and civilians gathered upon the Ridge for the signal rocket
that would start the big bombardment.

* Not Captain Octavius Anson, but his cousin.

They waited and watched and fidgeted, and complained again about the Engineers ("Fine fellows, but they wanted to make themselves out to do impossibilities!") and still the signal did not go up. Down below, the battery was already unmasked and revealed to the enemy, who were desperately trying to get its range before it could get theirs.

No sooner had the masking screens been removed than a roundshot crashed through the embrasure of one of Fred Roberts's guns and knocked him and two or three others to the ground. Roberts scrambled to his feet unhurt, but found that the young Horse Artilleryman whose job it was to serve the vent while Roberts laid the gun had had his right arm taken off by the shot.

The mutineers had at last realized something serious was afoot. They were trying to mount guns along the curtain wall itself instead of merely in the bastions—as they should have done long before. But, fortunately for the besiegers, in one day the mutineers had time to set up only a few light guns.

Now the day of the British was at hand. At eight o'clock in the morning of 11 September the order to fire was given. Major Edward Kaye, transferred from the burnt-out side of No. 1, was ready in charge of the right nine guns; Major Campbell was on the guns to the left; and Fred Roberts stood over Campbell's two right-hand guns. The Artillery were all at their places, together with the men from the Carabineers and Lancers who had volunteered to help pass up the shells. Medley, who had been up for two nights in succession and was almost dropping with weariness, watched in a trench as Major Campbell's nine 24-pounders crashed out with their first salvo. As the shells burst from the mouths of the cannon and the guns jerked back in recoil, the artillerymen gave a tremendous cheer which was taken up by the watchers on the Ridge, and repeated, and repeated. It was a moment the men would remember all their days, and live again in memory a thousand times.

The first salvo struck the point where the wall was to be

breached. With a thundering roar and a billowing cloud of red dust, huge blocks of stone fell in all directions and a great piece of the curtain masonry clattered in the ditch below. The shells had not penetrated the wall, which was 13 feet thick, but they had marked out a great circle in it. The guns on the Kashmir Bastion began to rumble now, throwing out gouts of flame.

The howitzers on Major Kaye's side fired again and again. After only ten minutes' concentrated pounding, the guns on the Kashmir Bastion ceased to answer.

From then on, the breach widened with every round from the battery. Its stone parapet and sides crumbled away every few seconds under the impact of the 8-inch shells, which burst as they touched and brought down yards of parapet at a time. Edward Thackeray, worn out, had lain down where he was the moment the first salvo struck the walls. He saw nothing of all this, although he was so largely responsible for it. For the next few hours he was sleeping peacefully behind the parapet, entirely unconscious of the roar and crash of the guns overhead.

All day long the firing continued.

The triumphant boom and roar of the howitzers and 24-pounders were echoed by the mortars behind. Shells poured down like rain on the ever-crumbling walls of the Red Fort. But although the mutineer gunners could not fire their cannon from the bastions, they were not at once dismayed. They kept up a strong enfilading fire from light guns set up in the open, plus a shower of musketry from their trench, and rockets from the martello towers on the walls. The sky was filled with shells and bullets coming and going; the noise was fearful. The ground trembled underfoot as though moved by a perpetual earthquake.

Except for the wounded, no one could leave their posts by night or day, except to slip away in turn for a few minutes to Ludlow Castle for a meal. An Engineer officer had to be in each trench on a twenty-four hour shift to maintain the batteries in working order, and since the expensive lesson of the fire in No. 1 Battery, buckets of water had been brought up and stored in the trenches, and the exposed parts of merlons and breastworks were protected by hides. The day was cool and cloudy, a relief for those panting at their reeking guns, but everyone agreed that there was nothing like real action to make them all feel fit again.

At night the exhausted gunners, faces and hands black with powder so that it was hard to tell Indian from British, slackened their fire. The mortar battery kept up its fire along the whole front, but in the hours of darkness No. 3 Battery had to be completed within a stone's-throw of the city walls. Again it took longer to finish than had been anticipated, and so work had to go on through the daylight hours next morning. Once it seemed as though the enemy guns had their exact range, and three times showers of grape rained down on the Pioneers. But, after what looked like total disaster, the area was left alone, and the work went on.

To arm this battery under cover of the Custom House, eight guns had to be dragged down in broad daylight, under fire all the way, to less than 200 yards from the walls. All these hazards added still further to the delay, and once the guns were hoisted into position the men had still to knock down the wall under whose protection they had built the platforms.

All this while, the batteries had been pounding on, so that almost the only heavy guns to be heard were those of the besiegers. The peppering musketry was largely from the enemy concealed behind walls and in trenches and pits—a form of warfare at which they excelled.

The infantrymen in the batteries were working under the Engineers officers' directions; replacing the sandbag parapets and embrasures knocked over by shot, and also taking their turns with the covering parties, one of the most unenviable duties among all the musketry fire. Charles Griffiths of the 61st was in the trench with his men when another officer unwisely looked over the edge of the parapet to see the effect of his fire, and was immediately decapitated by a shot from a 3-pounder gun the enemy had set behind a hole in the curtain wall. His mutilated trunk, spouting blood like a fountain, fell back among his horrified companions. The rest kept their heads down.

Nicholson, seeing how successfully the batteries were doing their job, wrote to Lawrence:

> The game is completely in our hands. We only want a player to move the pieces. Fortunately, after making all kinds of objections and obstructions, and even threatening more than once to remove the guns and abandon the attempt, Wilson has made over everything to the Engineers, and they and they alone will deserve the credit of taking Delhi.
>
> I have seen lots of useless Generals in my day, but such an ignorant croaking obstructive as he is I have never hitherto met with, and nothing will induce me to serve a day under his personal command after the fall of this place.

The cavalry were equally busy on their protective duties, for, thinking that the camp was probably left unprotected, a party of the enemy climbed over the canal drain and tried to make off with some of the pack-camels and bullocks, but they were safely cut off by the Guides and Hodson's Horse near the rear picket.

The mutineers, 200 of them, in full dress cavalry uniform, lined up bravely to take the Guides' charge, but suddenly lost heart and fled and were routed by forty men. And all the while the guns rumbled and thundered until, at the Custom House, the outer wall came tumbling down. When it was levelled enough to reveal the guns, it was found that the embrasures, built "blind" behind the wall, had been wrongly sited, and instead of being trained on the Water Bastion, they faced several degrees in the wrong direction. And so the digging and heaving and levelling had to be begun again, with another delay of several hours.

This meant that there was no chance of an assault that day; it also meant that the General, who was enraged by this last setback, had an opportunity to call a meeting of the Brigadiers and officers in charge of regiments, and to describe the plan of assault.

A special tent, without sides, was pitched for the conference, guarded by sentries posted at 100 yards' distance and patrolling to and fro, while beyond them the curious multitude stood gazing in with great interest, since there was nothing else to be seen but the legs of the initiated few. Nicholson, who was to lead the assault, had still no idea when it might be. "Gentlemen," he said, "I do not myself know the day nor the hour of the assault, and if I did I freely confess I would not tell you, for fear that in some happy moment . . . the secret might casually and unwittingly escape." But it was now common knowledge that once the breaches could be pronounced practicable, the assault was on.

The mutineers realized that the assault could not be long delayed, and had manned all their advance trenches. Crowds of skirmishers were scattered over the jungle and rough ground ahead of the battery, and their musketry was like a hail-storm overhead all day. No one dared stir a step beyond the parapets, and the only temporary slackening of the fire came when the Artillery in the battery occasionally substituted grape for round shot and so ploughed up the ground for some distance. But the martello towers never ceased firing, nor did the few guns mounted behind holes knocked in the city walls which could not be dislodged.

The mutineers had almost unlimited ammunition at their disposal and they meant to use it. At last Medley lengthened the epaulement to the right side and in the end they were forced to drag one of the guns from its position against the Kashmir Bastion and remount it to reply to the enfilading fire. Up on the Ridge, the General was so worried by the additional danger that he was ready to send down Reid and his men in a counter-attack to try to spike the enemy's guns in the suburbs, but at last he decided that the risk of loss was too great—the enemy were ensconced well within range of the walls and the approach was appallingly dangerous. It was all a matter of hanging on for another twenty-four hours or so.

The inflammable structure of the British batteries took fire several times from the firing of the guns. Medley leapt up on his parapet at least half a dozen times with a *chattie* filled with water, feeling such an extraordinary kind of excitement as he stood there knowing that every musket in the vicinity was probably turned straight towards him that he scarcely found time for fear.

So the blazing day passed with no one even stopping to think how hot it was. In the late afternoon, food arrived over the road between camp and the Kashmir Gate, a range the enemy guns over the river had long discovered; they kept shelling the pack-animals bearing arms and provisions. The men had their dinner and beer, and then out on the road a stream of frightened white-clad figures with pots and dishes came running. They were the faithful *khitmutgars* whose etiquette forbade them to fail to deliver their officer's dinner, no matter what was going on or where.

Then pipes were lit; a desultory firing by a skeleton party was ordered during the night, and the rest lay thankfully down to sleep within a few feet of the roaring guns, whose thunder was now so familiar that they did not notice it at all.

In the seven days between starting work on the batteries to the moment of assault, 327 officers were killed and wounded.

Up in camp, Colonel Greathed had been arguing in vain with Brigadier William Jones of the 61st, who was to command his assault column, against dividing up their storming party among several regiments, urging that "all military history points to the disasters which have occurred from frittering corps away by detachments," and that on so dangerous a duty the men were entitled to be kept together. But the Brigadier insisted that "both danger and honour must be equally shared among all regiments of the column." However, in all other respects, Greathed agreed with Colonel Campbell of the 52nd that the assault plan was thoroughly satisfactory. He ordered his servants to pack up everything of value to avoid possible looting while the camp was almost emptied of protection.

All that day the siege batteries had crashed out their disorder and death upon the city walls. All that night fatigue parties built up new embrasures. Casualties continued to be heavy, and to the dead and wounded were added men who collapsed from heat and exhaustion. The danger was that if new guns were successfully set up behind the curtain, and if the galling enfilading fire were still more aggravated, the batteries might be made untenable, and the assault could yet become impossible to carry out. It was essential, then, that the breaches already made should be practicable at least by next morning.

While the commanding officers studied their copies of the assault plan, Brigadier Nicholson visited the batteries with Alex Taylor, and together they surveyed the breaches in the walls. Much to the relief of the artillerymen, who had declared that they could not survive another such day under the deathly, mangling fire from the Kishengunge battery as they had just been through, Nicholson announced that they appeared "perfectly practicable."

However good these looked from a distance, they still had to be inspected more closely, and this task fell to Arthur Lang, a tall, good-looking fellow of about twenty-three, who had only one objection: he could not see in the dark as well as some. Could he, therefore, as a favour, make his trip to the wall at once—in daylight? Taylor nodded. "All right," he said, and scribbled a note for Lang to give to Captain Johnson at the Kudsia Bagh wing of the battery, so that the guns would cease firing as he set off. Johnson let him have four riflemen as an escort, and the little party at once set off on their mission under the dense cover of the orange groves, which shielded them for part of their journey.

Once opposite the breach by the Kashmir Bastion, Lang left his four men and ran up the bullet-swept slope and to the crest of the glacis, a distance of about 60 yards, over every inch of which he presented a long-legged target for the shot hailing through the air.

On the top he flung himself down and made himself as small as possible while, still exposed to all the muskets on the ramparts and in the breastworks of the bastion, he examined the breach. The berm on which the scaling ladders would have been supported had been almost covered by the piles of fallen debris which had crashed in tons from the walls, but the ditch was quite open and the breach was so wide that scaling ladders might not be needed. Without the slow business of ladders, the storming parties would present less of a target to the defenders above.

All this flashed through his mind during the two or three minutes he lay there, panting for breath. The mutineers held their fire and waited for the moment when he should run off again. Then, leaping to his feet again, as he said afterwards, he "legged it down the slope for all he was worth," pursued by a storm of bullets which whizzed and screamed harmlessly past his ears.

His hazards were not quite over, because as he was returning to the Kudsia Bagh with his escorting Riflemen, the sentries, who had meanwhile been changed, began to fire on them, not having been warned of the little expedition; but luckily their aim was no better than that of the enemy on the walls, and Lang survived to tell his story to Taylor and Maunsell, who had recommended him (though in vain) for a V.C.

Meanwhile, Jules Medley, who was sound asleep after his twenty-four hour duty in No. 2 Battery, was woken up and sent for by Baird Smith. From some lack of co-ordination in the staff work, he was ordered to undertake the very same reconnaissance that Lang had just completed! He ordered a

short, light bamboo ladder from the Engineer Park, and
then rode down towards the Kudsia Bagh and tied up his
horse at the last safe place before the batteries. When Lang
found that Medley was actually expected to mount the
breach, he decided to join him, relying on him to be his eyes.

The heavy firing, which had started up again once Arthur
Lang's trip was safely over, thundered on long after dark,
and Medley, in his turn, now asked the battery commanders
to cease fire at ten o'clock. Back again at the Kudsia Bagh,
he and Lang took an escort of six picked Riflemen and a
Rifles officer and twenty men to wait on the edge of the jungle
cover, which extended within 60 yards of the breach.

Once the ladder had arrived, there was nothing more to
do but wait, and they sat down in the bright starlight to eat
their dinners with the best appetite they could muster. Only
the roar of the batteries and the sharply defined, abrupt
sound of the mortar explosions broke the stillness of the
night. Above their heads in the moonless sky the repeated
flashes of rockets and fireballs burst like showers of fireworks. And then suddenly it was ten o'clock, and equally
suddenly, almost eerily, the batteries ceased their fire. It was
time.

The little party drew their swords, checked their revolvers,
and left the shelter of the picket to begin their stealthy
advance.

Once at the edge of the cover, they halted, talking in
whispers, under a large tree; they could see the flashes of
enemy muskets like spears of flame among a party of skirmishers only about 30 yards to their right. Shells and rockets
bursting in the air would illuminate them in a dazzling glare
for a second and then would be no more. Medley and Lang
crept forward with their half-dozen supporters across the
open ground which stretched between them and the dark,
crumbling mass of the wall ahead.

Within five minutes they had reached the edge of the ditch
before the Kashmir Bastion, and there was the breach yawning straight ahead, with no one else in sight. Lang quickly

slid down the steep counterscarp and stood at the bottom of
the ditch 16 feet below, and reached out for the ladder which
Medley passed down to him. Another two minutes, and they
could have been over the breach and examining the guns
defending it; but the slight noise they had made was enough
to have roused the enemy sentries on the wall, who came
running towards the breach from the opposite side.

Hearing their voices and footsteps rapidly approaching,
the little party scrambled back up the steep bank as fast as
they could. They had just time to throw themselves flat in
the grass when, clearly defined against the sky, bright with
stars and flares, a number of mutineers armed with muskets
appeared not 20 yards away on the broken ramparts.

They lay there in the rough grass scarcely daring to
breathe, pressing themselves into the ground and hoping
that the irregular surface would provide enough shade to
keep them invisible from their foes, whom they could see
clearly.

Medley whipped up his hand as a signal for retreat, and
the whole party leapt up and were racing off down the slope
of the glacis pursued by a whizzing volley which screamed
harmlessly round their heads.

Listening to Medley as he sketched the state of the breach
later, the Chief Engineer determined that no further time
could be lost. The British artillerymen were already on the
point of exhaustion. Who could tell what extra defences the
enemy might throw up if assault were deferred a further day
merely in order to destroy the musketry parapets on the
Water Bastion? He made his recommendations to the General accordingly.

Wilson refused to receive Baird Smith's reports direct, but
this did not prevent him from bombarding the chief with
agitated enquiries and reminders. ("Fifty pieces of ordnance
with three hundred rounds of ammunition per piece had to
be placed in No. 2 and 3 Batteries on the same night, between the time the Batteries are reported to receive them
and daybreak. Is this possible? I say it is perfectly *impossible*.

. . . I hope you are giving the Battery the protection of an epaulement. If an Engineer officer had to stay in the battery until it was done, it would soon be run up.") Actually, of course, Medley and then Lang had been continuously on duty there, and Medley had been making that very protection.

Even Baird Smith was obliged to admit that "we don't get on quite so fast as I wished," but *he* was inclined to blame the Artillery for their slowness in bringing up the guns and powder, and in mounting the guns. This was an additional thrust at Wilson, whose regiment of course it originally was; but Wilson would have none of it.

> My dear Smith [he wrote exasperatedly on the 12th], I send you a report from Scott of the state of his battery. I must request you will insist upon your officers having this battery properly repaired tonight. Considering that the Artillery officers perform ten times the work yours do, I do not think they ought to make the excuse of being tired, to save the lives of their brothers blue. Yours sincerely, A. Wilson.

Although it had become a slanging match, it was still contained within the bounds of etiquette.

Wilson was hovering on the brink of tears and disaster. Where his colleagues saw the state of the breaches as positively inviting assault, the General was writing back to the Engineer: "I should say the assault on the Water Bastion is *hopeless,* there is no approach to it apparently. What do *you* propose? . . . You are determined I shall not have a moment's sleep tonight. Please reply quickly to this, as it may change all our plans."

But he was satisfied at last. Baird Smith came to see him and convinced him that every hour that now passed added to the danger, since the pressure of the last week must be eased if the gunners in the batteries were not to collapse.

It was nearly midnight when the General put out the order so many had awaited for so long: they would proceed with their plan to assault Delhi.

CHAPTER VII

The Last Battle

THERE WAS small chance for sleep in the Delhi Force that night. Once the word had gone round, everyone set about reloading pistols, cleaning rifles, and filling their powder-flasks. Others thought out ingenious ways of protecting their heads from the enemy, who would fire down on them from the top of the walls.

Richard Barter, Adjutant of the 75th Regiment, wrote in his diary: "I wound two *puggris* or turbans round my old forage cap, with the last letter [from my wife] in the top, and committed myself to the care of Providence." He survived.

Like many others, he tried to snatch some sleep while he had the chance, but there were too many anxious considerations fighting for mastery in every head, so that anyone who did doze off for a few minutes soon awoke with a start to see lights still moving in other tents, and to hear the low buzz of excited conversation and "the snapping of a lock or springing of a ramrod sounding far in the still air, telling of preparation for the coming strife."

Reginald Wilberforce of the 52nd, one of the many nineteen-year-old subalterns with the Force, was given a shake by the Adjutant and warned of the time of march. He tumbled out of bed at once, and commenced an earnest argument

with his tent-mate about the right clothes for the job. Wilberforce also took the rather belated precaution of hastily swal-
lowing his castor-oil and opium drops, which had been prescribed for the inevitable dysentery and fever.

Thus fortified, he and a friend decided that the occasion
called for the best clothes they possessed, and Wilberforce
was obliged to lend his friend one of his two treasured flannel
shirts. He never received it back, because it was torn by a
bullet and thus appropriated by the borrower as a lifelong
memento.

When everything was ready, they all gravitated to the mess-
tents, where the General had ordered a double ration of
rum to be served out. All the 52nd, thanks to the foresight
of their Colonel Campbell, were provided with soda-water
bottles covered with leather to sling round their necks, so
that they could carry their reserve of courage with them.

The Engineers had drawn up plans of the operations on
oiled paper for each of the commanding officers of the columns, and these were distributed as the troops assembled.
The General and his Staff would await the result of the
storming on the roof of Ludlow Castle, where they could
view the proceedings uninterruptedly. General Wilson had
already privately commended his future and that of his army
to God; failure was too terrible to contemplate.

Taylor was busy with last minute arrangements until the
hour of assembly; Medley reported to Baird Smith that all
seemed ready, and then rode back to the batteries to call in
the Engineer officers on duty—including Arthur Lang—to
be ready at their posts with the various columns. Lang got
back to the Engineers' mess at about two in the morning.
All his friends were reading their instructions or poring over
a big map of Delhi on which the various routes were marked,
buckling on revolvers, filling haversacks with flasks and bread
and snatching a snack by candlelight.

Most of them, he noted later, were in the high spirits of
overtensed nerves, giggling with great glee over "an arrange-

ment of little wheels used for sharpening carving knives, on
which the youngest and most hilarious pretended to sharpen
their swords." Others were writing their last letters home,
wondering (either to themselves or to their wives) whether
they would be still alive twenty-four hours from now. Although no one had had any sleep from two o'clock onwards,
the various columns had been taking shape in camp, and at
about three o'clock, before they marched off to take up their
positions before the city walls, commanding officers read out
by the light of lanterns their orders for the assault.

No wounded of any rank were to be taken up from where
they fell by anyone in the ranks, but left to the offices of the
doolie-bearers, who would come up in the rear—should the
assault be successful. If the assault failed, however, wounded
and unwounded alike must be prepared for the worst.

No plundering was to be allowed and no prisoners were to
be taken. All prizes were to be put into a common stock for
fair distribution, and all women and children were to be
spared. ("No fear, sir," came from the ranks at this.) The
officers, drawing their swords, pledged their honour to abide
by these orders; the men followed by taking their oath.

The significance of the orders both to leave the wounded
to their fate and to kill any enemy captured was simply that
with all possible men who could bear arms pressed into
service the assaulting columns were still ludicrously small to
attack this vast rabbit-warren of a city with 30,000 desperate
defenders. None could be spared for guard or first-aid duties.

The organization and plan of the attack were simple on
paper, but complicated on the ground. Out of five assaulting
columns, three would storm the breaches in the first surprise attack, another would attack the suburbs, and one
would stay in reserve.

Nicholson commanded the first column, which consisted
of 1,000 men of H.M.'s 75th Foot, the 1st Bengal Fusiliers,
and the 2nd Punjab Infantry, under their commanders,
Lieut-Colonel Herbert, Major Jacob, and Captain Green.

Alex Taylor accompanied this column and so did the Engineers Medley, Lang, and Bingham. Its object was to storm the main breach near the Kashmir Bastion, which to Medley and Lang was already familiar ground, and to escalade the face of the Bastion.

The parade state of the 75th Foot showed how heavy had been the toll of sickness and the enemy guns. Only one sergeant, five drummers, and thirty-seven other ranks were marked as fit. But on parade in full marching order at three o'clock in the morning, ready and willing to storm the bastions were 361 men, twenty-nine sergeants, and six drummers. They had crept from their beds for this last battle. Everyone who could drag himself along was out on that tremendous morning.

Nicholson also had the ultimate command of the second column under Colonel W. Jones of H.M.'s 61st, which contained H.M.'s 8th, or the King's Regiment, under Edward Greathed, the 2nd Bengal Fusiliers, and the 4th Sikh Infantry, under Captains Boyd and Rothney respectively; in all 850 men, with Wilberforce Greathed and Lieutenants Hovenden and Pemberton as Engineers. They were to assault the breach near the Water Bastion.

The third column, under Colonel George Campbell of the 52nd, would enter by the Kashmir Gate, after its destruction by a party whose operation had been planned to the last detail. This column included 950 men from his own regiment, the Kumaon Battalion of Gurkhas and the 1st Punjab Infantry (Coke's Corps), under Major Vigors, Captain Ramsay, and Lieutenant Charles Nicholson, John Nicholson's brother. Three Engineer Lieutenants—Home, Salkeld, and Tandy— had the special and seemingly suicidal duty of blowing up the gate, so that the column could go through. After its entry, the column was to fight its way to the Jumma Musjid, a point of especial significance in the Moslem city. Once this could be captured, then much of the Moslem resistance might fade. After scaling the breaches, the first two columns would reassemble and march on the Lahore Gate, on the west side of the city, which Nicholson was to have opened to admit the fourth column. Their task was to capture the enfilading guns in Kishengunge and Paharipore, and then join in the main attack. Major Reid was especially pleased. At last he would fight in the suburbs over which he had for the past three months looked down from Hindu Rao's. He had under him 860 men from the camp, his faithful Sirmoor Battalion of Gurkhas, the Guides Infantry, the Dogras, and the men drawn from the various pickets. He had also approximately 1,200 men of the Kashmir Contingent, who were to be assigned to a post of their own, and Lieutenants Frederick Maunsell and James Tennant, the "Objector-General" of the Engineers.

In reserve, to be drawn up outside the walls and called in wherever required, was Column 5 under Brigadier Longfield of the 8th, with H.M.'s 61st, the 4th Punjab Infantry, and a wing of the Beloochi Battalion, commanded by Lieut-Colonel Deacon, Captain Alfred Wilde, and Lieut-Colonel Farquhar; 1,000 men in all, plus 300 of the Rajah of Jheend's troops, which had been brought in for the assault by their master's special request and were commanded by Lieut-Colonel Dunsford. Ward and Thackeray were the Engineers, and, as juniors, they had to resign themselves to the prospect of cooling their heels in the unglamorous position and hope that enough action would come their way to satisfy their bounding enthusiasm. Two hundred men of the 60th Rifles, under Lieut-Colonel Jones, would cover the No. 1 column's advance and then retire and join the reserve.

To make up these columns, every man who was not absolutely prevented by sickness was brought in, yet still the total added up to only 5,000, excluding the Kashmir troops, who were an unknown quantity. The camp would be left to the care of the sick and wounded, with a small Artillery and cavalry force, including Captain Octavius Anson, while the bulk of the cavalry under Hope Grant—the 9th, the Dragoons, Hodson's, and the Guides, with Tombs's Horse Artillery—

was called out to form up on the right of the first siege battery facing the Moree Bastion, to oppose any flanking attack
or sortie the enemy might make from the west side of the
walls.

If the entry of the first three columns was successful, the
ramparts were to be cleared as far as the Kabul Gate and the
columns halted until the result of the third column's movement against the Mosque should be known. Then, with Reid's
column safely admitted, the four bodies of troops would con-
verge and so gradually clear the town from north to south.

The Queen's infantry regiments, one of which was allotted
to each column, had been reduced by death and disease to
travesties of their former selves. The 75th could muster less
than 400 men, the 8th 250, and the 52nd 200. Yet the whole
force was wound up to such a pitch of desperate endeavour
that to have held back any longer would have been unthinkable.

As the first column stood drawn up ready to march down
to its prearranged position, Father Bertrand, the Roman
Catholic Chaplain, came up robed in his vestments, and
begged Colonel Herbert for permission to bless the regiment.

"We may differ, some of us, in matters of religion," he
said, "but the blessing of an old man and a clergyman can
do nothing but good."

The Colonel agreed at once and the priest raised his hands
and called down the blessing and the mercy of Heaven on
those who should survive and those who were to die. The men
stood silently in their ranks, the solemn words of prayer em-
phasizing the terrible task that lay ahead and the certainty
that many would not survive it.

In Column 3, Major Vigors of the 52nd, who was actually
commanding his regiment, since Colonel Campbell was responsible for the entire column, made a mess of his orders to
proceed.

The Major, a popular Irish officer of the old school, an excellent rider and a good drinker, knew nothing about such

regimental affairs as marching off a body of men. He shouted a few obscure orders which caused chaos, and then called to the nearest Captain: "Get them right, there's a good fellow! Get them right!"

Since by then the confusion was past ordering, he halted the men, and amid their laughter, called cheerfully, "Fifty-second, *get yourselves as straight as ye can!*"

And so the great assault began.

The sullen roar of our batteries, which fired with redoubled fury, to cover the advance of the troops [wrote Medley afterwards]. The noise of the answering shells, rockets and round-shot from the enemy as they burst, or hissed, or rushed over our heads, lighting up the dark but clear atmosphere with livid flashes; and the silent steady tramp of the columns as they advanced—all made a scene which filled one with a mixture of awe and anxiety, and formed a striking contrast to the maddening excitement which so quickly followed it. . . .

The parties carrying the scaling ladders marched at the heads of the columns, and with the first Medley and Lang went as guides. The three columns were to advance at once on the explosion of the gate. Medley, feeling the weight of his own responsibilities, saw Nicholson a little way off, looking "quiet but anxious," and then the General, equally care-ridden, rode up and overtook them.

Behind the battery trenches opposite Ludlow Castle they all halted, and those who were riding dismounted. Then they all wheeled off to the left to await the signal in the Kudsia Bagh.

Further still to the left, the second column had formed up behind the Custom House battery ready for their advance on the Water Bastion breach, and Colonel Greathed, who had been on duty down there all night, took over the command of his regiment. The third column remained where it had halted, on the high road.

General Wilson and his Staff, including Baird Smith and

young Chesney, Colonel Young and the A.D.C.s, went on to Ludlow Castle, where they took up their positions as spectators on the roof. But even they were not out of range, and a large shell harmlessly tore up the ground right in front of them just as they approached.

It was now between three-thirty and four in the morning, and the assault was expected to begin at any moment, for the day slowly began to grow light. But the first two columns, quietly assembled round Ludlow Castle and the Kudsia Bagh, and the third a mile or so farther back on the road, were still kept waiting without any clear idea why. Many of those who had forced themselves on parade, and had crawled from sickbeds to put on their uniforms and be helped into their equipment, could stand no longer; they began to fall out of line and were dragged to one side and lay moaning with fever and the agonies of dysentery.

There was a grave reason for this delay: in the growing daylight the officers could see that the mutineers had filled in the trenches with sandbags, in order to remount their guns. There was nothing to do but to continue the artillery duel, and blow the sandbags out again. Thus the columns which had marched down from the Ridge without a whisper were now forced to lie flat on their faces and possess their pent-up impatience as best they could until the crash and thunder of the guns ceased at last, and the way was open again.

For nerves already frayed to breaking, the wait down there by the walls was wearing; and also for Wilson and his Staff drawn up anxiously on the roof of Ludlow Castle; and, three miles farther back, for Chamberlain, Daly, and Khan Rosa Singh, a wounded Sikh officer, watching from the battle-torn top of Hindu Rao's, with the feebly guarded camp and its hospitals behind them and the unmanned Ridge batteries below.

At last, when the sun was high overhead, Nicholson prepared to give the warning to attack.

"Is everything in order and ready?" he asked Brigadier Jones, who commanded the column.

"Yes," replied Jones. Nicholson explained that the immediate signal to advance would be seen by the sudden rush forward the Rifles would make; and then, in a spontaneous gesture which expressed an emotion rarely seen by anyone outside his most intimate circle of friends, he put his arm round Jones's shoulders for a moment and hurried back to his own post. On the third anniversary of the Battle of Alma, the assault was on.

The roar of the batteries ceased gradually, and the smoke blew away from the mouths of the guns. A strange silence followed the thunderous din which had made hideous the past few days. The first sound to break it was a tremendous cheer, as, at Nicholson's signal, the covering Rifles ran forward steadily through the low jungle in skirmishing order. On they ran at the slow, loping pace of well-trained soldiers. The mutineers saw them coming, but because of the continuous pounding of the British batteries they had not been able to lay and fire their cannon. They opened up with a barrage of musket fire from the whole length of the walls. Some Riflemen went down, but the rest closed in and went on running; there was something inexorable and terrible about this charge; these were men who could never be beaten.

Medley waved his sword, and as the men with the bamboo scaling ladders saw his blade glitter in the sunshine, they also started to run forward over the rough, tufted ground, two men to each ladder. As they reached the crest of the glacis they met the hail of Indian bullets and fell in dozens. The only covering fire they had came from the Rifles, who were themselves under heavy fire from the mutineers on the walls. Within the first ten minutes nearly 100 men fell as they struggled to place the ladders so that their comrades could cross the ditch. The slaughter was terrible and chaotic, but not a man faltered or fell back. As they died and dropped forward into the ditch their bodies hampered the work of those who were still alive, and the ladders fell out of reach of those to whom it was death to be without them.

As the ladder-men fell, men of the storming parties rushed out on their own initiative to take their places, seizing the ladders, and dragging them along anyhow, tumbling after them into the ditch. Another check—while the defenders flung down rocks and stones and pieces of masonry on their heads—as they found that the ladders were too short. They did not reach high enough up the wall.

But with torn and bleeding fingers, the British seized stones and debris already in the moat, and dozens of the bloody and mangled corpses of their comrades and piled them in heaps and stuck the ladders on them until they reached up nearly to the berm. Thus even the dead helped in the assault of Delhi.

Farther to the right, Lang and Nicholson ran forward with the ladder parties, followed by the Fusiliers. At the Custom House they turned and raced up the glacis to the face of the Kashmir Bastion.

"It was most gloriously exciting; the bullets seemed to pass over us like a hissing sheet of hail, and the noise of the cheering was so great that I could hardly make myself heard," Lang wrote later in his diary. He was shouting to Nicholson: "To the right, sir. Keep to the right!"

To the right they went, swords out, racing for the ditch. They were held up by the same delay with the ladders, for their bearers had been nearly all shot down, and Nicholson impatiently ran over to the left again and scrambled up behind the 75th. Lang and the rest, equally impatient, started to swarm up to the berm eight feet above their heads. Almost unconsciously, Lang noted that the level berm was—just as he had reported—too narrow with accumulated debris to allow ladders to be fixed safely, and, anyway, the way was practicable without them.

Climbing hand over hand up the crumbling face, he nearly came to disaster as the broken masonry gave way under his hands, and he was saved by two little Gurkhas from a ghastly death of impalement on the bristling bayonets now following up below. They had miraculously materialized miles away from where they ought to have been—back with the covering parties—and held him forcibly against the wall till he recovered his balance and climbed on.

Medley, meanwhile, had already been wounded by a musket ball which struck him on the right arm like a sharp blow, but he was too excited to notice it. Under the screams and curses of the defenders, who fired their muskets and then, lacking time to reload, hurled stones and blocks of rubble on their heads, daring them in a frenzy to come on, two ladders had been thrust into the ditch, and Fitzgerald, an officer of the 75th, was already climbing. Medley and the soldiers slid after him and then Fitzgerald, who received a mortal wound, and Barter were over the breach, and the whole column streamed through and down the ramp up which Edward Vibart and the other officers of the 74th had run so desperately —also under fire from the mutineers—four months ago.

Farther over to the left, No. 2 column had strained their ears in vain for the noise of the explosion which was to be their signal to advance, but although it was lost in the deafening noise all round, they advanced to the assault as if by an intuitive impulse.

Just before they rushed out from the cover of rose bushes where they were concealed, Wilberforce Greathed had introduced Lieutenant Pemberton to his brother as the officer who was to lead them in. The two brothers shook hands solemnly, wished one another luck, and then within minutes Wilberforce was struck, half-way over the glacis at the head of the ladder party, with two infantry officers. A bullet broke his right arm and passed round his ribs under the skin. As he fell, his one feeling was thankfulness that the whole thing was over for him and there was nothing more for him to worry about. He crawled back painfully and lay on the ground under a rose bush. He was quite surprised when instead of dying he was rescued and made a good recovery.

Of the thirty-nine ladder-men leading the column, twenty-nine were out on the ground, wounded or dying. No matter; the troops were in the city now.

Sliding down the grassy counterscarp among the rain of bullets and the flying stones hurled on them by the enemy standing shoulder to shoulder and three deep on the walls, Colonel Greathed found to his surprise that his chief anxiety was that he should not sprain his ankle.

Forward and up to the berm they went, sobbing for breath, and then to the jagged edges of the breach in the Water Bastion. Greathed scaled the top and then heard a voice calling from below. He was just in time to stretch a hand to the struggling Colonel Jones, who had hastened ahead of his reserve and found that his enthusiasm had outrun his physical ability to climb a vertical face.

On top of the walls the two senior officers stopped to look round and Greathed found the moment quite lyrical.

> The sight . . . was beautiful [he wrote afterwards]. We could see the two columns on our right climbing up the breach like a swarm of bees, or rather like the horses of the sun all abreast, then like hounds topping the fence into a gorse cover they disappeared into the town; it was really a glorious thing to see, and I rarely remember a happier moment in my life than that.

But not many people were finding anything romantic in the occasion. Three-quarters of the Grenadiers of the 8th had been burdened with the ladders, and so, of course, had not been able to fire, and had fallen under the barrage of musketry on the glacis and in the ditch. George Baynes, because of the confusion in which many of the Fusiliers had crossed over the other breach, found himself in front of the bastion with only twenty-five men. And further along to the right the explosion party who were to blow up the Kashmir Gate were racing forward, heads down and stooping as men run when under fire, yet still able to muster a cheer as they ran like madmen through the showers of grape and musketry.

Theirs was the most spectacular entry of all.

Two Engineer Lieutenants, Duncan Home and Philip Salkeld, who had escaped cross-country from Delhi with Vibart in May, led this explosion party with three sergeants from the Bengal Sappers, Carmichael, Burgess, and Smith, plus four native Sappers and a havildar. Each carried 25 pounds of gunpowder in a bag. They also had a bugler to give the signal when the breach was blown so that the waiting troops could follow them in. They all knew that theirs was probably the most dangerous task of the whole assault. None of them really expected to survive; and yet this thought did not weigh them down. Rather did it seem to inspire them.

The Kashmir Gate stood in a salient, facing west near the western angle of the walls; its heavy wooden framework was flanked on three sides by masonry. They started to run towards it, strung out in a wide line, eyes fixed on the gate, ignoring the hail of bullets that came over their heads, the tufts of weed under their feet, and the wild shouts of encouragement from their own men.

The gate had an outer wicket, and as they approached they saw to their surprise and alarm that this was open—a further and unexpected hazard, because it meant they could be fired upon at point-blank range by anyone inside.

On they ran, hearts bursting, lungs tight with the unaccustomed effort in the heat after months of waiting. They were very near now, and could see the startled faces of sepoys at the loopholes, amazed at these mad *sahibs* running on to certain death with what looked like sandbags in their hands. The mutineers seemed quite staggered by the audacity of their advance, and called for others to look out and see this astonishing sight for themselves. In their amazement, they quite forgot their own duties and only fired a few straggling shots at them. All went wide. The men ran on.

Home led the Sappers over a couple of ragged beams which were all that remained of the gate's wrecked drawbridge, with the ditch yawning beneath. They laid down their precious powder bags against the timber gate and ran for cover.

To those watching from the British position, they seemed to be moving deliberately, like people working in slow motion. As they ran, a hail of musket fire followed them, the bullets striking up little puffs of dust on the ground. The sepoys on the wall had realized too late what was happening and were firing with everything they had from the open wicket, from the top of the gate, as well as from loopholes. The havildar fell wounded, but Home and the bugler leapt down into the ditch in front of the wall, unhurt. Although they were not hit, all element of surprise had been lost. Salkeld, who was to run out with his party and light the fuse on the powder-bags, faced the worst possible conditions for the task. However, there was nothing he could do to alter things; he had to go as agreed, and drawing his sword to bolster up his own and his party's confidence, and carrying the portfire in his other hand, he led his followers over the broken beams of the bridge with the second lot of bags.

Carmichael was arranging his bags of powder when he fell dead from a musket bullet fired by a sepoy through a loophole. One of the Sappers was killed and another wounded, and by the time Sergeant Smith, who brought up the rear, had crossed the skeleton drawbridge with his bag, only Salkeld and Burgess were still on their feet. Smith put down his bag by the gate and then seized Carmichael's, which had fallen near the wicket, and put it by his own. The rifle fire was now intense, but they were working so close to the wall that the sepoys found it hard to train their muskets on them. They were leaning out of loopholes, almost falling off the top of the wall, in their desperate eagerness to kill the Engineers before they could light the fuse.

Salkeld crouched by the bags as close to the warm red stones of the wall as he could get, one leg stretched out behind him to keep balance. This was his undoing, for a sepoy, firing from the open wicket gate, put a bullet in his thigh just as he bent with his slow match to light the fuse.

For a second he crouched in agony and then, dizzy with pain, lost his balance and began to roll over into the ditch beneath him.

In that split second of falling he held up his hand for the nearest man to take the match. Burgess seized it automatically, but as he applied it to the fire he turned.

"It won't go off, sir," he cried. "*It's gone out, sir!*"

Smith, standing behind him pressed against the wall, thrust a box of lucifers at him, but as he put out his hand to take them Burgess was shot through the body and fell backwards after Salkeld into the ditch. Smith, left alone, crouched over the bags and struck a match, shielding the tiny flame in his hand. And then, with a hiss and a puff of smoke, the fuse went off in his face. It had taken after all. He had just time to seize his rifle and jump before the whole gate went up in smoke—even before he reached the ground.

The other Sappers had jumped too, and they were all together shambling about in the smoke and falling stones at the bottom of the ditch calling out each other's names, anxious to know they were not alone. Smith groped his way round in the choking gloom, momentarily dazed by the shock of the explosion. He found that he had only a small bruise on the leg, for his head was protected by a leather helmet, and so he set off, feeling his way along the wall till he touched someone. Lieutenant Home, also unhurt, had been helping Salkeld to cover when the explosion occurred.

And then, as the smoke cleared, they could see Salkeld and Burgess, covered with dust, lying in the middle of the ditch. Although masses of debris had toppled over them, they were still alive, arms and legs threshing feebly.

By now the survivors were being fired on from the walls, for as the smoke and dust blew away the sepoys could see them plainly.

Bugler Hawthorne and Smith dragged Salkeld, whose arm
had been broken by the fall, under the drawbridge, where
Smith begged Home to rejoin his column; he would stay with
the bugler to look after Salkeld and the wounded sergeants.

Home agreed, but first he ordered Hawthorne to sound his
bugle. Hawthorne stood up and sounded the advance, but
the noise of mortars and muskets was so tremendous that
Home ordered him to sound off twice more, but still there
was no sign of advancing troops.

To the men hunched up in the ditch with their dying comrades, red with brick-dust and shaking with reaction, it
seemed that their sacrifice had been in vain.

Back on the road, tensely awaiting the result, the column
had been exposed to a terrible storm of musketry from the
walls, and Colonel Campbell ordered everyone to lie down
and seek what cover they could. One man flung himself
straight on to a cactus plant and was up again "in no time."

As they waited and listened, the officers peered hopefully
towards the corner which hid the Kashmir Gate, but still
there was no sound of the bugle. And then, at last, a column
of smoke billowed up slowly beyond the wall. Could that be
the explosion? It was impossible to tell; the roar of the gunpowder bags had been unheard, owing to the bellow of their
own mortars just behind them. Had the Sappers succeeded or
hadn't they? The situation was growing desperate, for Campbell knew that they could not wait indefinitely. He decided to
charge and see for himself what had happened. He gave the
order, and at once, from the ditch, from old shell-holes and
craters, the men were on their feet, bayonets fixed, running
in extended line towards the walls of Delhi. As they started,
the barrage on both sides increased, so that the racing figures
were wreathed in a fog of gun-smoke and dust from shells
that landed short.

"You never heard such a row," wrote Alfred Wilde afterwards, who was drawn up with the reserves. "The fire of

guns, mortars, rockets and muskets was positively deafening."

When the first wave reached the gate, they saw that the explosion had blown in only one side of it. The hole was just wide enough for one man at a time to go through. The first man in was Captain Crosse of the 52nd, with Corporal Taylor of his own company behind him.

(Afterwards Reginald Wilberforce claimed that the Corporal eagerly thrust him aside at the entrance, and so he was the *third* man in.)

The rest came streaming in over the wrecked drawbridge above the explosion party and inside the gate they faced the sunlit open square of the Main Guard—quite empty. Under the arch of the gate a cannon was set, loaded to the muzzle, and round this lay the corpses of those who had killed so many of Salkeld's party, and who had within minutes been killed themselves.

The assault party threw open the gate as wide as it would go—for half of it was blocked with debris—and in streamed the 52nd, Coke's, and the Kumaon Battalion, who formed up as directed in the open space. Then came the first column swarming up and over the nearest breach and on their heels the Reserve Column.

Well, they were in.

There were exclamations of astonished delight at their splendid success so far: it all seemed far too easy; if the assault was as simple as it had been, then why had they not attempted it before? It seemed too easy, and so it was. The three columns quickly reformed, and Campbell's men, guided by Sir Theo Metcalfe, moved off to the left, past the Water Bastion, to the Jumma Musjid.

With them went some of the 1st Bengal Fusiliers who had become separated from their column, and the whole force surged forward to storm the church and its surrounding buildings.

Alex Taylor, so far attached to Nicholson, now took charge of the Engineer Corps as "Director of the Engineering Oper-

ations in the city" until evening, when it was expected that
Baird Smith would be down and in command.

The momentary impression of having swept back the enemy at the walls soon faded, for storms of musketry from
side-streets and from the ramparts above the narrow lanes
began to mow them down, even as they ran, cheering and
shouting. But even so nothing could depress them now; on
they swept, seizing guns as they went, and at the Moree, where
the besiegers had many an old score to pay off, men of the
8th stormed the bastion. The mutineers' gunners, who had
been firing at Hindu Rao's to support the sepoys' attack on
Major Reid's column outside, put up a fight, but they were
overpowered, shot or bayoneted, and thrown into the ditch
below.

Soon afterwards Lang and the others of the first column
came pouring past the Moree, and Lang shouted eagerly that
they ought to line the parapet to give three cheers.

"Bad advice," he recorded laconically afterwards in his
diary—for they were at once fired on by their own batteries
outside. In the fog of confusion, anyone who showed himself
must be an enemy. They ripped strips of red, white, and blue
cloth from the uniforms of the dead sepoys and stuck up an
improvised flag on a bayonet, and the firing stopped.

They did not seem to be killing or shooting many of the
enemy, except at some bend or on a turret, where a few stragglers were dispatched. The houses were practically empty of
inhabitants, since most of them had taken refuge on the other
side of the city, and so the impression of tremendous progress
was kept up until Colonel Jones reached the advance party
and suddenly called out to Lang: "Where *are* we?"

They were, suddenly, in a very bad position—right before
the Lahore Gate, where a barricade had been set up and, as
they paused, a gun behind it began to pour shells into their
midst.

Their proper objective had been only the Kabul Gate, said
the Colonel, horrified, and they had passed that some way

back. The Lahore Gate was Nicholson's affair, and just where on earth was Nicholson?

The men, excited by the speed of their advance, clamoured to go on, but the most Jones could allow was that they should hold their ground. Their zeal had led them into a trap, and now, as they paused uneasily, grape-shot from the cannon and bullets from snipers hidden in upper rooms began to pick them off, and as the men were kept crouching in the arches below the ramparts or hid behind walls, they began to make for the comparative safety of the Kabul Gate.

Nicholson had come on with a small force directly towards this gate. It took him a couple of hours to catch up with the remnants of the two columns.

Major Reid's plan of campaign was to send part of the Kashmir Contingent with their four guns to occupy the Idgah on its hill before dawn. With the main body of his troops and with the other Kashmir men in reserve, he meant to form up on the Grand Trunk Road outside the Subzi Mundi picket and march down on Kishengunge at daybreak, to capture the enemy's heavy guns and turn them on the mutineers.

By this time he expected that the Kashmiri guns at the Idgah would be in action in his support, so that by a crossfire he could drive the enemy from the suburbs and be free to march down the dry canal bed which would lead him straight to the Kabul Gate and then on to meet Nicholson.

Unfortunately, Reid was delayed, because his first guns did not arrive.

At last a harassed Artillery commander arrived with the news that though the four guns were available, he had only enough men to serve one and so had not brought along any.

This was grievous news indeed, but while Reid was considering what to do, the batteries ceased firing—the signal for him to advance—and so he was forced to set off. Then, to his horror, he heard the sounds of shots and shouting in the direction of the Idgah. The Kashmir troops had seen deserters

swarming out of the city, and, unable to contain their enthusiasm at such a target, had engaged the enemy prematurely.

At last Reid reached the canal bridge, and from there he
could see streams of sepoys approaching from the Kabul Gate,
completely filling the dry canal bed up which Reid had
hoped to advance with his 860 men. With even one gun,
Reid could have massacred them; with none, his position was
desperate. He jumped up on the parapet of the canal bridge
to see how to deploy his force, and while he was talking to
his engineer officer, Frederick Maunsell, a bullet struck him
on the head and he fell down stunned. A Gurkha carried
him away to the rear, and almost at the same moment Maunsell was knocked to his knees with a shot between the eyes.
Fortunately, it was a spent bullet and, though a fairly serious
wound, did not kill him.

Deprived of their commanding officer, the column was in
confusion. No one knew what Reid's orders had been or who
should take command, and to make matters worse the Kashmiri troops, fighting now in open ground, were breaking
completely under a mutineers' charge. They fled in disorder,
losing many of their men and four of their guns—whose capture the survivors were afterwards at some embarrassment to
explain to their Maharajah.

The mutineers were so elated at this unexpected success
that their officers rode along the lines to urge the men to press
home their advantage, and they came on cheering, in redoubled fury. Then the Lahore Gate opened to let out hundreds
more, so that a mass of infantry and cavalry swarmed towards Reid's column.

He recovered consciousness long enough to hand over the
command to Captain Richard Lawrence, the youngest of the
Lawrence brothers, but in the meanwhile many other officers,
seeing the impossibility of holding their position, and knowing Reid was wounded, had begun to fall back. A section of
the 60th Rifles, which had been advancing in skirmishing
order on the left, were even given conflicting orders by their

officer, who did not realize that Lawrence was the new commander. Slowly, and in disorder, the column began to
retreat towards the camp—a rout seen by Colonel Jones, powerless on the top of the Moree Bastion, and by Brigadier Chamberlain, on the top of Hindu Rao's. If the mutineers were
victorious in the suburbs, he realized that they might attack
the camp, and even turn the flank of the assaulting columns
in the city.

Chamberlain was still suffering from his wounds and could
walk only a few paces, so he ordered a *doolie* and was carried
down to the scene of the defeat to take command. Daly, who
could also neither run nor ride, went with him in another
doolie and took command of a picket.

There was no question of the column's breaking into the
city now in the originally planned flank attack, but at least
the rout was stopped, though at great cost in lives. All this
continued until late in the afternoon, but the repercussions
on the course of events inside the city were felt long before
that.

In Delhi, Brigadier Campbell's column, advancing from
the church towards the heart of the city to assault the Jumma
Musjid, had lost a number of men who dived enthusiastically
down various streets in pursuit of different parties of the
enemy, and did not return.

This third column, pushing its way into the depths of the
city under Metcalfe's guidance, rapidly came to narrow streets
with houses filled by armed soldiers firing down on them.
Through the Begum Bagh, the Queen's Garden, they advanced to a gate opening on to the Chandni Chauk, the main
thoroughfare which ran in a straight line from the Lahore
Gate on the west to the palace, a distance of more than a mile.
A small party of volunteers of the 52nd burst open the gate
and, apart from some musketry, they ran up the street un-
opposed, although Charles Nicholson—the Brigadier's brother
—received a bad wound in one arm. Captain Ramsay and the
Kumaon Gurkhas occupied the Kotwali, and the rest of the

dwindling column went on to within 100 yards of the Jumma Musjid. They saw that its gate was closed and the side arches bricked up for defence, so that to assault the building was obviously a matter for powder-bags or artillery—and certainly required more than a regiment which, starting with 240 men, had now dwindled to about 150. The column's Engineers had been killed; no one had any powder-bags. They might have used big guns against the defences, but they had no guns, either, for they were too wide to pull through the smashed Kashmir Gate. Up at this end of the street, the houses were filled with enemy soldiers, waiting for them, and it seemed that before long the column would be cut off in the Chandni Chauk.

For a long time Campbell refused to consider retiring without orders. He had never done so yet, he declared, and he was not going to do so now. His orders were to await the arrival of the first two columns, which, presumably after their advance along the walls, would soon be working their way up to him, and wait he would.

As they waited in the growing heat of the morning, parties of single-minded *ghazis* from the mosque, in white linen robes and waving their glittering *tulwars* above their heads, made suicidal charges at them, literally flinging themselves on the bayonets of the men with great shouts of *"Allah Deen!"*

Finally it became clear that the other columns were not going to appear in support, and so at last the Colonel gave the order to fall back on the Begum Bagh.

Before setting out on their perilous retreat, they all solemnly shook hands, put their dead on *charpoys* and window-shutters, which they brought out from empty houses, and set off under fire.

The smoke from burning houses was as thick as fog, and young Wilberforce and another ensign, who were bringing up the rear, missed the canal bridge over which the others had crossed, and in making a desperate sprint along the street to find another, they unwittingly put to flight a crowd of the

enemy who were approaching from the direction of the Lahore Gate. Seeing two youths coming full tilt towards them,
they supposed they were the advance-guard of an attack which
the lingering smoke hid from them, and fled.

But when the two youths crossed over a little bridge and
turned back to join the rest of their party some sowars spotted
their error, and chased after them furiously. They escaped
only by dodging the horses and slipping down a side street
and doubling back up filthy alleyways.

Once back at the Begum Bagh, the column faced an even
hotter fire from houses directly opposite. They stuck it out
for well over an hour, fired on by grape and canister as well
as muskets, until eventually a Staff officer from Headquarters
told them that the first and second columns had been checked
at the Kabul Gate and therefore they should retreat again on
the church, half a mile away.

At this point, things began to go seriously wrong.

Greathed's men reached the Kabul Gate, and halted there
while he went along the ramparts checking that the small
gates and the bastions so far were held by guards. On his return about an hour later, he was astonished to learn that
Jones, who had been there with his men when he left, had
gone on again, thinking that he had not reached the right
gate! Jones learned his mistake and fell back again. From
then on, a smart fire from the Lahore Bastion rained down
on them, for the enemy had seen that their advance was halted
and meant to make the most of their indecision. None of the
British troops had any protection for their heads against such
fire from above—unless hats stuffed with rags and turbans—
and so their casualties were nearly all fatal. Seeing this, some
of the Sikhs began to trickle away towards the Kashmir Gate.
Greathed, observing it, asked their native officer what he
thought his men were doing.

"Are we not to leave Delhi?" asked the Sikh innocently,
looking straight at him.

"Never!" replied Greathed dramatically, looking straight back. "Not till the heavens fall!"

This proved a satisfactory answer; the Sikhs began to return.

Nicholson now arrived at the Kabul Gate and they checked on their progress so far. It was not at all encouraging.

Nearly 100 men and eight officers had been killed and wounded, and still there was no word of the fate of the third column. Rumours of setback, retreat, and failure were now going round from unit to unit, and it seemed clear that the attackers could press no farther forward that day. They therefore occupied houses that commanded the approaches to the gates, and started to brew up tea as fires were made from broken doors and panels.

But Nicholson did not mean to give up the capture of the Lahore Gate so easily. He had to control the Gate because it commanded the main street of the city. The only way of reaching the gate was along a narrow lane under the wall, never more than 10 feet wide, which had an arcade of buttresses on the low rampart side and a blind wall on the other, preventing the progress of more than two men at a time. Nicholson left the rest of Jones's column in their positions and advanced with the 75th, the 1st Fusiliers and the Sikhs. The fire against them was intense, and, on top of the strain and danger of the storming, this terrible barrage from an unseen enemy behind wall turrets, window-shutters, and roof parapets checked them completely. Forced into a bottle-neck of a lane where they could not properly defend themselves, the tired men hung back.

Nicholson was at the rear of the column, and when he saw the men waver, he rushed to the front, his sword above his head, as he had rushed to lead them against the Sealkote mutineers on the march to Delhi.

He turned round and shouted: "I never thought that Europeans would quail before *heathens!*" As he spoke he suddenly

bent forward and fell; a bullet had smashed a rib and penetrated one of his lungs.

A sergeant rushed to his side and pulled him into cover by
a buttress, while an officer hurried forward with his brandy
flask, but Nicholson waved them away. He refused to be
moved till the lane was carried. Still the shot was pouring
down on them like white-hot rain from the housetops; there
was no longer the means of advancing, and at last he had to
allow himself to be taken back, and the command devolved
on Colonel Jones.

At least fifty men and eight officers of the Fusiliers had
been killed in minutes; barely a quarter of Delhi had been
penetrated, and that quarter was only being held with the
utmost difficulty.

Back at the Kashmir Gate there was also trouble. The explosion had blown only half of it in—enough to admit infantry, but no more—and the crash of rubble had choked the
passage. At the bastion, dismounted guns lay smashed among
the wrecked platforms, surrounded by torn and mutilated
corpses. Medley was sickened by the sight and smell of the
charred and smouldering bodies of the sepoys killed by the
explosion, and the gateway was jammed with shouting, angry
men trying to get their artillery and ammunition wagons in,
while camp-followers with *doolies* full of wounded men were
trying to get out.

Taylor supervised the arrival of the equipment and stores,
coaxing order out of a chaos of carts, rearing pack-animals,
elephants, camels, and ammunition arriving from all directions. Debris and glass from the church were thick underfoot,
and the smell of gunpowder and clouds of smoke poisoned
the air. As a background to the shouting and the shambles,
there was the unending crackle of musketry and the thunder
of shells as the various columns, their fate still unknown,
fought their way into the city.

Nearly all the Engineer officers had now been either

wounded or killed. By the afternoon, only Home, who had so miraculously survived the explosion, with Geneste, Thackeray and Lang remained on their feet.

Before this, however, General Wilson had ridden down into the city from his vantage-point, and, map in hand, dispatched officers to discover the situation among the various columns. Their reports were not encouraging. The harassed General learned with dismay of the fate of Reid's attack; of the galling fire which the cavalry, powerless to reply, were suffering outside; of Campbell's failure; and, worst of all, that Nicholson was mortally wounded. More, a rumour came in that both Hope Grant and Tombs had been killed outside with the cavalry. In anguish, Wilson sent out Fred Roberts to find out whether these reports were true.

Roberts had just reached the Kashmir Gate when he saw an abandoned *doolie*, left by bearers who had gone off in search of loot. He dismounted, and went over to see if he could do anything to help. He lifted the curtain and found to his horror that the man within was John Nicholson, the leader of the assault, left there helpless, although death was near. He explained faintly that his bearers had left him and that he was in great pain and needed to get to the hospital as soon as possible.

"He was lying on his back," wrote Roberts years afterwards. "No wound was visible, and but for the pallor of his face, always colourless, there was no sign of the agony he must have been enduring."

Roberts said nervously that he hoped the wound was not serious. Nicholson replied flatly: "I am dying. There is no chance for me."

It was almost more than Fred Roberts could bear; Nicholson had been his hero and the pattern of what a leader should be. ("To lose Nicholson seemed to me at that moment to lose everything.")

He ran off to find the bearers, and tracked them down ransacking shops and houses with other camp-followers who were making the most of their opportunities. Then Roberts chased out a sergeant of the 61st, put him in charge—telling him who was in the *doolie*—and sent them off to the field hospital. He never saw Nicholson again. Then, riding on with a heavy heart, he came up with Grant's brigade.

About 400 of his men had been left in camp under Octavius Anson to swell the slender force protecting it; the remainder the General had ordered Hope Grant to keep drawn up on the Ridge in front of the Mosque to await the result of the assault for further orders. Grant had nearly 600 men, 200 of the 9th Lancers and the Sikhs of the Punjab Cavalry, Guides, and Hodson's Horse.

He had just taken up a position in a dip on the slope at about five in the morning when he was warned that a large force of mutineers were advancing through the Lahore Gate, apparently to attack the camp. At once the Horse Artillery and cavalry galloped through the batteries, where the gunners stood up and cheered as the riders put their charges at the sandbag parapets; and reined up below the Moree Bastion.

The Horse Artillery unlimbered, but, of course, they had no infantry support, and once Major Reid's attack on the suburbs had gone wrong, the enemy poured out fresh troops from the Lahore Gate, riddling them with musketry.

The wait became a costly piece of passive heroics. They remained mounted, drawn up in line under fire, with the textbook object of preventing any possible flank attack from the Gate or the suburbs on either the siege batteries, or, worse still, on the columns inside the city. They sat motionless, as if on parade, only the horses tossing their heads wearily and whinnying and pawing the ground at the hail of roundshot and grape.

For over two hours the horsemen sat patiently, powerless to take any action except to fire their ten Horse Artillery guns, which were blazing away in the front until the barrels glowed with heat. It was a fearful, meaningless test of discipline. In front of the horsemen stretched a row of gardens in which it was impossible for them to manœuvre. They dared not now retire—even if the order were given—for then they would lose their guns; and they could not take back their guns as well for fear of losing the position and laying the rest of the artillery and the infantry fighting inside the walls open to the danger they were supposed to prevent.

"Rather a mad act, *I* think," was Fred Roberts's comment as he heard of this morning's work. Out of Tombs's fifty gunners, twenty-five were hit, and seventeen of the horses.

Hope Grant and four of his staff lost their horses, and both he and Tombs were struck by spent bullets. Soon the officers of the troop were forced to serve the guns themselves, for they had so few men left. Everyone agreed that the cavalry stood up splendidly to this entirely unnecessary massacre, and one officer wrote home when it was all over that Hodson "sat like a man carved in stone, and as calm and apparently as unconcerned as the sentries at the Horse Guards," while all around cannon-balls fell like hail.

Young Gough was having a severe exercise in self-discipline, but he kept telling himself that "it seemed not much worse than being out in the rain without an umbrella. . . ."

After a time he lit his pipe to show how calm he was.

The failure of Nicholson's repeated attempts to attack the Lahore Bastion freed more of the mutineers for the offensive against these stoic horsemen, and eventually a 24-pounder was turned on them from the walls of the bastion Nicholson tried so hard to capture. Under the savage fire of grape, forty-two Lancers—a quarter of their little force—were killed or wounded, with sixty-one horses. The Lancers had never given up their white jackets, and Dighton Probyn's troop were actually in their scarlet—brilliant targets for the gunners: John Watson's troop, who wore slate-coloured uniforms, suffered comparatively little.

Suddenly a rebel sowar galloped full tilt towards the Lancers, sword in hand. They imagined he was riding up to surrender; and then he started cutting and hacking his way through their ranks, and killed four men before someone lanced him. Doggedly, the rest of the troops closed up their ranks, dug their knees harder into their horses' flanks—and stayed where they were.

At last Hope Grant pushed his nephew Frank, who was also his A.D.C., off to Hindu Rao's on a borrowed horse to implore Chamberlain to send down some infantry to help them retire from this inferno. The Brigadier obliged with eighty men of the Guides.

They cleared the gardens where the cavalry could not manoeuvre, and then were so hard pressed themselves that they had to be relieved by the Beloochi Battalion, which Chamberlain belatedly sent down with Frank Grant. With their arrival, the enemy fire gradually slackened, and at last the remnants of this other gallant 600 were able to fall back towards Ludlow Castle, where they were ordered to remain on call. This order was only of academic significance, for scarcely a man or a horse was left unharmed to drag the guns away—and for no gain at all. They had sat for hours, living, breathing targets for the sepoys, for no one liked to give the order to withdraw.

Fred Roberts learned that at least Grant and Tombs were still alive, and at once he galloped back to the city to tell the General. But although he brought good news, he was greeted with gloom at the church. Campbell's column had just reappeared, driven back, with Campbell wounded; Nicholson was now known to be dying. This, with the news of Reid's repulse, made up a cumulative tale of loss and disaster that crushed Wilson's resolution and energy, and he began to look anxiously at his Staff and suggest that they ought to withdraw.

"We *must* hold on!" exclaimed Baird Smith angrily. He was now so contemptuous of his General's military capacity and his timidity in emergency that he was convinced his mind was unhinged. Nicholson, wounded and in agony, shared his opinion. When he was brought up from the bloody strife below to learn of Wilson's indecision, he muttered, "Thank God I have strength yet to shoot him, if necessary!"

To the combined weight of their insistence, Wilson found himself obliged to defer. For better or worse, they would hold their position in Delhi.

But, despite this decision, it was a gloomy little party that gathered round the church from midday onwards. The church itself was only a shell, riddled with shot, where officers snatched what breakfast they could while round-shot crashed through the open windows above their heads and broken glass was ankle deep in the aisles.

"Such a number of woebegone faces I think I never saw before in my life," thought Roberts, looking round him as he wolfed down his breakfast. "All the old officers completely at their wits' ends!"

Young Reginald Wilberforce, though, came back with Campbell's column, and was delighted to see the mess servants in their white *dhotis* near the church with stocks of food and drink. He and a friend helped one another to brandy-and-soda, but when it was poured Wilberforce's spirit failed him at the thought of drinking off this stiff peg on an empty stomach and in such a state of exhaustion. He looked around to see who might benefit by the drink. A group of senior officers were talking animatedly on the steps of the church, and so he walked over to them, tumbler in hand.

One of them looked very old and worn and desolate. Wilberforce's own Colonel was speaking to him angrily: "All I can say is, I *won't* retire, but will hold the walls with my regiment."

The old officer was silent, pulling his straggling goatee beard, and then suddenly a glass was held before him and a boyish subaltern was saying, "Would you care for this brandy, sir?"

The old man took it abstractedly and drank it down, and after a moment or two the subaltern heard him say more cheerfully: "You are quite right. To retire would be to court disaster! We *will* stay where we are!"

Thus did General Wilson recover his resolution—or so Wilberforce liked to think.

After his meal, Wilberforce and the rest bedded down on empty sandbags in the church. Two hours later, his Adjutant shook him awake; a shell was blazing away on the floor not far away. The mutineers were shelling the church again and everyone else had left it. He had slept through a heavy bombardment and he was so tired that as soon as he was outside the building he dropped to sleep again.

Medley had been shot in the arm earlier on, but such was his excitement at being in action that he forgot all about his pain until, up by the magazine, he suddenly found himself almost falling with nausea and faintness. He turned back to make for the camp, but at the Kashmir Gate met two of his servants bringing down his breakfast. Medley drank off a bottle of lemonade in one gulp, the best drink he had ever tasted, and offered another to a soldier lying in a *doolie* in helpless agony with a shattered thigh.

Outside the gate his *syce* waited for him with his horse, as if he had just been in the city on a casual call, and he rode back to camp to find a doctor. On his way he overtook a seemingly endless procession of *doolies* that slowly jogged up to camp with their loads of wounded and dying, groaning and screaming in their agony.

Up at the hospital Medley was greeted by a surprised doctor with: "What, *another* of you?" For ten out of the seventeen Engineers on duty that day were wounded or killed. At last, his wound dressed, and hardly able to focus his eyes any more, Medley reeled back to his tent and fell sound asleep.

All this time there had been feverish activity at the field hospital, which had been set up at a house about half a mile from the walls, a little above the edge of Metcalfe's park. *Doolie* after *doolie* shed its burden, until every room was packed with *charpoys,* and before noon many of their occupants were hastily carried out to a little tiled outhouse in the courtyard to await burial, while the beds were immediately filled by the next casualties.

Soon there was no room inside the house, even on the floor, and the wounded were laid on heaps of straw on the ground. The straw was running with blood. On verandas, on rough wooden tables, other soldiers lay with uniforms torn, sodden with blood, and crawling with flies, all waiting their turn to go on the operating table. Surgeons and even their apothecaries were pressed into service for the many amputations. Bearers ran in and out carrying away arms and legs; the shattered limbs the surgeons were sawing off in such numbers were piled in heaps on the ground. All round the hospital the earth was trodden into a mud reddened with blood that stank and steamed as the sun warmed it.

Vultures and other carrion birds wheeled round the sky in wide, cautious sweeps, settling on the roof of the hospital and then flying off again uneasily, distrusting the noise of battle, and yet greedy for its fruits.

The Chaplains, Mr. Rotton, Mr. Ellis, Father Bertrand and an Italian priest, spent nearly the whole day at this ghastly spot, but were far too few for the work which faced them.

At the end of his long day, in which he had never paused for a moment, Ellis was unexpectedly struck down with fever. Mr. Rotton was more fortunate, but had to carry on single-handed with the Church of England troops, raising the screen of *doolie* after *doolie* to give his help to those within.

He fell exhausted into bed at last, but was roused to go with a party of coolies, which had been sent up to him, to supervise the digging of a vast common grave at the edge of the cemetery, over which in the small hours of the next morning he was repeating the burial service for the hundreds of corpses laid side by side.

While he was at the hospital, John Nicholson was brought in with the rest, and for the first time the Chaplain spoke with the man who was a legend in the north-west. At last Nicholson was taken on to the camp and put in Daly's tent. His friend, Chamberlain, came in to find him lying helpless in his tent on a *charpoy*, mercifully half stupefied with morphia. He could speak only painfully, in jerks.

"Just what has the surgeon said about my wound?" he asked slowly.

Chamberlain explained carefully that the bullet had broken a rib and penetrated the lungs, and admitted that it was serious.

The Brigadier pressed him for news of their position in the town and of the next move. Chamberlain, who had just been dictating to Wilson's A.D.C., Captain J. R. Turnbull, an answer to the General's latest appeal for advice ("Our numbers are frightfully reduced, and we have lost so many senior officers that the men are not under proper control. . . . If the Hindu Rao picket cannot be moved, I do not think we shall be strong enough to take the city"), reassured Nicholson that he had told the General that "we had no alternative but to hold the town until the fall of the last man."

Even as he spoke, Nicholson seemed to slip into a semi-coma from the pain and the drug, and Chamberlain, remembering guiltily how he had been warned that talking was discouraged, withdrew. Late that evening he visited Nicholson again, and found him cold from his weakness and the loss of blood.

During the following evening Hope Grant, back in camp, made the rounds of his men in hospital. He thought he would look in on Daly and see how he was after his day's activity. The camp, now almost empty, had an eerie and unaccustomed stillness about it, and Daly's tent looked dark and gloomy, with only one tiny candle dimly burning within.

He went in and saw a motionless figure stretched on the couch, with an Indian servant standing beside him. Even by the candle's light he saw on Nicholson's face the marks of approaching death. He had last seen him on the walls, advancing triumphantly with his men, and now, thought Hope Grant, "he was a noble oak riven asunder by a thunderbolt."

As he gazed, Nicholson asked hollowly: "Who are you?"

The last words Hope Grant ever heard him speak were thanks which, after a long pause, he painfully uttered in response to Grant's offer to help him in any way he could.

While Nicholson was still lying at the field hospital, his brother Charles, whose shattered arm had been amputated by Dr. Buckle of the Punjabi force, was brought in a litter and set down beside him, and for some hours the two brothers lay side by side, hardly less quiet than they usually were together. Their conversation in camp had often only consisted of "Hullo, John!" and "Ah, come in, Charles!" followed by silence, with an exchange of affectionate looks which betokened the depths of a brotherly love, possibly stronger for being driven under by their Puritan discipline regarding their emotions.

Down in the city, with many of his best officers already killed or incapacitated, and everyone worn out with exertion as well as with the continued strain of knowing that their position was at best precarious, the General faced a new trouble: the increasing drunkenness of his troops. Just behind the advancing columns had come the plunderers, camp-followers of all kinds, men who had become detached from their troops, and Sikhs who regarded looting as the natural object of the assault. They ran into shops and houses, bursting open the doors and scattering their contents over the streets as they ransacked the rooms for prizes.

Very soon some came upon the abandoned shops of wine and spirit merchants, and at once great vats and tuns of liquor were split open, and eager hands dipped every available container into their depths. After an hour or so of swilling beer and brandy, dozens of the overdriven men were reeling about no longer understanding or caring where they were or for what purpose. Deaf to the shouts of their officers who came upon them, lying half insensible in corners or stumbling about trying to prise open doors, past any amenity to discipline, they lacked all desire to go on and complete the capture of the city against which they had set out so confidently that morning.

Wilson and his staff were distracted. As the hours passed, it became clear that nearly the whole surviving force could be written off for further service for the rest of the day and night. It was a trick of the enemy, many of them said angrily, to place such temptation in the way of the *Feringhee* to bring him to this doom.

The only way in which the officers could act was to see that no more liquor fell in the way of their men, and so parties were dispatched in all directions to smash the jars and bottles and allow the precious alcohol—which would have been invaluable up in the hospitals—to pour away to waste, mingling in the streets with the blood that had already flowed there in such quantities that day.

A cry of "Poison!" helped a little with those not too stupefied with drink to grasp its meaning; but it was well into the next day before many of the troops were fit for duty again, and then, red-eyed, thick-mouthed, and heavy with sleep, the edge was off their endeavours; they were sullen and unwilling to advance.

Towards sunset the General determined to send out a mounted party to sound the position of the advanced columns, and he asked Norman, Johnson, and Fred Roberts, as the most responsible of the junior officers still available to him, to lead it. Roberts, like many others, had been sleeping the sleep of exhaustion through the racket of the past two or three hours, using his saddle as a pillow; but he leaped up to join the little expedition. He felt secretly astonished that he had survived untouched so far; the appalling losses of the 1st Fusiliers were enough to sober any man.

The three young men and their troop passed through the half-wrecked and littered streets towards the advanced posts, and found them much as they had expected. Although the officers' servants had come to the temporary headquarters with food and wine for their *sahibs*, no rations at all had reached the unfortunate men. Their cooks could not be persuaded to venture so far into the city with enemy fire battering down on them from nearly every house, and the only food the men had was what they looted from the shops.

Most of the Europeans Roberts met were drunk, reeling about, singing, waving empty bottles at him in greeting. The Indians were plundering (which the British would have been doing had they not been too drunk), and, save in a few places, officers and men had become separated from each other, and were broken up into small parties in the maze of narrow lanes. Even where this had not happened, nobody had any orders or instructions and, because of the over-rapid advance during the morning and its almost catastrophic conclusion, nobody could say what was happening even a couple of streets away. The best the reconnaissance party could do was to try to cheer them by saying that if they held on till morning "all would be right." With this optimistic view, General Wilson would not have agreed.

Ahead of them stretched miles of still unpenetrated streets and lanes: the main street, Chandni Chauk; the Mosque to which it led and, on their left, the centre of the whole revolt —the Magazine, the Palace, and the Red Fort, behind whose high walls no one could even guess what might be now going on. Looking around at the chaos that had come on their weak columns of assault, Roberts thought—and never saw any reason to change his opinion—that they would have done better not to attempt such an advance, but to have limited themselves to establishing a base where the Headquarters now was. With command of the Kashmir and Water Bastions on the north side, they would have avoided much bloodshed and loss of life.

During their progress, the little party fell in with a troop of sepoys who had been concealed up a side lane waiting for just such a chance. It was only a "small scrimmage," Roberts wrote modestly to his father, for luckily a neighbouring picket heard the firing and came to their rescue. Unfortunately, Roberts's mare was shot in the exchange, a greater blow to him than the "slight crack near the hip" which he himself received. It was soon over, and they made their way back to the General to make their report.

Colonel Greathed, who was at his advanced post still and who did not come into the party's orbit, had fared better than many of those whom Roberts and his friends had visited. His servants managed to bring up some food by the afternoon, though he was still so keyed up by the morning's excitement that he felt neither hunger nor fatigue.

They were holding their position without great difficulty; the end of their street was swept by a gun which fired at regular intervals, but they avoided its attentions by taking care to cross the street immediately after it had fired and was being reloaded. As darkness fell, the officers assembled on the roof of the large house they had taken over for the picket and had their supper. Later an emissary came from the General, Colonel Burn (an officer not attached to the Force, but who had joined it while on leave), to discuss further movements, but it was agreed that these must wait till the morning, and Greathed turned in on a captured cot in the street outside the house door, for it was too hot to sleep inside, and fell asleep.

During the middle of the night he was shaken awake again and hurried indoors by the Sikhs on guard and, still half asleep, fancied that at least thirty or forty lunatics were rushing down the street shouting and hallooing.

Before he could grasp exactly what was happening, there was a shot or two, and then all was still. He went back to sleep, too tired to investigate. In the morning, he discovered the noise had been caused by one man who had flung himself down the street towards the Kabul Gate, presumably in a forlorn attempt to recapture a gun taken in the morning.

The men sleeping near at hand jumped up and shot him down, but unfortunately in the dark and confusion they also shot a young officer of the 2nd Fusiliers.

So the night passed.

Sixty-one officers and 1,104 men had been killed and wounded—nearly one-third of those who had taken part in the assault. The wounds, someone noted, were either very slight or very severe; there was nothing in between—possibly attributable to the grape-shot the mutineers were using, which could inflict a small graze or blow a man to pieces, depending on how near he was to the explosion.

Daly, away up in the comparative safety of camp, wrote in his diary that had it not been for the failure of Column 4 "all would have been glorious"; but then Daly had not been there and seen the shambles, the losses, and the tenuous position so determinedly held by those who were continually bolstering up the exhausted General's confidence.

General Wilson, for his part, was in a wretched state of worry and indecision. "I have not a Queen's officer under me worth a pin, or who can preserve any sort of discipline, except Jones of the 60th Rifles," he wrote to his wife. "In fact, the men are so badly officered they will and can do nothing. Altogether our prospects are not good."

For once Hodson agreed with him. "You may count our real officers on your fingers now," he wrote.

Next morning the sun beat ruthlessly down again and the air was heavy and oppressive. All those who had been in the batteries were burnt as black as coals; their friends could hardly recognize them.

The Staff moved into Skinner's house, which was more comfortable than the church, which was now "swarming with junior officers and soldiers."

Many of the Staff had nothing at all to occupy their time. and so they wrote letters to their wives in the hills.

A few chairs were available, but no tables either for meals or any other purpose, and Colonel Young found himself balancing his writing paper on top of a stove-pipe hat, "a regular fashionable ventilator," which someone had plundered.

Swarms of men, women, and children came over to beg permission to leave the city, which was granted, though no sepoy who tried such a request met with anything but death. Hundreds were already fleeing through the southern gates, and over the bridge, with as many loaded pack animals as they could gather together.

While an attempt was made at restoring and continuing the campaign against drunkenness, plans were put on foot for the extension of the front. Guns and mortars had been brought in from the siege batteries and set up against the strategic points of Magazine and Palace.

Roberts was put in charge of a section between the Kabul and Lahore Gates, where losses had been heaviest. Advance by rushing up the streets was out of the question, for this had been the cause of so many deaths the previous day. His only chance was to storm one house after another and to try to gain possession of the wall connecting the two gates, and this slow progress was to occupy him for several days to come. Many of the houses were built round garden courtyards with no windows on the lane front, but richly appointed inside, and the men sacked and destroyed systematically as they went. The Prize Agents were not likely to be on their rounds for some little time to come, and most people made the best of their opportunity while it lasted. Many things they seized had already been looted by the mutineers, such as women's bonnets, artificial flowers, miniature portraits, and pieces of luggage. Roberts was saddened when he came upon a portmanteau bearing the name "Miss Jennings," whose fate he recalled with a shudder, remembering obliquely how pretty she had been.

By the end of the second day the position was very much as it had been at the end of the first, but on the third day—16 September—the artillery made a small breach in the wall of the Magazine. An infantry party, led by Colonel Deacon of the 61st, set off early in the morning to storm it.

The Magazine was within a high enclosure, inside which were various buildings and an artillery park. Sepoys lined the top of the wall, but they did not expect the British to attack, and so the place was rushed with comparatively little resistance.

They found about 120 guns, with huge quantities of shells and ammunition (including thousands of powder-caps which wishful rumours had for weeks insisted were running short in the city).

At noon, however, the real excitement over the Magazine took place, for the mutineers made a determined counter-attack and the besiegers became the besieged. In the afternoon the mutineers caused a fire by flinging poles tipped with lighted rags on to the thatched roofs of some of the sheds.

It was a fearful spot for a fire to break out. Lieutenant Renny, an Artillery officer, climbed on to the roof to hurl over half a dozen live 10-inch shells, which Lieutenant Vicars of the 61st was handing up to him. Thackeray climbed up on the roof, too, and, to prevent the fire spreading to the gunpowder and other explosive stores below, he flung canvas bags of water on to the flames as a servant passed them up to him. He and Renny were targets for the enemy outside, whose missiles included not only bullets, but stones and bricks, and both knew that at any moment the fire might set off either the shells or the explosives underneath. At last the fire began to die down, and just as Thackeray was preparing to leap down again the heads of three sepoys appeared over the top of the wall 10 yards away and three muskets deliberately took aim at him. To Thackeray's intense astonishment, they all missed. So great was his surprise that he fired back and missed them, too.

Since Thackeray was the only Engineer officer present, he did not think it fit to mention the affair to his senior officers, but Maunsell got to hear of it at last, though not for some time, as at the moment he was lying wounded up in camp. Two years later, he recommended Thackeray for the V.C., and in another three years Thackeray was awarded this decoration. He was so modest, however, that even forty years later, in writing his memoirs of the siege, he did not mention the incident.

The welcome news of the capture of the Magazine reached Colonel Greathed, far on the west side of the city; things were improving at last.

His brother Hervey, the Commissioner, also paid him a visit, coming along cautiously under the ramparts, carefully stepping over the bloated bodies of sepoys, bullocks, and mules that were already making the city smell worse than the camp.

While he was in the district he looked in at a looted European shop near the gate. The British troops were happily breaking open crates of provisions with bayonets, and helping themselves to whole cheeses and sides of bacon to improve their limited commissariat. The Commissioner took the liberty of purloining a wine-glass to replace a borrowed one which he had broken.

Even under these very changed circumstances, Hervey Greathed's day was leisurely. "I go down early to the city, breakfast there, see all that is to be seen, pay Edward a visit, and return about one to write letters," he wrote in his diary. "I dine and sleep in camp. . . ."

His brother, the Colonel, led a more active life. He kept a strict watch on his men, and once was only just in time to stop them shooting a harmless-looking old Indian who had found himself a musket to try to protect his life from the invaders.

"But he isn't a sepoy!" he protested.

"Oh, sir!" was the reply. "Didn't they *all* murder the young ladies?"

Many of the troops had private accounts to settle. One very quietly behaved Sergeant, who rarely said a word, was saving his energies for an opportunity for revenge. During a reconnaissance he disappeared with a small party of men to fight a little battle of their own in another quarter.

Wigram Clifford, who had been Assistant Commissioner (in the Bengal Civil Service) at Goorgaon, seventeen miles from Delhi, had a terrible debt to pay.

On 10 May, he had taken his eighteen-year-old sister to Delhi to stay for a few days with Mr. Jennings, the Chaplain, and then returned to Goorgaon.

On 12 May he heard of the mutiny, and when the Goorgaon natives also rose, he escaped in disguise across country to Meerut, and deliberately came down to Delhi with the force.

His old school-friend, Lieutenant Charles Griffiths, always remembered his obsession that his sister, before being murdered, was outraged by the rebels. He had become a changed being. All his passions were aroused to their fullest extent, and he thought of nothing but revenge. Armed with sword, revolver and rifle, he had been present at almost every engagement with the mutineers since leaving Meerut. He was known to most of the regiments in camp, and would attach himself to one or the other on the occasion of a fight.

Yet, although quite careless of his own life, Clifford survived the siege unharmed.

Then, on 14 September, Griffiths met Clifford in a street. "He shook my hand," he wrote afterwards, "saying that he had put to death all he had come across, not excepting women and children, and from his excited manner and the appearance of his dress—which was covered with bloodstains—I quite believe he told me the truth."

A few nights later, when Delhi was fully in their hands, Griffiths met him again at dinner and learned that he meant to accompany a small force next morning in attacking a neighbouring village. "He vowed to me he would never stay

his hand while he had an opportunity of wreaking his vengeance. Poor fellow! that was his last fight; advancing in front
of the soldiers, he met his death from a bullet in the heart
when assaulting the village. . . ."

That same morning the General, in a vain endeavour to
restore something of his strength, had in desperation arranged for Chamberlain to come down and take over command for a day in the city while he went up to rest in camp.

He had slept only for five hours since the assault began,
and found that his limbs were so weak and stiff with nervous
tension that he could scarcely walk. He was so over-anxious
that even the capture of the Magazine could not in his mind
outweigh the slow advance. If *only* he had insisted on waiting
for more troops! If *only* he could place *any* dependence, not
only on the broken reeds of the Kashmir Contingent, but
even on the Queen's men! So many troops, Europeans and
Asiatics, were, in his words, "making beasts of themselves
and incapable of doing their duty." And his officers! "Such
a set left, no head, no control over their men. . . ." So the
poor General, his hair turned grey with his few months of
command, crept slowly and painfully back to his tent in the
almost empty camp.

Baird Smith tactfully suggested to Chamberlain that he
might make the offer to relieve the General himself, which
should give no offence and might do all the good in the
world. Chamberlain accordingly wrote to the General, who
replied that he was indeed very grateful, but he felt anxiety
on his Adjutant's account, in case he was still too weak after
his wound to take over any active work. "You must keep
here and not move about," he wrote. *"Head* is what is
wanted. . . ."

Wilson profited very little from his rest. He was not like
Hodson, who could sleep for an hour in the saddle and wake
perfectly refreshed; nor like Wilberforce Greathed, who
could present himself with a prescribed time for sleep and
spend it in deep unconsciousness; nor like Alex Taylor, who

was just awakening from thirty-five hours of continuous sleep after eight days of uninterrupted activity. Now that General Wilson had the opportunity for sleep, he could not sleep at all.

Next day he returned to the city, and a telegram arrived for Henry Norman at Skinner's, which, fearing some catastrophe, he opened as Norman was not there. A moment later he sealed the envelope again with a relieved smile; it was from Norman's wife, and announced the birth of a girl.

During the day a report came in that the heavily fortified suburb of Kishengunge had been evacuated. Parties rode through the place which for months past had meant only danger and death to them, and looked with astonishment at the strength of the breastworks and emplacements which, right up to the time of Reid's battle there on the 14th, had proved so fatal to the Delhi Force. Now there was no sign of life; all the defenders had gone, and had abandoned their heavy guns.

By evening, the line of the attackers was still bounded by the Kabul Gate, the Bank, and a line of posts between the Palace, and Fort, the Jumma Musjid, and the Chandni Chauk which were still in enemy hands. Guns in the gardens commanding the Palace had begun to shell both it and the Fort, with very little opposition, but nobody knew how many were inside, and a likely guess was that it contained at least a regiment who would fiercely contest their entry when that was attempted.

Three times men of the 60th Rifles and the 52nd charged the Bank—a large square pseudo-classical building with a row of pedimented windows and a Corinthian colonnade —before it was finally carried. Twice it was cleared at the point of the bayonet, and men with sandbags followed up to make defences, and twice the stormers were dislodged by grape-shot from a 9-pounder the sepoys had set up.

Many houses contained only dying mutineers or putre-fying corpses of men who had crawled in wounded from the streets to die alone. Where defenders were found, they were often on the first floor, and as the Sappers climbed in at basement level, their plan was to rush upstairs in a body, batter in the door of the main apartments, and then fall on their faces to avoid the volley which would pour from the inside.

Young Wilberforce of the 52nd, on one such occasion was greeted by no volley, and so he peeped into the room and found it was apparently a hospital ward; all the beds were filled with women.

"Turn out," he said to the men who had eagerly followed him in. "We'll go upstairs."

But one of the more eager lingered to slip his arm around a pretty neck and make the most of his opportunities. Wilberforce shouted at him angrily as he heard the snap of a matchlock, but, in the act of embracing the girl, the soldier had encountered a bristling moustache beneath her in the bed. Quickly the girls were ordered out and the slaughter began.

When women were found, they were usually gathered together and passed down the street in single file to the nearest gate out of the city. Occasionally a guard, not entirely guided by military zeal, would lift a veil to appraise the face underneath. More than once that face was unexpectedly whiskered. Eventually it was ordered that no women were to pass without close inspection, and several disguised sepoys were thus unmasked and executed.

Nevertheless, the overall lack of progress was enough to fill the General with misgivings. And, although the enemy had disappeared in such numbers that Hodson estimated there could not be more than 3,000 or 4,000 remaining, their huge camp outside the Delhi and Ajmere Gates to the south was still held, and he even imagined that those who had fled might return when they discovered how slow the advance of the besiegers really was. On the other hand, the bombardment of the Palace and Fort continued steadily, and nearly all the guns and ammunition, except in the bastions still in enemy hands, had been captured.

"I trust in God," the General wrote again to his wife. "It may yet prove successful, but we are and always have been too weak for the work to be performed. It has been a hard task imposed upon me, dearest, harder than I can bear. Both mind and body are giving way. . . ."

Over in the camp things were now so quiet that Major Reid, whose wound soon healed, walked across the Ridge, marvelling what he and his men had endured at Hindu Rao's for so many weeks. He walked round the battered walls, from which almost every inch of surface had been pounded, looking up at his old position for the first time as an observer. He saw an enemy's-eye-view of the ground ploughed up by shells, with rocks torn by bullets, and the house riddled through by shells, whose fragments still lay on the ground, despite cartloads that had been carried away. He scanned the houses of Subzi Mundi below, which to him had always symbolized danger, death, the hiding-place of snipers and guns, the firing of musketry in blazing sun, and bold advances against thousands of enemy. "Can it be? Is it *possible?*" he burst out. "Am I *really* a living being, after all I have gone through!"

This attitude of humble amazement was shared by many of the Delhi Force. So many had died that the survivors could hardly believe that they had been spared.

Those fighting their way through the city were living under appalling conditions. They took cover in hovels among the swollen corpses of the dead mutineers, while firing swept the streets outside, for in order to conserve their lives it was strictly forbidden to engage the enemy in the streets. One night, Reginald Wilberforce and his men were driven beyond endurance by a 9-pounder—one of those seized from the British at the start of the Mutiny—which a party of sepoys had in action at the end of the street. This gun was on the end of a rope; they would load it in safety round the corner, and then give it a push so that it fired up the street, and then they pulled it back and started all over again. Wilberforce ignored the order about engaging the enemy, charged this gun, and captured it. But next morning, when his senior officer came to inspect the position, he had some explaining to do.

"What's that?" the officer asked, indicating the gun.

"Please, sir, it's a 9-pounder."

"Who did it belong to?"

"Her Majesty, sir!"

"How did you get it?"

"It came down the street," said Wilberforce unblushingly, gazing straight before him.

"Lose any men?"

"No, sir. . . ."

"H'm!" said the officer at last. "Well, don't do it again!"

The stench in the streets was now overpowering, for corpses were lying on every corner and inside houses and huts, and nobody could be spared to move them. The ranks of the attackers were now so thin that a concerted assault by even a fraction of the mutineers could have driven them out of Delhi. Many of the men were so sickened by constant smells of decay and putrefaction that they were quite unable to eat. The nights were stifling hot, and so they lay out in the streets trying unsuccessfully to sleep despite the foul atmosphere.

None of the troops had changed their clothes or even been able to wash for at least five days, and this, and the filthy looted *charpoys* on which they lay, had infested them with vermin.

The liquor stores were now under strong guard, with camp-followers engaged all day in smashing the bottles, relieving each other at very short intervals because they were constantly turning dizzy with the fumes of alcohol. Outside in the streets leading to the gates went marching processions of women refugees and men who had been pronounced harmless. Everybody else was searched for plunder, which was flung down by the side of the road ready to be handed over to the Prize Agents.

The Magazine now furnished fairly comfortable quarters for those who could get back to them, with a mess table made out of boxes and shutters, and even facilities for a bath of sorts—merely the opportunity to have a *mussuk* of water showered over a man's back while he squatted on the ground. At Skinner's house, the Staff were all crowded together, nearly twenty of them sleeping on the open veranda, for although there were numerous rooms, these were really too dirty to use. One or two were cleared for writing and messing; but all the gossip and social life took place on the veranda.

On the morning of the 18th, Colonel Greathed announced his plan for the capture of the Lahore Gate, and, having secured General Wilson's consent to put it into action, he assembled his storming party for the attack. He had about 300 men in all, and two guns, and they set off at dawn down a long, twisting lane, which led into another, which in turn led straight to a small gate that opened on to the Chandni Chauk, about 150 yards ahead.

Unfortunately, this gate was guarded by a party of sepoys, and an unexpected fire came rattling in their faces as they advanced.

Greathed, bringing up one of his guns, made an unsuccessful attempt to blow it open, and then suddenly the gate flew open, as if on its own accord. Right in its mouth was another gun, loaded with grape, which was instantly fired, killing one of his officers and several men.

Greathed fired *his* gun, and so prevented the mutineers from reloading or from slamming the gate shut, and after a second round, he called on the men of the 75th—who were out in front—to charge.

But to his astonishment, as he said afterwards, "nothing would bring the men on." No orders or entreaties that either he or anyone else could make would induce them to move forward. There was no panic; indeed, quite the reverse. The gun was barely ten yards ahead, and nobody was near it except an old gunner, who was pelting them with stones and rubble at such a rate, and with such senile fury, that the British troops actually began to laugh so much that they could not even take aim and shoot him down. Yet they would not go on.

They explained that there was far too much danger of a crossfire when they got beyond the gate. But the sepoys will flee if *only* they would charge, protested their Colonel, but in vain. He had to let them fall back. They were not pursued; but the Colonel was so astonished by the men's reactions that he could scarcely believe that they were the same troops who had with such verve and enthusiasm stormed the breach a few days earlier. That was really the trouble; they were.

General Wilson was disheartened at this story of failure, and privately he wondered how they could ever advance at all. By now he had only 3,100 infantry in all the city and there was no chance of any further reinforcements.

Greathed shrugged off his disappointment at the result and went in search of his brother Hervey to tell him of the setback. Hervey was as full of energy as ever, and they went off on a little sightseeing tour of the captured bastions. Nothing had altered much since the storming of the walls. Some ladders still lay where they had fallen when the men carrying them were struck down; others, safely carried over the ditch, were still planted against the ramparts. In the Water Bastion, now reduced to rubble, the overturned guns lay with whole pieces gouged out of them. All the trees round about had been cut to pieces, and a deathly silence hung over the place like a blanket. The only birds were vultures; nothing could frighten them away for long. They thrived on war.

There was a slight advance during the day, about 300 yards nearer the Palace, and all next day the process continued.

Taylor now tried out a plan of his own against the Lahore Bastion.

He had spent some time prowling round the quarter contained between the Kabul and Lahore Gates, and Canal Street, a main thoroughfare leading in from the former gate and the Chandni Chauk. From his wanderings he found that although certain points were strongly held and fortified, most of the houses were either deserted or occupied only by families. From a window of an empty house facing on to the Chandni Chauk he had actually looked down on the head of a sentry on his beat.

Taylor thus put forward the idea of seizing some large houses which commanded the approaches to the bastion, and then attacking it from strong points. This was accepted by the General, who gave Taylor the necessary authority to borrow a few hundred men from Colonel Jones and occupy various houses near the bastion.

Only one door separated them from the ramp that led to the back of the bastion. Darkness fell, and about fifty European soldiers and fifty Sikhs, commanded by Captain Gordon of the 75th, waited to charge. Like Greathed's men, however, tired out, hungry, and filthy, they were, as Roberts wrote home later, "anything but eager for a fight."

Roberts had reconnoitred ahead and assured them that it was only a matter of seizing a bastion which was virtually empty, although he admitted "a sentry or two might be below who would have to be knocked over."

All was ready. Lang hastened forward and with a fierce thrust of the shoulder burst open the door, and was all for rushing out at once at the head of the soldiers when he found himself seized and pulled in again by Taylor.

"No more of that, young fellow," said his senior officer. "Those days are over."

Reluctantly Lang stood aside, and Gordon led his party out into the dark and lowering lane.

They broke into the bastion, overpowered the surprised

guard and carried it without loss; but, like the General, their
overstretched nerves were ready to give way at any check,
and a scare that the place was mined was nearly enough to
cause a stampede. Roberts looked round and found that he
and Gordon were the only two present; "every other soul had
bolted!" Hurrying back after them, he soon got them to
come back, however, "and away we went and took the place
as jolly as possible."

Once the bastion was secured, Lang took out a working
party, and they dismantled the sandbag parapet to supply
the materials for a traverse across the street, behind which
they drew up the captured guns from the platforms. It was
quite dark by now, and suddenly a furtive figure came running up the ramp, bent on getting inside the bastion. A hand
fell on his shoulder and an ominous voice said: "Who are
you?"

The poor fellow started back in almost ludicrous astonishment, for he had no idea that the bastion had thus quietly
fallen to his enemies. He had come to warn his comrades
that an attack was rumoured. He came too late, and was
stood up against the wall and shot.

At dawn the reconnaissance parties formed up again, and
continued forward to their further objective, the Chandni
Chauk, again by means of the large houses, hoping to seize
the Lahore Gate. Roberts and Lang were together, with
twenty-five of the 2nd Fusiliers, of whose fighting quality
Lang had a very high opinion, and twenty-five Sikhs. From
time to time Lang kept a check on their direction in the
maze of alleyways by taking a sight on the ramparts of a
distant mosque.

Bursting into a walled court on their way, the two young
men suddenly found themselves in the midst of some forty
or fifty fat and terrified grain-merchants who had taken
refuge there, as much from the sepoys as from the besiegers.

They leapt up, quaking with fright as the warlike party
rushed in, and not without reason, for the Sikhs were all

for cutting their throats at once, harmless though they were. Lang and Roberts hastily intervened, for they realized that they could use the men.

Looking as fierce as he could, Roberts announced that they regarded all as traitors, and in face of their tears and entreaties, he at last appeared to relent to the extent of offering to spare their lives—if they would lead them safely to some vantage-point from which they might survey the Lahore Gate.

After an anxious discussion, two of the merchants agreed to act as guides, and Roberts pointed out that he would treat the rest as hostages until he and Lang returned in safety. He left the rest of the party as guards, and followed their trembling guides through ways so secluded that they did not see anyone at all. Finally they reached a house that looked out on the Lahore Gate, only 50 yards away.

There, wrote Roberts to his father, "I saw the scoundrels of sepoys lolling about and loading a couple of guns, as if they were going to remain masters of Delhi for ever. They were talking about us and seemed quite happy."

Some were cleaning their rifles, and others stood sentry over the gateway "in a lackadaisical manner." One gun was pointed out towards the Subzi Mundi, the other northwards along the wall. Roberts could see the numbers on the men's caps; they had belonged to the 5th Native Infantry.

Roberts and Lang returned to their hostages, but were so delayed by the caution of their guides, who, in their fear lest their captors fell victims to the enemy, made such careful surveys of every turning that by the time they reached the courtyard again, the patrol was on the point of giving them up for lost and was preparing to shoot the merchants.

Arthur Lang gathered together as many Europeans as he could find and as many Sikhs as he could entice from the more absorbing business of looting, and then led the party into the Chandni Chauk, and charged the Gate. Within minutes it was theirs.

This was great progress; they now had in their hands the

main entrance and the main thoroughfare of the Mogul City, whose final collapse could not be long delayed. Only a few wounded sepoys, deserted by their comrades, remained in the Chandni Chauk. The only sound was of their own footsteps. The atmosphere was eerie and unreal. It was as though the heart of Delhi had already died.

Now, as the final assault was about to be made on the Palace in the Fort, sepoys began to fire from the parapets above the Fort. There was a slight delay while Duncan Home arrived, for General Wilson, in recognition of his noble services at the Kashmir Gate, wished him to have the honour of blowing in this last gate. It was a simple matter. When the smoke cleared, the Rifles and Wilde's Punjabis rushed through the broken gate into the arched entrance to the Palace of the Great Mogul.

They forced open a second gate, which was chained and barred, and ahead stretched a long passage whose recesses were filled—not with defenders, but with wounded men, lying in blood-soaked rags on the tiles.

Beyond lay the courtyard of the Palace, and a few loyalists still ready to die for their cause.

One of these, a Moslem grenadier of the 37th Native Infantry, stood at his post, about 30 yards up the passage from his enemies, holding his musket on his hip. He waited as they advanced, watching them, and when the range was shortened he deliberately raised his musket and fired, striking an officer on the helmet. Then he charged the British in one last endeavour, and fell in a moment, riddled by bullets.

So ended the last siege of the city of the last Mogul. With the fall of the King's Palace and the Red Fort of Selimgurh, all effective resistance ended.

The King had fled to Humayon's Tomb, some way beyond the walls.

The troops poured through into the sacred Palace, seizing eagerly on whatever they could find, tramping in their war-torn and filthy uniforms into the splendours of the throne-room, admiring the marble baths, sitting on the Mogul's own throne, turning over the delicate fabrics and jewellery in their powder-blackened hands, breaking open caskets, laughing and joking both over the victory and over the vanquished.

Roberts rode out with Alex Taylor to the Mosque, where Taylor exuberantly rode his horse up the steps in the best tradition of heroics. He and Roberts and Arthur Lang climbed one of the towering minarets and had their first view of the wrecked city, smoking, charred and foul with the smell of thousands of unburied dead; a sad, brave, forlorn sight. Someone had run up the Union Jack above one of the bastions, and as they watched, the wind took the flag, stiffening it like a board. Under it, the parties of looters swayed about, yelling triumphantly as they burst into houses and unearthed some new treasure. Along the streets passed a continual procession of refugees, all trying to escape to the desert and the hope of a new life. The officers could hear the shouts of looters in the Palace, and immediately below them a crowd of soldiers in a courtyard of the Jumma Musjid were toasting themselves in mugs of beer and rum.

Hardly able to bear the sights and sounds, they climbed down. Victory was theirs, but it had been bought at a terrible price.

That night there was champagne at the Engineers' mess, where the worn-out survivors came off duty for their first wash and their first glimpse of anything resembling civilized life since 13 September. And at sunrise, in honour of the Queen across the water, the guns of the Palace fired a royal salute.

General Wilson wrote piously to his wife: "The more I see of the strength of the place the more I am astonished at our success. Most certainly to the Lord of Hosts can be ascribed the victory."

But now that the most pressing danger of defeat was removed, others came crowding in its place; 3,300 were sick and wounded, and elsewhere in India other commanders expected him to come and assist.

In Agra, for instance, they knew he had seven European regiments and would "immediately put them down as 1,000 strong"—but in fact most of them were barely 200 strong. "I wish I could have that exultation that everyone else seems to have at my present success," wrote the General.

And then, in the midst of victory, came a great personal loss—Hervey Greathed, one of the strongest of men, died of cholera. His brother Edward reached his bedside only a few hours before his death. Colonel Greathed had just learned that the General had given him command of the column of 2,700 men which was to follow up the enemy, and he found his belated triumph turned sour and flat.

"I have indeed found out how vain everything in life which we wish for most, turns out when it is grasped," he mourned. "There is nothing in the world which I wished for as much as an independent command. I have obtained a brilliant one, and have been hitherto successful, but he who would have shared so entirely all my feelings is gone."

This feeling summed up the attitude of many. They had endured so much, suffered so much, and overcome so much, that victory was itself an anticlimax.

Hodson was also in the midst of eventful days.

On 19 September he went out on a reconnaissance with a troop of cavalry through the streets of Kishengunge and Telewara. They put to the sword about fifty stragglers and looters they met scattered along the way. The enemy camp was abandoned. A few wounded men lying there helplessly were quickly put out of their pain by the representatives of a force which could afford no mercy.

Then Hodson and his Lieutenant, MacDowell, cautiously approached the Delhi Gate, ready for any surprise. But the gate stood open; all was silent. Suspecting a trap, they entered the city, some with carbines cocked, others with revolvers in their hands. Suddenly, among a heap of plundered treasure, Hodson saw two bottles. Beer!

"We uncorked and drank the Queen's health at once," he later told his wife.

Hodson was very popular when he brought in quantities of mess plate, and the standards and drums of the Company's Army, which the mutineers had seized. But during the next three days he put all this popularity in jeopardy, and became the most controversial figure in all the Delhi Force. The change in his fortunes came about this way.

No provision had been made by the General or anyone else to apprehend the King of Delhi. On 21 September, Hodson learned that the King and his Princes were all hiding at Humayon's Tomb, some three miles farther out than the Kootub, and he hastened to the General with this news, and begged to be allowed to take out a detachment and seize them, lest the continued freedom of the King endanger their hard-won victory. General Wilson pointed out that he had not a European to spare, but finally allowed Hodson to take fifty men and to offer the King his life and personal safety, "solely on the ground," Hodson wrote afterwards, "that there was no other way of getting him into our possession. . . . His name would have been a tocsin which would have raised the whole of Hindustan."

The place where the King was concealed with many of his followers was among the ruins of the old city which had been abandoned when the grand city of the Moguls had been built on its northern fringes in the seventeenth century. The tomb of the Emperor Humayon, a building with a cluster of milk-white domes in a huge garden, surrounded by a wall with a splendid arched gateway, was approached through ruined fragments of buildings and over ground which lent itself admirably to ambush or guerrilla fighting. It concealed an unknown number of armed and desperate mutineers, who watched Hodson arrive and stood by in silence while he sent emissaries in to the Begum with his offer. The rest of his party waited outside in the hot, still air trying to look unconcerned. The horses pawed the ground, the sun beat down, and a vast crowd began to gather. This was, Hodson confessed afterwards, the most nerve-racking suspense he had ever experienced.

Two hours passed and the crowd was immense, thousands and thousands of people all watching his little force impassively. At last the messengers reappeared. The King, they reported, would deliver himself to Hodson and to no one else. Hodson nodded: he would take his surrender. Alone among the hostile throng, Hodson rode to the gateway, sword in hand. A crowd of armed retainers stood inside, the gigantic mausoleum towering behind them. He shouted that the Government promised that the prisoners would be safe.

There was a pause while their decision seemed to hover in the balance; and then slowly a procession emerged, headed by Queen Zeenat Mahal in a closed *palki,* and then the old King himself.

The trembling old man and his son, Jumma Bukht, handed over their weapons to Hodson, who had his own sword drawn in his hand, ready for any emergency, and then they all started off for the city. Behind the little group came a vast throng of refugees who might at any moment start a riot. But Hodson (though every step of that five miles seemed to take an age) wore his habitually unmoved look. His confidence worked here, as it had always worked elsewhere; gradually the mob thinned out, and by the time Hodson reached the Lahore Gate only a few hangers-on remained.

When the party arrived, the Duty Officer wanted to know who were in the litters.

"Only the King of Delhi," answered Hodson offhandedly.

The guard pressed forward and begged to be allowed to give a cheer. But no. The King would certainly take it as an honour to himself: permission was thus refused.

Thus the defeated monarch, heir to all the Moguls, entered his city again and was taken by his captors up the deserted main street which, a couple of weeks ago, had been thriving with all the life and trade of his capital. At the Palace gate, Hodson formally handed over his charge to Mr. Saunders, the civil officer, who exclaimed, "By Jove, Hodson! They ought to make you C.-in-C. for this!"

Hodson went into the Palace to report to the General, who had moved his Headquarters to the Dewan Khas, and Wilson was delighted with the success of the operation.

"Well, I'm glad you have got him, but I never expected to see either him or you again!" He allowed Hodson to keep any of the King's weapons he fancied, and so two magnificent swords passed from the keeping of the last of the Moguls to that of William Hodson, a leader of light horse.

Hodson had learned that the Princes were also hiding in the tomb, but the General did not wish to be saddled with such difficult prisoners, and it was only after prolonged argument that he agreed to allow Hodson to seek them out.

"But don't let *me* be bothered with them!" he added.

So Hodson and MacDowell rode off for the second time through the old city, where he had been credibly informed 3,000 armed men were hidden, while another 3,000 were within the huge enclosure and among the cloisters of the tomb with the Princes. He sought the two sons of Shah Bahadur—Mirza Mogul and Mirza Kishere Sultanet—and a young grandson, Abu Bukht. These three degenerate characters had ordered—and witnessed—the wholesale murder of the surviving European and Eurasian men, women, and children who had been held captive in the Palace. Abu Bukht was also said to have "stripped our women in the open street, and, cutting off little children's arms and legs, poured the blood into their mother's mouth." Hodson was not envied his task of bringing these men back to Delhi.

As ever, though, his task lay lightly on him. His cavalcade halted half a mile from the tomb. One of the King's nephews had been captured, and Hodson promised him his life in return for his help. This unhappy man was sent in with the

message that Hodson had come to seize the Princes, dead or
alive. After half an hour of anxious waiting, a messenger
came out to ask whether, if the Princes surrendered, they
would be promised their lives.

"Unconditional surrender!" snapped Hodson; and the wait
continued.

The two young officers debated what to do should their
orders have no effect. It was clearly impossible to take the
Princes by force with their 100 men against several thousands. They could already hear the fanatical shouts of the
Mohammedan soldiers, urging the Princes to lead them out
and cut up the little force. Yet, as the suspense lengthened,
the Princes made a craven decision. If they led a charge, it
might go ill with them, whereas if they surrendered they
would not only avoid having to fight, but might even placate
the enemy. Their skins primarily concerned them; they had
no thoughts of a greater victory. The messenger was sent out
again, this time to say that they were coming to surrender.

Hodson took no chances. He sent ten of his 100 men forward to bring up the prisoners, and at his orders MacDowell
drew up the rest across the road with instructions to shoot
the Princes at once if there were any treachery. Soon after,
they saw approaching a small bullock-cart, with five of his
troopers riding on either side. Behind it swarmed an excited
crowd of about 2,000 or 3,000 armed Moslems, servants,
hangers-on of the court, and rough characters, all spoiling for
a fight, for they had nothing to lose but their lives. In the
bullock-cart sat three richly-dressed figures—Mirza Mogul, a
handsome, short, but powerful and muscular man of about
thirty-five; his brother, aged about twenty-five; and his eighteen-year-old nephew. Hodson and MacDowell rode forward
to meet them. There was some stiff bowing on either side,
and Hodson ordered the driver to proceed.

This was the minute [wrote MacDowell on his return].
The crowd behind made a movement. Hodson waved them
back; I beckoned to the troop, which came up, and in an

instant formed them up between the crowd and the cart. By Hodson's order, I advanced at a walk on the people, who fell back sullenly and slowly at our approach. It was touch and go.

Meanwhile Hodson galloped back, and told the ten sowars to hurry the Princes along the road, while we shewed a front and kept back the mob. They retired on Humayon's Tomb, and step by step we followed them. Inside they went up the steps, and formed up in the immense *harden* inside. The entrance to this was through an arch, up steps. Leaving the men outside, Hodson and myself (I stuck to him throughout), with four men, rode up the steps into the arch, when he called out to them to lay down their arms.

There was a murmur. He reiterated the command, and (God knows why, I never can understand it) they commenced doing it. . . .

Again Hodson's display of personal magnetism had worked. It took two hours to collect the weapons, which had not only prevented a rescue, but also allowed time for the cart to get away. MacDowell, inwardly tense and expecting every moment that the crowd would rebel and set upon them, kept up a nonchalant air by smoking his pipe. At last, about 500 swords and even more firearms were piled in the centre of a throng of horses, bullocks and covered carts, where they were left under an armed guard.

The two officers rode off at last in the rear of the captive Princes, with their diminished troop at their heels—a cautious departure, for the crowd were still behind them. By now they looked to MacDowell like 6,000 men, and he thought that never, even under the hottest fire of the siege, had he been in such danger.

In this way they rode for about a mile, and at last Hodson, who had been thinking his own thoughts, turned to his Lieutenant and said, "Well, Mac, we've got them at last!" And as they looked at one another they both grinned with a sigh of relief.

Near the city they began to catch up with their charges. It was not a moment too soon, for here among the inner suburbs the crowd was pressing close in on the cart, jostling the riders, and looking every moment more threatening.

Hodson glanced again at MacDowell.

"What shall we do with them?" he asked. It was a rhetorical question, for he had already made up his mind, and had been more than half inclined to the decision before he ever set out.

"I think we had better shoot them here. We shall never get them in," he said slowly. He had already got them out, against terrific odds, even worse than these; but still he was persuaded that this was the only course.

He halted his little troop. Here were the villainous Princes, he said, the butchers who had murdered and ill-treated so many helpless women and children, and whose punishment was now ordered by the Government. (He put that detail in on his own account.) His Moslem soldiers seemed taken with the idea of retribution, and the Sikhs openly shouted their approval. As for the mob, they began to move off. Now the moment for action had come, they had no stomach for it.

Hodson ordered the three prisoners down from their cart and, in order to complete their degradation, made them strip off their outer clothes. When he ordered them back into the cart again they were wearing only loin cloths. Then, taking a carbine from one of his troops, he deliberately shot them dead, one after the other.

The mob watched in silence as the bodies fell in the bottom of the cart.

Suddenly a man dashed out of the crowd and raced away, the sun glittering on his flaying arms. A sowar and Mac-Dowell rode after him, and cornered him. He was the King's favourite eunuch, renowned since the Mutiny began for his cruelty and treachery. The trooper ran him through with his sword.

Once more Hodson rode through the city gate in triumph,

and at his order the bodies were taken from the cart and displayed on the stone terrace in front of the Kotwali, the spot where murdered women were said to have been exposed in the early days of the Mutiny. The bodies lay for three days, and by then all those who remained in the city, and the whole of the Delhi Force, had come to view the dishonoured corpses of three of the men who had profited most from the Mutiny.

"In twenty-four hours," Hodson wrote to his wife, "I disposed of the principal members of the house of Timur the Tartar. I am not cruel, but I confess I did rejoice at the opportunity of ridding the earth of these wretches. I intended to have had them hung, but when it came to a question of 'they' or 'us,' I had no time for deliberation."

It was the most embarrassing action which had been performed by any of the British since the Mutiny began. Argument raged through tent and mess at headquarters, in picket houses, and along the wrecked streets. There were plenty to condone Hodson's action as the just reward for traitors; but there were at least as many who, while feeling glad that the business was over and the Princes dead, either condemned the manner of their precipitate execution or wished that Hodson had awaited the judgment of a court.

His story of the exigencies of the moment was greeted with a good deal of well-founded scepticism, and Hodson's arguments savoured too much of an apologia. Hugh Gough regarded it as "one false step" in his hero's career—an unworthy descent to the rôle of executioner. Roberts, a perspicacious young man, deplored the shortsightedness of Hodson—such a brilliant soldier in so many respects—in laying himself open to hostile criticism. Hope Grant condemned Hodson's act as over-rash, and down to ensigns like young Edward Vibart there were voices to condemn.

The General was too thankful that the business was over to analyse it too much; in his opinion, Hodson was a "brilliant partisan officer" and his work was invaluable. As for

Hodson, while gratefully receiving the congratulations of his friends, he declared himself as "too conscious of the rectitude of my own motives to care what the few may say while my own conscience and the voice of the many pronounce me right."

Plenty of officers were now gratifying their curiosity by having a look at the wretched old man in whose name so many atrocities had been committed. They visited the prison of Shah Bahadur in the miserable small house belonging to the Begum where he was confined. Nearly all spoke with reverence of his great age—he was said to be ninety years old—his venerable white beard, and his almost total blindness. Hope Grant was struck by his general appearance, "short in stature, slight, very fair for a native, and with a high-bred, delicate-looking cast of features." He was always seated on a common rope *charpoy*—a bed with a rope mattress—with his legs crossed in front of him, rocking himself to and fro as he intoned verses from the Koran in a low murmur, his eyes fixed on the middle distance and his mind evidently far away. He seemed neither happy nor unhappy; adjusting himself with a kind of religious resignation to the fearful changes of destiny and the contrast between his dubious power of a week ago and his complete helplessness now.

The Begum always hastened to prevent her husband speaking to the Europeans, lest he make some compromising remark. If anyone asked him a question, she would reply.

The old King was given an allowance of 2 annas a day—about 3d.—for his food. Mr. Saunders, the Commissioner, noted that he was "treated with disrespect by the officers and soldiers," who boasted that they made the King stand up and *salaam* to them. Several even pulled the King's beard to see what he would do. He did nothing.

The Begum and the Princess who had stayed with him had little more privacy. Soldiers came into their rooms whenever they wanted, and ignored the gilt slippers which were placed at the door as a sign that they wished to be alone. But still

they preserved what dignity they could. Soldiers who pushed
their way in at these times said that the women at once turned
their faces to the wall and refused to look at them, or even
admit their presence.

The city was now being systematically occupied. Daly
thought that it was

> a wondrous sight: doors and windows broken open, here
> and there a cat peering. Bottles, boxes, bedding, furniture,
> and articles beggaring description cast about. Soldiers of all
> colors searching and plundering. The inhabitants roaming
> about helpless and hungry in every direction. Nobles and
> delicate women, still carrying jewels and wealth, without
> food and almost without covering. The desolation no lan-
> guage can paint. . . .
>
> Walking about the streets of Delhi one could only wonder
> how we had acquired it. The rebels in some places were
> ready for a stiff resistance. Sandbags in piles, guns loaded
> to the muzzle and placed in position, all betokened that
> which they had no leadership or heart to carry out.
>
> We have struggled and reeled through our trials [he con-
> cluded thoughtfully]. Had we to depend on Home succour,
> what would our hold on India have been worth?

From the day after the final capture of the strong points of
the city, an attempt to set it in order again was begun. Thousands of corpses were carted away and buried, but many were
still hidden in houses and down alleyways and took days to
find.

Colonel Burn, occupying the position his great-uncle had
held after Lord Lake's capture of Delhi in 1803, was appointed Military Governor, guards were placed at all the
gateways and strategic points, and the light artillery were all
withdrawn to Ludlow Castle.

Regimental messes were being set up, and the Rifles found
themselves a house which Colonel Young thought one of the
finest he had ever seen in India. It was so large that it accom-

modated the entire regiment, officers and men, and still several rooms were left empty.

It had belonged to a nobleman named Ahamed Ali Ahan, and was furnished with splendid chandeliers, couches, and large looking-glasses, most of which had been smashed by Sikhs during the occupation. The carpets were so rich and soft that men of the Rifles slept on them happily.

Headquarters was now established in the Palace, and the General allowed himself a moment of astonished pride that he, Archdale Wilson of the Artillery, and late of Norfolk, should be seated on the throne of the Great Mogul. He was nearly a wreck, in body and mind, but he could still feel gratification at not having disgraced his native county and at the letter of congratulation he had received from John Lawrence.

Senior officers were examining the splendours of the Palace with its combination of riches and filth, and its cluttered buildings which had housed thousands of retainers and servants.

To those who had known Captain Douglas and Mr. Jennings, his chaplain, and his daughter, the climbing of the stairs to see their former apartments had a special poignancy. George Bourchier of the Artillery looked round the room which had been stripped of all traces of their previous occupants, and recalled with a stab of sorrow a happy week he had spent with them only that spring.

Anson found a little drawer full of trinkets and elegantly made trifles, which he persuaded himself would be just the thing for his young children. Hope Grant and Brigadier Showers, with equally innocent faces, regarded carved sandalwood necklaces and illuminated Persian books.

About the harem there still lingered the heavy, subtle perfume of attar, proof even against the stench which rose from the ruined city outside. In his wanderings Anson was surprised to find a pair of forceps, which he also pocketed with a practical view to home dentistry in the future.

The new Headquarters mess was the Dewan Khas, its marble walls inlaid with flowers of cornelian, around which ran the motto, now so ironic: "If there is a Paradise on earth, it is this, it is this, it is this!"

The murder of the Princes was only the prelude to a series of killings by official decree. Many of the British expressed regret in after years for the innocent victims who fell along with the many sepoy stragglers in these days. So few of the responsible officers were left, as the General was bemoaning, and the men had got so out of hand—being so scattered among the vast city with its closely packed houses, hovels, and narrow lanes—that it was impossible to keep track of even a quarter that was going on.

Every now and then a little nest of mutineers was discovered, and all would be surrounded and put to death. Looting, despite orders, had become almost indiscriminate, and sometimes newly-arrived troops actually waylaid others and took from them at pistol point the plunder they had already seized from the dead or the fleeing.

The main guard at the Kashmir Gate was stacked with junk seized from camp-followers leaving the city: mostly brass pots and old clothes.

The road outside was thronged with women and children and aged refugees. Many of them had never left their homes before, and now they wandered out into the country with no clear idea what would happen to them. This sight depressed even the ebullient Fred Roberts.

"Kicking men out of house and home matters little," he wrote afterwards, "but I cannot bear seeing unfortunate women suffering—and yet it can't be helped."

He was actually within a few days of his twenty-fifth birthday, but his first campaign had given him the insight and the experience of a much older man. Indeed, the siege changed everyone for good or for evil.

Nicholson sank slowly towards his death. For a few days his

condition seemed to improve, until on the afternoon of 22 September Dr. Mactier went to see Chamberlain and told him that there was no longer any hope for his friend.

Chamberlain, who had done all he could to ease Nicholson's sufferings and who had anxiously listened to daily bulletins on his state, now hurried to the wounded man's tent and found him looking much altered, his face fallen in, and so weak that if left alone he would fall at once into a coma and could only be roused by stimulants.

He had long accepted the thought of his death, and was now so far removed from the things of the world that he said his life held no more interest for him.

He was sorry only that he had neglected to make his will before the assault, and now he was so fatigued and weakened that he could not attempt it. He spoke of his friend, Herbert Edwardes, and added: "Say to him that if at this moment a good fairy were to give me a wish, my wish would be to have him here next to my mother."

Chamberlain left him promising to visit him again in the evening, but by then Nicholson was too weak to talk. He died that night. Chamberlain reverently bent down and cut off a few locks of his hair to give to his friends.

No one in the Delhi Force had fired the enthusiasm of everyone like this man, ageless despite his youth, of whom Herbert Edwardes had said to Lord Canning: "If ever there is a desperate deed to do in India, John Nicholson is the man to do it." Now his deed was done.

His fierce Sirdars of the Mooltani Horse and others of his followers were admitted to the room to see him, and as they stood by his bedside or filed reverently past, their devoted praises were interrupted by their tears. Even his servants and orderlies broke out into sobs at the death of their master.

The following day no cannons were fired at the subdued funeral ceremony, which had neither music nor martial accompaniment. Only the friends of the dead man stood about his graveside, Chamberlain chief among the mourners. Farther off stood the Pathans, the Afghans, and the Mooltani Horse; and some of them, as the coffin was lowered, flung themselves to the ground and wept.

Afterwards, men of the Mooltani Horse packed up their plunder, and, when ordered to further duties, replied proudly that they owed no allegiance to any Government. They had come down to the accursed plains only to serve Nicholson and to loot Delhi; this they had done, and farewell. They took no pay, but, well satisfied with their winnings, were off to the hills again.

Some time afterwards young Philip Salkeld also died. Crowded though the days were, everyone found time to praise the tremendous sacrificial courage that had marked him and his companions in their blowing of the first gate, and General Wilson sent word to him that he was to be awarded the Victoria Cross. He even let him have the red ribbon of the order in advance, hoping to strengthen in him the will to recover.

But Salkeld was past all encouragement. He could only whisper: "It will be gratifying to send it home." His award was posthumous.

All the survivors of the exploit at the Kashmir Gate—Duncan Home, Smith, and Hawthorn—also received the V.C., and all the Sappers, after the familiar long delay, received honours and grants of land.

Later in the day on which Nicholson died the General issued from his Headquarters an official return of all the killed, wounded, and missing in the Delhi Force from 30 May, when they had fought their first action at the Hindun, until 20 September, when the last enemy stronghold in Delhi had fallen.

Nine hundred and ninety-two were killed, 2,795 were wounded, and thirty were missing. Out of this total of 3,817, there were 2,140 Europeans. Casualties among horses amounted to 378. Nobody ever knew how many sepoys had died; and nobody ever calculated how many lives might have been saved on both sides had the chief British authorities, both military and civil, acted with decision and vigour while the whole outbreak was in its infancy. Or, indeed, how many more might have been sacrificed had not John Lawrence shown just these qualities in the Punjab.

The Prize Agents had now begun their task of systematically gathering together all the plunder to be found in the city which had been left by the many predatory hands at work on their own account.

Despite the strict orders against looting, so much had filled the pockets of both officers and men, Europeans and Indians, that later an unusual number of N.C.O.s and men bought their discharge after their return to England, and a remarkable amount of oriental jewellery appeared in the shops of those towns where men of the Delhi Force were later stationed.

Both Edward Vibart and Charles Griffiths volunteered for the job of searching for loot on behalf of the Prize Agents, and although some days yielded very little for their pains, others brought rich hoards to light.

In a back-room of a shop off the Chandni Chauk, for instance, they found a wall evidently recently plastered over. They hacked this away with pickaxes and discovered more than a dozen crates, stuffed with gold, silver, coins and precious stones, hidden away in a hollow place.

When this splendid prize was turned in, they were invited to choose "a few little things" for themselves. Vibart was so dazzled by the extent of the wealth before him that his powers of judgment were affected, and he made the prosaic choice of "a handful of carbuncles" which he had set in gold for gifts to friends and relations at home.

Griffiths, who was with an officer who spoke fluent Hindustani, reaped the benefit of their being able to question their way round, and after being directed to a mansion already despoiled, they found hidden under the earth floor of

its privy a large jar full of gold coins, jewellery, golden orna-
ments, pearls, and other gems, to the value of many thousands of pounds. With the utmost regret, they handed this
over to the authorities, and Griffiths contented himself with
"a few trifles," which he stuffed into his cummerbund.

Men who raided temples found that underneath the "idol,"
which they were at pains to smash and overturn, were often
hidden caskets of jewels.

Those entering houses tried to discover the religion of the
owners by looking at any books. In a Moslem house they
would dig under the floor; in a Hindu house, behind the
walls.

The rooms allotted to the Agents were so full of splendid
jewels, gold mohurs, finely wrought gold and silverwork,
precious cloths and silks, that they overflowed. The plunder
was almost mediaeval in its richness. At last, as the population were allowed to trickle slowly back to their homes, whole
streets were sold to them by the Agents for thousands of
rupees; thus actually selling to the citizens the right to look
for treasure themselves.

The amount in the Agents' hands was estimated as worth
some half or three-quarters of a million sterling; and this was
only a fraction of what could have been discovered or what
had already been spirited away. After the expeditions of discovery were over, the army sat back to await its official share
as promised by the Government. They had to wait a very
long time.

Long before the Agents had got into their stride with their
search for the treasures of Delhi, the Movable Column had
been sent out in the rear of the fleeing mutineers to continue
the campaign towards Agra. Those who were ordered out
with it considered themselves the lucky ones to escape from
the sink of sickness and decay which had undermined their
health for so many months.

Colonel Greathed was given the command—"Not," so

Henry Daly wrote somewhat acidly, "on account of his capacity, but because the men of capacity were either killed or wounded."

Fred Roberts, whose abounding energy had never failed him even in these most exacting of days, was delighted at the opportunity of going out with the column as D.A.Q.M.G.—and scouring the country ahead of it with 150 cavalry.

Hodson, who after numerous changes of plan among the Headquarters, found himself ordered to stay on at Delhi while his regiment rode off with the Column, expressed indifference.

"The business is so mismanaged that I have ceased to care whether I go or stay," he said. "I fancy they find me too useful here."

Young Hugh Gough found himself appointed, after only four years' service, to his first independent command at Hodson's instigation. The 9th Lancers also were ordered out. Their officers were thankful to get away, as several had broken out in painful sores all over their faces from general debility, inadequately balanced food, and tainted water.

A few days away from the poisonous air of Delhi and a life on the move once again improved their health, but among them, as among the whole Delhi Force, there were many who were to die, prematurely aged, within a few years.

Early in the morning of 24 September the Column marched off to its comparative freedom—the morning of Nicholson's funeral. This cast a gloom over them.

"Not a sound was heard," wrote Captain Bourchier, "save the deep rumble of our gun-wheels, or the hoarse challenge of a sentry on the ramparts. Here might be seen a house denuded of its contents, there a jackal feeding on the half-demolished body of a sepoy, arms, carts, shot, dead bodies lay about in the wildest manner. Outstretched and exposed to the public gaze lay the bodies of the two sons and grandson of the wretched King. . . . The air of the city seemed dense and uncomfortable to breathe. . . ."

Uncovered and decomposing limbs, worried by dogs; vultures, too gorged to seek for further prey or even to fly, sickened even eyes now fully accustomed to the horrors of war. Some corpses, Fred Roberts noted with horror, looked even in their putrefying state hideously alive. Their contorted limbs were locked as they struggled in death, stretched or uplifted as if in movement. The horses, terrified at the sight and stench of death, snorted and reared, trembling under their riders. The atmosphere was poisonous, loaded with mortification and decay, and foul with disease.

Once the canal bridge was crossed and the country came in sight, every step seemed to bring them nearer to freshness, air, and life, every heart quickened, and several of them, despite the solemn morning, were ready to sing.

But the dark and evil shadow of Delhi stretched far across their path; and that night cholera claimed its victims.

Those who remained still had their problems. Mr. Rotton was chagrined to find that he was to be appointed Chaplain of the Force, even after it was reduced to the level of a "garrison" the following January, and it was long before he left the city for a new appointment.

At General Wilson's request, he held a service in the Dewan Khas to celebrate their thanks for the victory so hardly won; Mr. Ellis read the service and Mr. Rotton preached on the text: "What shall I render unto the Lord for all the benefits which He has done unto me?"

For the few survivors, it was a fair question.

The General was fully engaged in writing his dispatches. After the thanksgiving service he sat down to write to his brother, George Knyvet Wilson, a Captain in the Royal Navy, a summary of the fortunes of his force, and reiterated the conviction he had always held: the real test was in holding Delhi once they had attacked the city:

And so it proved. . . . Had the fellows had any pluck, our small force must have been annihilated, after getting into the city, which is built of brick houses each a fortification with few exceptions.

But now it was all over, and he felt out of place, for Delhi now needed a diplomat, not a soldier:

> Such a heterogeneous force as I command was certainly never before gathered together [he wrote to his wife]. Beloochees, Afghans, Sikhs, Pathans, Dogras, all of whom have been bred and taught to consider plunder of an enemy legitimate and will not be restrained. The Europeans so badly commanded from the loss of most of their old officers as to be quite as bad, if not worse. . . .

A week later, on 2 October, he heard the inexpressibly welcome news that he was to be relieved by General Penny from Meerut, and granted two months' sick leave.

Even the prospect of the honours which the success of his campaign would bring upon him was an additional burden. Wilson hated displays and elaborate ceremonies; he was a retiring, quiet-natured man; and now he was also to be a famous one. Hanging over his future were the penalties of his success: "lots of speechifying and suchlike nonsense."

"Thank God it is all over," wrote young Thackeray to his brother. "I am sick of bloodshed and seeing men killed."

Roberts, already away from Delhi, was having similar thoughts of future and past: "I am so glad I came to Delhi. Such service I may never see again, and I have done my best to profit by it. Do you think *Major* Fred Roberts will do? For the present, perhaps!" Indeed, after that he hoped to go on to become "a General, K.C.B., and all sorts of things"; he never for a moment wished he had taken up another profession. He was a happy young man; and he achieved all his ambitions.

Baird Smith was at last free to indulge his bottled-up fury and impatience against the General. ("The Mutiny is now virtually a matter of history, for its neck has been broken here.") He was never sorry that he had served at Delhi, but after his three months of "bad water, bad food, bad every-thing," he was now able to confess himself "rather gravely dilapidated, and about as weak as a child."

His mouth had broken out into sores, his joints were weak, and his foot still suppurated. He observed philosophically that "at Sebastopol people suffered in precisely the same way, and I don't think my case is a bad one." On 26 September he had the happiness of being able to set off on the road for Meerut, still, and ever after, contemptuous and full of con-demnation of the General.

Others of the wounded were less fortunate. Brigadier Chamberlain was forced to stay on in the foetid city, his wound so neglected during the climax of the siege that he became an invalid again. When he recovered, he was made President of the Special Commission to try the State prison-ers, but not until December was his wound sufficiently cured for him to be reappointed Brigadier Commander of the Pun-jab Irregular Force. Henry Daly, less ill, was able to leave in a week or two after the departure of the Movable Column for Simla, and then for England.

Young Turnbull, one of the General's A.D.C.s, left behind with the Staff when his regiment, the 75th, had gone off in another of the small forces pursuing the enemy, hoped that he too might be granted a prolonged sick leave, but to his disgust, in answer to his claim that his constitution was "shaken" by his recent hard work, the doctor replied cal-lously that he "had not looked so well for a month."

Early in October he was appointed to join a pursuing col-umn, and at the end of the month he had the opportunity of carrying dispatches to Lord Canning in Calcutta. Feeling very out of touch with the gay and fashionable world of the Gov-ernor-General's capital, he appeared at a glittering dinner and showed his sketchbook of Delhi, to the great admiration of the gentle Lady Canning. ("It is like seeing a man who has made the great North-west Passage," she breathed, "to see one actually from *before* Delhi!") She admitted that neither she nor anyone else in her circle had "even conceived what tremendous fighting it was."

Alex Taylor found himself immobilized in Delhi, too valuable to be allowed to leave, especially since the Chief Engineer had gone away sick. His friends and all those who knew of his untiring work on the batteries gave him credit for the fall of the city. One of Nicholson's last injunctions had been: "Remember to tell them that Alex Taylor took Delhi."

Had Nicholson survived, that honour would probably have been more hotly contested with Baird Smith; but Nicholson was dead, and the supporters of the two men, the organizer and the field executive, both eagerly claimed that their hero was entirely responsible.

There was great talk of the utter destruction of that city, and plenty of revengeful spirits who argued that just retribution demanded that it be razed to the ground—Palace, Jumma Musjid, and all.

Some said that the Mosque was the gathering-place of the heathen, and the proselytizing spirit of the time urged its demolition; others argued that the holy places, even of the enemy, must always be respected.

In Calcutta, Lady Canning, as far as ever from apprehension of all the implications, wrote home to England with a flutter of fond regret: "I am afraid most of the Palace at Delhi must be pulled down, for example's sake. . . . C. is going to employ [Dr. Murray of Agra] to photograph all that is to be demolished. I want any transportable parts of the Great Mogul's Palace to go to London. It would have a grand effect, and they could be floated down the Jumna in the rains with ease. . . ."

Fortunately, these ultimate barbarities of Western civilization were not visited on the city of the last Mogul. John Lawrence, from reasons of humanity and justice, came down firmly on the side of preservation.

"I am myself averse to destroying the city," he wrote to Chamberlain. "There were hundreds and tens of hundreds of its inhabitants who had nothing to do with the rebellion. Many of them would also have sided with us if they had dared."

But if the buildings were to be spared, many harmless citizens were shot down or put to the sword for no better reason than that they had lived in Delhi throughout the siege. The general feeling in the Army was that they were natives, traitors, rogues, and scoundrels; their colour and their race condemned them.

Brigadier Chamberlain did his best to prevent the continuance of these wholesale murders.

"I am ready to pass sentence of death against all rebels and mutineers against whom any single murder or participation in any act of gross cruelty can be proved," he said, "but I would sooner resign my commission than stand a passive spectator of indiscriminate slaughter."

He had behind him the weight of the dead Nicholson's support. Even before the siege began, while the Delhi Force was still being gathered together, Nicholson had written to John Lawrence: "I would not pardon a single Pandy in a regiment that had murdered its officers or committed any other atrocity. I think, however, that there are Corps to which it would be neither just or polite to refuse pardon. . . . Some regiments were positively the victims of circumstances, and could not have held out any longer. We cannot, if we would, annihilate the whole force now in arms against us . . . and it is not wise, all things considered, to make every man desperate. . . ."

With the fall of Delhi, the heart of the Mutiny died. Cawnpore had still to be avenged and Lucknow to be relieved; there were still slaughter and bitterness and bravery on both sides. But the King was captured; the citadel of the Moguls had been taken. It was only a matter of months before all India was again at peace.

The King of Delhi stood trial before a military commission in his own palace, charged with having ordered the mur-

der of forty-nine Christians in Delhi, with waging war against
the English Government, and with urging the people by proclamation to subvert it.

He was found guilty, but Lord Canning—"Clemency Canning"—determined to save the old man's life; he was sentenced to exile and taken to South Africa. There, the colo-
nists in the Cape of Good Hope refused to have him, and so
the last of the Moguls went begging for a prison.

He was brought back across the Indian Ocean to Rangoon,
where, with his Begum and a few retainers, he ended his days
in a tented camp, dreaming of the glories that were gone.

And yet, out of all the blood and bitterness, much good
was born. As early as 26 July, the Prince Consort had written
to Prince William of Prussia—later Emperor William I: "If
we get over the crisis, which I firmly believe we shall, the
general result may possibly be good."

The prophecy that had promised the end of the Company's
rule in 1857—the centenary of the Battle of Plassey—was right,
after all. In December, Lord Palmerston informed the Court
of Directors that a Bill for placing India under the direct
authority of the Crown would be brought before Parliament,
and in November of the following year Queen Victoria formally assumed the government of India. Lord Canning, the
last Governor-General, became her first Viceroy.

Years before, in 1833, when the Company's rule seemed
unchallengeable, Macaulay had asked in Parliament what
India's far future might be. His questions and his answers
provide the last words for this tale that started long ago on a
hot Sunday in Meerut.

"Are we to keep the people of India ignorant in order that
we may keep them submissive?" he had asked. "Or do we
think we can give them knowledge without awakening ambition? . . .

"The destinies of our Indian Empire are covered with
thick darkness. . . . It may be that the public mind of India
may expand under our system till it has outgrown that system;

that by good government we may educate our subjects into a capacity for better government; that, having become instructed in European knowledge, they may, in some future age, demand European institutions.

"Whether such a day will ever come I know not. But never will I attempt to avert or to retard it. Whenever it comes, it will be the proudest day in English history. To have found a great people sunk in the lowest depths of slavery and superstition, to have so ruled them as to have made them desirous and capable of all the privileges of citizens, would indeed be a title to glory all our own.

"The sceptre may pass away from us. Unforeseen accidents may derange our most profound schemes of policy. Victory may be inconstant to our arms. But there are triumphs which are followed by no reverse. There is an empire exempt from all natural causes of decay. Those triumphs are the pacific triumphs of reason over barbarism; that empire is the imperishable empire of our arts and our morals, our literature and our laws. . . ."

New Delhi—London.
October 1953*—April* 1956.

Bibliography

The Indian Mutiny, by a former Editor of the *Delhi Gazette.* Rout-
ledge, 1858.
Letters from Delhi, 1857. Published 1903. (India Office Library pam-
phlet P/V 449-54.)
Life and Services of Major-General W. W. H. Greathed, C.B., by H. Y.
Privately printed in London, 1879.
My Journal, June-November 1857, by A Volunteer, 1858.
Narrative of the Indian Revolt, George Vickers, 1857–58.
*Agra in the Mutiny and the family life of W. and E. H. Muir in the
Fort, 1857.* Privately printed, 1896.
The Army Purchase Question. Ridgway, 1858.

ADYE, GENERAL SIR JOHN. *Recollections of a Military Life.* Smith, Elder
& Co., 1895.
ANNUAL REGISTER, THE, 1857.
ANSON, BREVET-MAJOR O. H. S. G. *With H.M. 9th Lancers in the In-
dian Mutiny.* W. H. Allen, 1896.
BAYLEY, J. A. *The Assault of Delhi.* A pamphlet, 1876.
BECHER, AUGUSTA E. *Personal Reminiscences in India and Europe,
1830–88.* Constable, 1930.
BENSON, A. C. (Editor). *The Letters of Queen Victoria, 1837–61.* Vol.
III. John Murray, 1907.
BERNCASTLE, DR., M.R.C.S., M.R.C.P. *The Revolt of the Bengal Sepoys.* A
pamphlet. J. R. Clarke, Sydney, 1857.
BOUCHIER, COLONEL GEORGE. *Eight Months' Campaign against the Ben-
gal Sepoy Army, 1857.* Smith, Elder & Co., 1858.
BROWNE, J. CAVE. *The Punjab and Delhi in 1857–1861.*
CAMBRIDGE HISTORY OF INDIA, THE.

CAMPBELL, SIR GEORGE. *Memoirs of my Indian Career.* 2 vols. Macmillan, 1893.

CHAMBERLAIN, GENERAL SIR CRAWFORD T. *Remarks on Captain Trotter's Biography of Major W. S. R. Hodson.* A pamphlet. Edinburgh, 1901.

CHICK, N. A. (Compiler). *Annals of the Indian Rebellion.* Calcutta, 1859.

DALY, MAJOR H. *Memoirs of General Sir Henry Dermot Daly, G.C.B., C.I.E.* John Murray, 1905.

DANGERFIELD, GEORGE. *Bengal Mutiny.* Hutchinson, 1933.

DANVERS, R. W. *Letters from India and China during the years 1857–58.* Hazell, Watson & Viney, 1898.

EDWARDES, LADY EMMA. *Memoirs of the Life of Sir H. B. Edwardes.* 1886.

FORBES-MITCHELL, WILLIAM. *Reminiscences of the Great Mutiny.* Macmillan, 1893.

FORREST, SIR G. *Life of Field-Marshal Sir Neville Chamberlain.* Blackwood, 1909.

—— *History of the Indian Mutiny.* Blackwood, 1904.

—— *Selections from Letters, 1857–58.* Military Department Press, Calcutta, 1893–1912.

FROST, THOMAS. *A Complete Narrative of the Mutiny in India.* A pamphlet. Read & Co., 1857.

FURNEAUX, RUPERT. *The First War Correspondent, William Howard Russell of "The Times."* Cassell, 1944.

GOUGH, GENERAL SIR HUGH. *Old Memories.* Blackwood, 1897.

GOVERNMENT PUBLICATIONS: Intelligence Branch Division of the Chief of the Staff Army H.Q. in India. *The Revolt in Central India, 1857–59.* Govt. Press, Simla, 1908.

—— *Further Papers relative to the Insurrection in the East Indies.* U.K. Parliament, London, 1858.

—— *Press List of Mutiny Papers, 1857.* Govt. Press, Calcutta, 1921.

GRANT, SIR J. HOPE, and KNOLLYS, SIR H. *Incidents in the Sepoy War.* Blackwood, 1873.

GREATHED, HERVEY H. (Edited by his widow.) *Letters written during the Siege of Delhi.* Longmans, 1857.

GRIFFITHS, CHARLES J. *A Narrative of the Siege of Delhi.* John Murray, 1930.

HARE, AUGUSTUS J. C. *The Story of Two Noble Lives,* Vol. II. George Allen, 1893.

HODSON, GEORGE H. (Edited). *Twelve Years of a Soldier's Life, or Hodson of Hodson's Horse. (Letters of Major W. S. R. Hodson.)* Kegan Paul, 1883.

HOLMES, F. M. *Four Heroes of India.* Partridge, 1892.

HOLMES, T. RICE. *Four Famous Soldiers.* W. H. Allen, 1889.

INNES, J. McLEOD. *The Sepoy Revolt.* Innes, 1897.

IRELAND, WILLIAM W. *A History of the Siege of Delhi.* A. & C. Black. Edinburgh, 1861.

JASON, DR. KURT (Editor). *The Letters of the Prince Consort, 1831–61.* John Murray, 1938.

JOCELYN, J. R. J. *The History of the Royal and Indian Artillery in 1857.* John Murray, 1915.

KAYE, JOHN W. *History of the Sepoy War.* W. H. Allen, 1864–76.

KAYE, JOHN W., and MALLESON, H. *The Indian Mutiny.* 6 vols. W. H. Allen, 1888–89.

MACAULAY, LORD. *Miscellaneous Writings and Speeches.* Longmans, 1889.

MCCARTHY, JUSTIN. *A History of Our Own Times.* Caxton, 1897.

MACKENZIE, A. R. D. *Mutiny Memoirs.* Pioneer Press, Allahabad, 1891.

MCMUNN, LIEUT.-GENERAL SIR GEORGE. *Behind the Scenes in Many Wars.* John Murray, 1930.

——— *The Indian Mutiny in Perspective.* Bell, 1931.

MALLESON, H. *The Mutiny of the Bengal Army.* Bosworth & Harrison, 1857.

MEDLEY, JULIUS GEORGE. *A Year's Campaigning in India, 1852–58.* Thacker, London, 1858.

METCALFE, CHARLES THEOPHILUS (Translator). *Two Native Narratives of the Mutiny in Delhi.* Constable, 1898.

MOTTRAM, R. H. *Trader's Dream: The Romance of the East India Company.* Appleton Century Co., Inc., New York and London, 1939.

MUIR, SIR WILLIAM (collected by), and COLDSTREAM, WILLIAM (edited by). *Records of the Intelligence Department of the Government of the North-West Provinces of India during the Mutiny of 1857.* 2 vols. Edinburgh, 1902.

MUTER, MRS. *My Recollections of the Sepoy Revolt.* John Long, 1911.

NEWTON, A. P. *A Hundred Years of the British Empire.* Duckworth, 1940.

NORMAN, MAJOR H. W. *A Narrative of the Campaign of the Delhi Mutiny* (published by permission of Governor-General Canning). W. H. Dalton, 1858.

PEILE, MRS. FANNY. *The Delhi Massacre, A Narrative by a Lady.* Calcutta, 1870.

Picture Post. 3 June, 1939.

RAMSAY, LIEUT.-COLONEL BALCARRES D. W. *Rough Recollections of Military Service and Society.* Blackwood, 1882.

REYNOLDS, REGINALD. *The White Sahibs in India.* Martin Secker & Warburg, 1937.

ROBERTS, FREDERICK SLEIGH, LORD ROBERTS. *Forty-one Years in India.* Richard Bentley, 1897.

——— *Letters written during the Indian Mutiny.* Edited by Countess Roberts. Macmillan, 1924.

ROBERTSON, LIEUT.-GENERAL SIR ALEXANDER CUNINGHAM. *Memoirs of*

General Sir Edward Harris Greathed, K.C.B. A pamphlet. Harrison & Sons, 1885.

ROTTON, REV. J. E. WHARTON. *The Chaplain's Narrative of the Siege of Delhi.* Smith, Elder & Co., 1858.

SEATON, MAJOR-GENERAL SIR THOMAS. *From Cadet to Colonel.* Hurst & Blackett, 1866.

SMITH, R. BOSWORTH. *Life of Lord Lawrence.* Smith, Elder & Co., 1883.

SMITH, VINCENT A., C.I.E. *The Student's History of India.* O.U.P., 1908.

TAYLOR, ALICIA CAMERON. *Life of General Sir Alex Taylor.* Williams & Norgate, 1913.

TAYLOR, JAMES (Editor). *The Victorian Empire.* (Div. IV).

THACKERAY, COLONEL EDWARD, V.C., R.E. *Two Indian Campaigns in 1857–58.* Mackay & Co., 1896.

—— *A Subaltern in the Indian Mutiny: letters of E. T. Thackeray, V.C. 1857–58.* Edited by Brevet-Colonel C. B. Thackeray. Royal Engineers' Journal, 1930.

TEMPLE, SIR RICHARD. *Men and Events of my Time in India.* John Murray, 1882.

THOMPSON, EDWARD J. *The Other Side of the Medal.* L. & V. Woolf, 1925.

The Times.

TREVELYAN, G. O. *Cawnpore.* Macmillan, 1865.

TROTTER, CAPTAIN LIONEL J. *The Bayard of India.* Blackwood, 1901.

—— *A Leader of Light Horse* (W. S. R. Hodson). Blackwood, 1901.

TURNBULL, LIEUT.-COLONEL J. R. *Letters written during the Siege of Delhi.* Privately printed, Torquay, 1876.

—— *Sketches of Delhi.* Maclean, 1857.

VIBART, COLONEL SIR EDWARD. *The Sepoy Mutiny as seen by a Subaltern from Delhi to Lucknow.* Smith, Elder & Co., 1898.

VIBART, COLONEL H. M., R.E. *Richard Baird Smith.* Constable, 1897.

WILBERFORCE, REGINALD G. *An Unrecorded Chapter in the Indian Mutiny.* Murray, 1894.

WILKINSON, MAJOR-GENERAL OSBORN, and WILKINSON, MAJOR-GENERAL JOHNSON. *The Memoirs of the Gemini Generals.* Innes, 1896.

WILSON, GENERAL SIR ARCHDALE. *Letters of Sir Archdale Wilson to his Wife during the Indian Mutiny.* Unpublished: privately stencilled copy made for Miss Knyvett Wilson, 1916.

WOODHAM-SMITH, CECIL. *The Reason Why.* Constable, 1953.

WOODRUFF, P. *The Guardians.* Cape, 1954.

YOUNG, COLONEL KEITH. *Delhi, 1857.* W. & R. Chambers, 1902.

The Author and Publishers wish to thank:

India Office Library, for permission to include the photographs of the Delhi and Lahore Gates (*frontispiece*), taken from *The Archaeology and Monumental Remains of Delhi*, by Carr Stephen;
Messrs. Macmillan & Co. Ltd., for permission to include the pastel drawing of Fred Roberts (*page* 64), by E. Grimston, which appears in *Letters Written during the Indian Mutiny*, by Field-Marshal Lord Roberts (edited by Countess Roberts);
Messrs. John Murray (Publishers) Ltd., for permission to include the drawing by Lloyd of the lane where Nicholson was wounded (*page* 289), taken from *The History of the Royal and Indian Artillery in the Mutiny of 1857*, by Col. J. R. J. Jocelyn. Also for permission to include the drawings of the Subzi Mundi and of the Jumma Musjid mosque (*page* 81), taken from *An Unrecorded Chapter of the Indian Mutiny*, by Reginald G. Wilberforce;
The East India and Sports Club, for permission to reproduce the portrait of Brigadier John Nicholson (*page* 288).

For permission to include all other photographs the Author and Publishers are indebted to *Picture Post*.

Index

379